IMAGES
of America

NISKAYUNA

I0792654

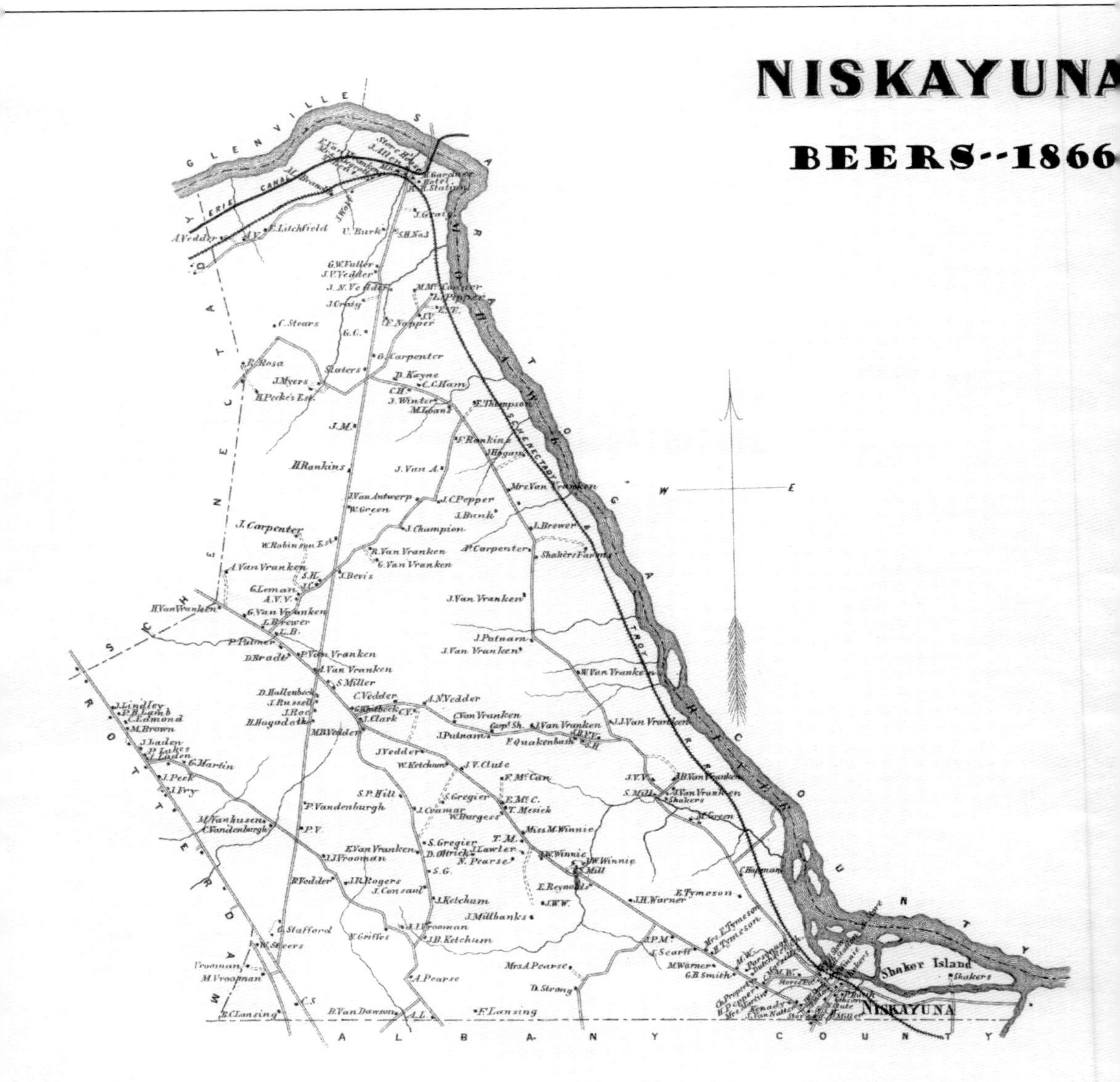

This image is a Beers map of the town of Niskayuna from 1866. (Schenectady County Historical Society.)

On the cover: The "Gingerbread House" on Balltown Road, built prior to 1856, was given that name because of its ornamental woodwork and gingerbread color. It was razed in 1964 to make room for the education wing of the Calvary United Methodist Church. (Schenectady County Historical Society.)

IMAGES
of America

NISKAYUNA

Schenectady County Historical Society

ARCADIA
PUBLISHING

Copyright © 2009 by Schenectady County Historical Society
ISBN 978-0-7385-6536-1

Published by Arcadia Publishing
Charleston, South Carolina

Printed in the United States of America

Library of Congress Catalog Control Number: 2008941205

For all general information contact Arcadia Publishing at:
Telephone 843-853-2070
Fax 843-853-0044
E-mail sales@arcadiapublishing.com
For customer service and orders:
Toll-Free 1-888-313-2665

Visit us on the Internet at www.arcadiapublishing.com

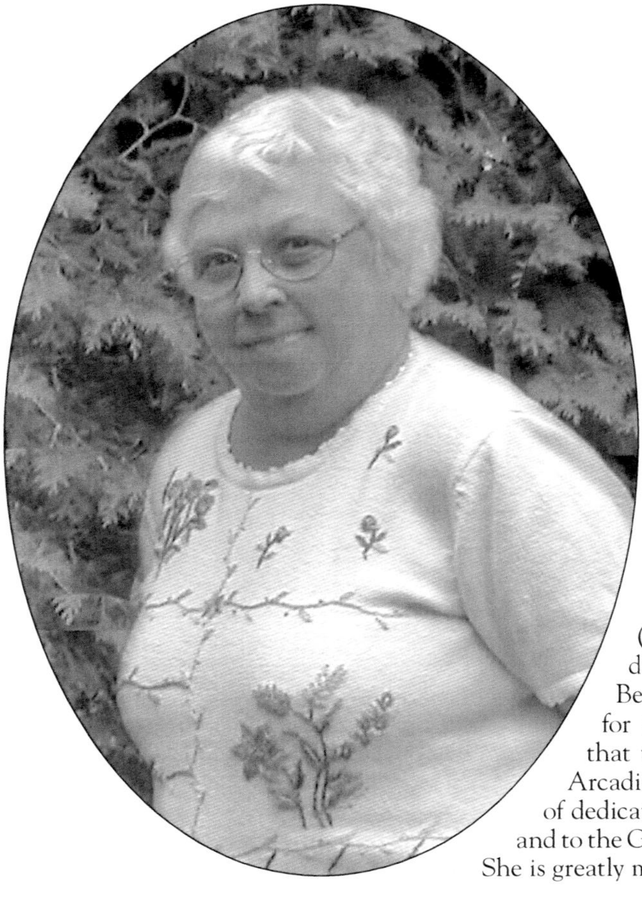

This book is dedicated in loving memory of Beth Pfaffenbach (1942–2008), editor-in-chief, who died during production of *Niskayuna*. Beth also served in the same capacity for the *Rotterdam* and *Glenville* books that the historical society composed for Arcadia Publishing. She gave many years of dedicated service to the society in general and to the Grems-Doolittle Library in particular. She is greatly missed.

CONTENTS

ACKNOWLEDGMENTS

The Editorial Committee of the Schenectady County Historical Society (SCHS) extends its profound thanks to all those who gave so generously of their time to help make this book.

Those who helped with research are SCHS trustee Ruth Bergeron, Bill Buell, Mel Burger, Linda Champagne, Guy Cregier, Margaret Denison, Howard Fiedler, Dianne Gade, Tom Gifford, Gary Gridley, Frank Griggs, Scott Haefner, Bud Halsey, Gary Hermanson, Nancy Holsberger, Bernice Izzo, Barbara Jeffries, Don Middleton, Frank Pidgeon, Peter Reilly, Sadie Schneider, Betty Denison Shaver, SCHS trustee Frank Taormina, Fred Thompson, Dick Waterfield, and Jeff Wilkin of the *Daily Gazette*.

Those who contributed photographs or illustrations are Robin and Donna Benaquisto; Carl Buell; Janette Burger; Rudy Dehn; Carl Derwig; Dan Elliott, Grand Boulevard Fire Company; Al Finke Jr.; Richard Flanders; Kevin Franklin, historian, Town of Colonie; Ralph Gasner; Chris Hunter, archivist, Schenectady Museum; Glen Huntsberger III; Leona Jeffes, St. Helen's School librarian; Karen Kast; Helen Kopke, Niskayuna town clerk; Andy Kulmatiski, director, Schenectady County Public Library; Jim Mancuso; Dick Masse; Carole McCarthy; Peg and Rick Mele; Bertha Guthan Pakan; Paul Pakan; Kathryn Reilly; Cynthia Seacord, archivist, Efner City History Center; Peter Sheehan; Skip Smith; Harry Steven, SCHS trustee; Nancy Stopera, Niskayuna Reformed Church; Frank Taormina, SCHS trustee; Carolyn Veeder; Dick Waterfield; and George Yager.

Where indicated in the body of this work, certain images are from the society's Laura Brown Collection, its Larry Hart Collection, or its John Papp Collection.

Serving on the society's editorial committee were Beth Pfaffenbach, editor-in-chief; trustee Ann Aronson, photographer; Katherine Chansky, librarian-archivist, SCHS Grems-Doolittle Library; Ann Eignor; trustee Jim Eignor, photography editor; trustee Carol Lewis; and Ed Reilly, president, SCHS.

Introduction

The name *Niskayuna* is said to be derived from the Connestigione Indians who occupied the locality at the coming of the Dutch around 1642, 20 years before Arendt van Curler founded Schenectady. The name, meaning "extensive corn flats," evolved from the original, "Canastagione."

What is now known as Niskayuna was once part of a much larger area. When the first settlers arrived here in the 1600s, Native Americans occupied land on both sides of the Mohawk River, including the current hamlets of Alplaus and Rexford, an area reaching as far east as Latham Corners in the town of Watervliet (now Colonie), and the Stockade area of the city of Schenectady. On February 9, 1690, when Symon Jacob Schermerhorn escaped from the burning Schenectady Stockade and rode to Albany to warn of impending danger to Fort Orange, he took the shortest possible route—right through the heart of Niskayuna.

When the county of Schenectady was carved from Albany County on March 6, 1809, much of Niskayuna's original area was ceded to other towns. Niskayuna, with just 681 residents, became one of the five towns and a city that comprised Schenectady County.

In 1664, Harmon Vedder built the first home in Niskayuna. In 1687, the Van Antwerp farm emerged at what is now 1727 Van Antwerp Road. In 1746, one of a group of blockhouses, ranging from Fort Massachusetts to Fort Hunter, was built in Niskayuna by Gov. George Clinton.

The Reformed Church of Niskayuna, organized about 1750, moved a short distance to its current location on Troy Road near the Colonie border in 1852. It is one of two Niskayuna sites listed on the New York State and National Registers of Historic Places. The other is the George Westinghouse Jones home on the corner of Troy Road and St. David's Lane, now the education center of the First Baptist Church.

In 1762, John Duncan (1722–1791) acquired an estate of about 800 acres of Niskayuna land in an area now known as Stanford Heights. It was named after the 1859 owners of part of that acreage. The Stanfords were the parents of Gov. Leland Stanford of California and state senator Charles Stanford of Niskayuna. Duncan's first home on the property was called the Hermitage, but it burned down in 1790. In about 1817, a second home was built 100 yards to the north by Hermanus Schuyler, who later became town supervisor. Called Locust Grove by the senior Stanfords, the Stanford mansion and a 1950 addition now sit on only 12.4 acres, all that is left of Duncan's original 800. The property became the Ingersoll Memorial Home for the Aged from 1922 until 2008, when the institution moved to a new home on Consaul Road.

In 1799, the Albany–Schenectady Turnpike (now Route 5) was built through Niskayuna, and tolls were still being collected in 1886. The route of the turnpike was laid out by surveyor Lawrence Vrooman, who became Niskayuna's first town supervisor in 1809.

When built in 1805, a bridge across the Mohawk River at Rexford was known as Alexander's Bridge, and two nearby mills were called Alexander's Mills, the earliest name for the center of what grew to become a hamlet. The person who built both was Revolutionary War veteran Alexander Alexander (1765–1809).

As of 1822, the Erie Canal crossed the river into Niskayuna at Alexander's Mills on an aqueduct 748 feet long and 25 feet above the stream. From that time onward, the hamlet became known as Aqueduct. There were two locks on the canal between Schenectady and the hamlet of Rexford in the Saratoga County town of Clifton Park.

In 1843, the Troy and Schenectady Railroad was built along the Mohawk River with one station in the Aqueduct hamlet and another, still standing, in the Niskayuna hamlet. Halfway between these was the Rosendale hamlet opposite Niska Isle. In 1975, the town acquired the railroad's abandoned right-of-way and converted it into a hike-and-bike trail.

In 1886, the Edison Machine Works was founded in nearby Schenectady when Thomas Edison bought the abandoned buildings of the McQueen Locomotive Works from the descendants of Niskayuna resident Charles Stanford and moved his factory from New York City to Schenectady. The electrical industry was born in Schenectady and led to a dramatic increase in the population of the city and of the town of Niskayuna.

Prominent in the town 150 or more years ago were families whose names are still used to designate streets and places in Schenectady County, including Bradt, Burger, Clute, Consaul, Craig, Cregier, Glen, Green, Groot, Lansing, Maxon, Pearse, Scheckelman, Schoolcraft, Schopmeier/Shopmyer, Spoor, Stanford, Van Antwerp, Van Vranken, Vedder/Veeder, Viele, Vrooman, Wemple, Winne, and Zenner.

Public transportation linked Niskayuna to areas to the north and east. By 1920, trolleys from Schenectady made their way up Union Street, previously called Niskayuna Street, and out Troy Road to the east past many stops on the way to Troy. Trolleys also ran along Van Vranken Avenue and up the newly created Grand Boulevard to Van Antwerp Road and along Aqueduct Road crossing the Mohawk River into Rexford and then north to Saratoga Springs.

The crossroads of Niskayuna, situated very close to its geographic center, is the intersection of two streets that are each named for a clergyman whose first name was Eliphalet: Nott Street and Balltown Road. Nott Street was named for Rev. Eliphalet Nott (1773–1866), a clergyman, inventor, and president of Union College for 62 years. In 1785, a few miles north of Niskayuna, Rev. Eliphalet Ball (about 1727–1797), a third cousin of Pres. George Washington, founded Ball's Town, known as Ballston in Saratoga County. The road south from there, Ball's Town Road, soon became Balltown Road. It comes into Niskayuna at the Rexford Bridge, crosses Nott Street and Union Street, and continues past the Stanford mansion to State Street.

After many years of meeting in an upstairs room of a fire station, the town government moved to a new building of its own on Balltown Road in 1950. It served the town for 44 years until a much larger town hall was completed on an extension of Nott Street in 1995.

Niskayuna is home to several institutions that have long and distinguished histories of their own, including television station WRGB, the Grand Boulevard Fire Company, the Mohawk Golf Club, Bellevue Woman's Care Hospital, the Schenectady Curling Club, GE Global Research, the research laboratory of Schenectady International, and the Knolls Atomic Power Laboratory.

In 1962, Niskayuna became a town of the first class, a formal state designation, and then in 1975, it attained a status of still higher autonomy, suburban town. Niskayuna now offers all of the services of a city, and with its population of 20,295 according to the 2000 census, the town is more populous than 35 of New York State's cities and is still growing.

Edwin D. Reilly Jr., president, Schenectady County Historical Society, and supervisor, Town of Niskayuna, 1970–1979 and 1989–1997
Francis Taormina, retired Niskayuna Central School District administrator

One

Aqueduct

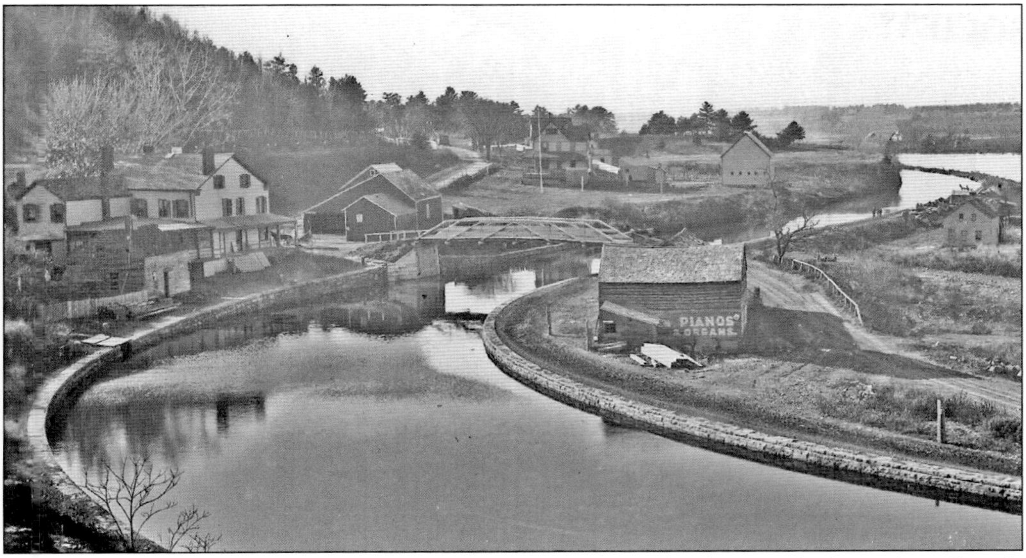

This view from the bank of the Erie Canal looking west toward Schenectady shows the Whipple Farm bridge that carried Balltown Road over the canal. In 1805, Alexander Alexander built a bridge across the Mohawk River and a dam to furnish power for Alexander's Mills, an early name for the hamlet of Aqueduct. At left is the Craig Hotel and across Balltown Road from the hotel is its wagon house. (Karen Kast.)

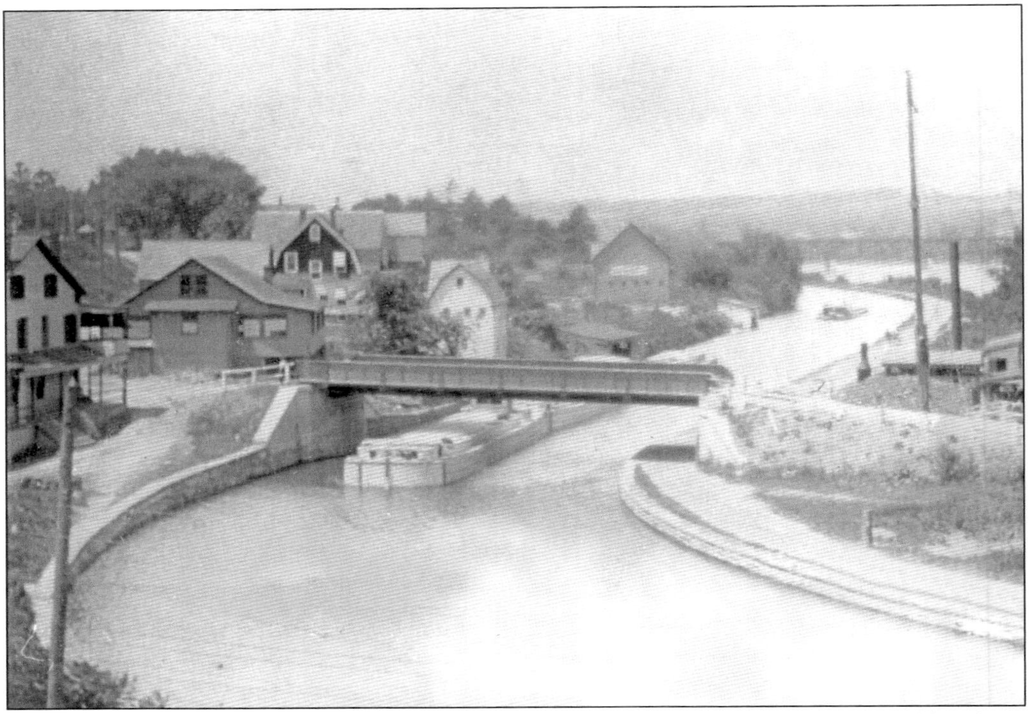

Here is a later photograph of the Erie Canal at Aqueduct. The bridge over the canal has been replaced with a steel girder structure. The Craig Hotel can be seen at the left edge of the picture with a remodeled wagon house, and more buildings have been built in the background. (Skip Smith.)

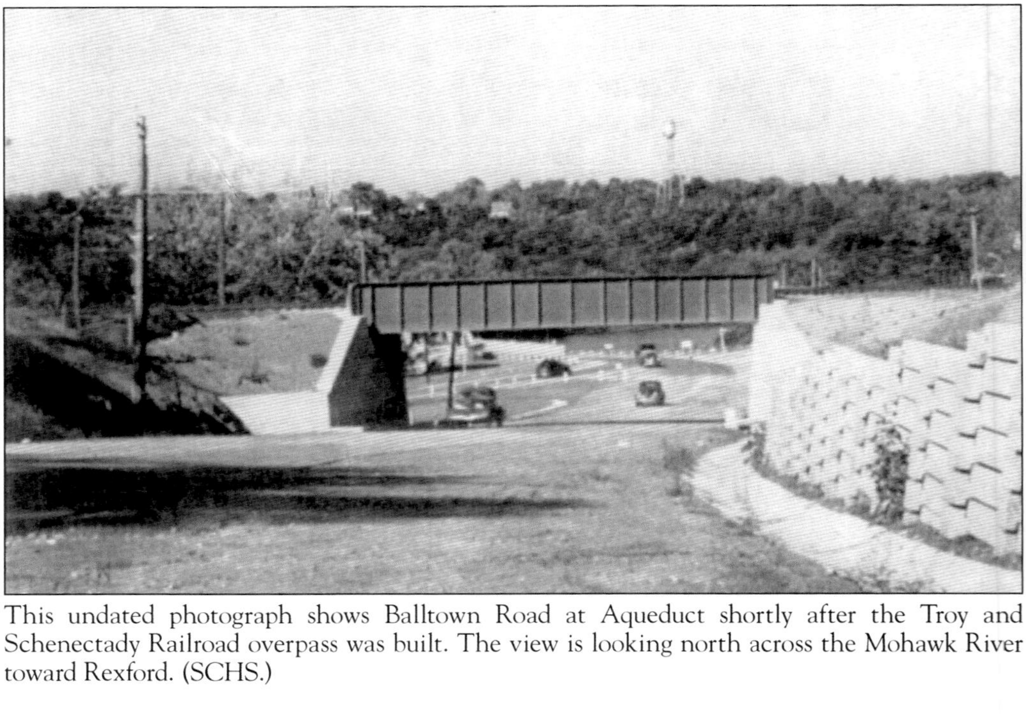

This undated photograph shows Balltown Road at Aqueduct shortly after the Troy and Schenectady Railroad overpass was built. The view is looking north across the Mohawk River toward Rexford. (SCHS.)

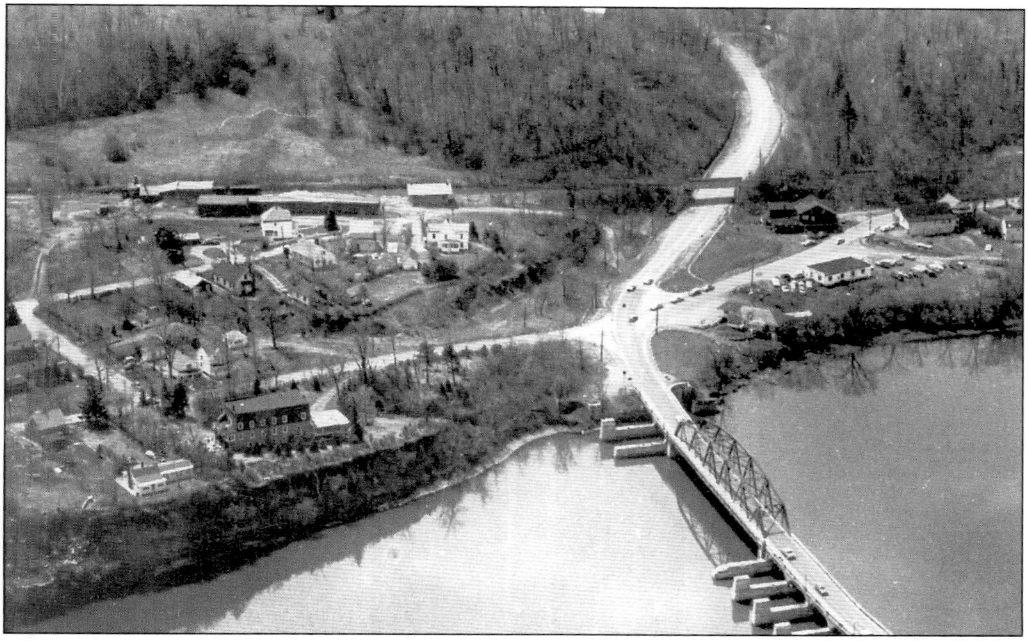

This is an aerial view of Aqueduct, taken prior to 1964, looking south along Balltown Road. It shows the bridge built in 1924 and the piers for the Erie Canal aqueduct. To the right is Smith's Garage, the Craig Hotel, and the Boat House. To the left near the overpass is the Aqueduct train station and accompanying buildings. (Karen Kast.)

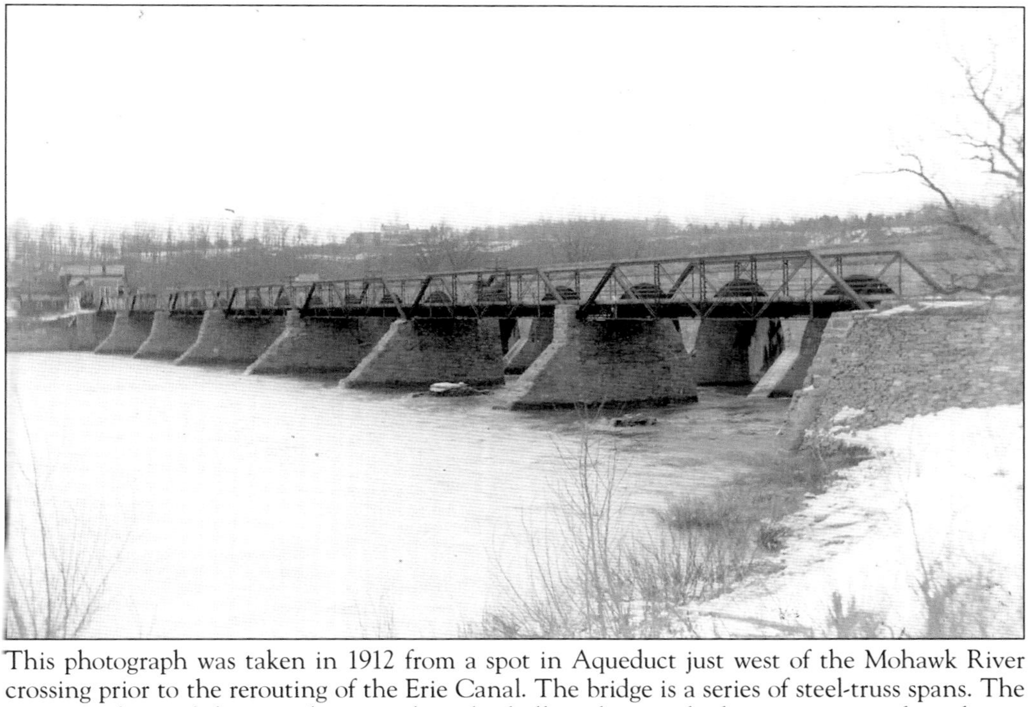

This photograph was taken in 1912 from a spot in Aqueduct just west of the Mohawk River crossing prior to the rerouting of the Erie Canal. The bridge is a series of steel-truss spans. The upstream faces of the piers have a relatively shallow slope with the expectation that, during spring runoff, ice floes would break over the sloped surface. (SCHS.)

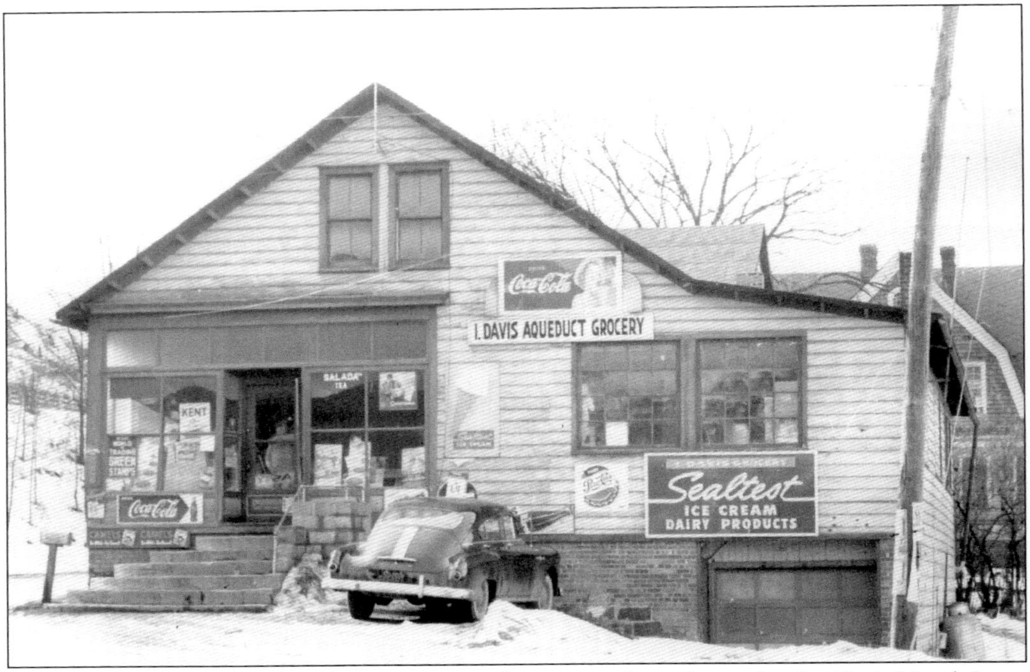

Dating back to 1835, this building was originally a wagon-horse livery for the Craig Hotel. Later known as the Izzy Davis store, it was Aqueduct's only grocery store up through 1957. Izzy was a nickname for Isaac. (Efner City History Center.)

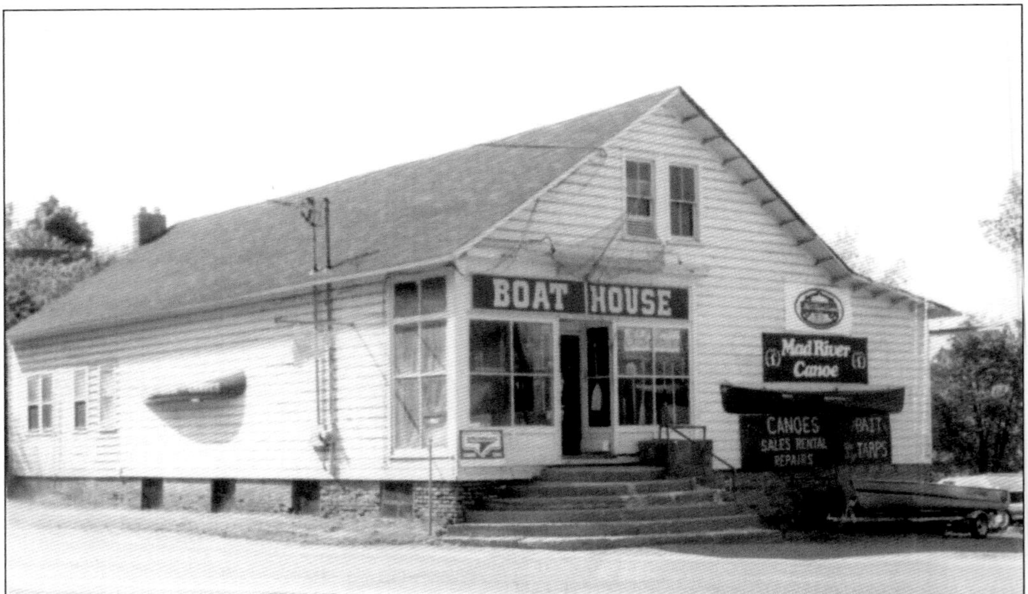

For four decades, this same building has been known as the Boat House, a business specializing in canoes, kayaks, and accessories. It is located at 2855 Aqueduct Road across from what was the Craig Hotel until 1980. From 1970 to 1981, the Boat House was owned by WRGB personality Ernie Tetrault and operated by him in partnership with Don Middleton. Current owners Bud and Sara Halsey continue to operate the Boat House. (Efner City History Center.)

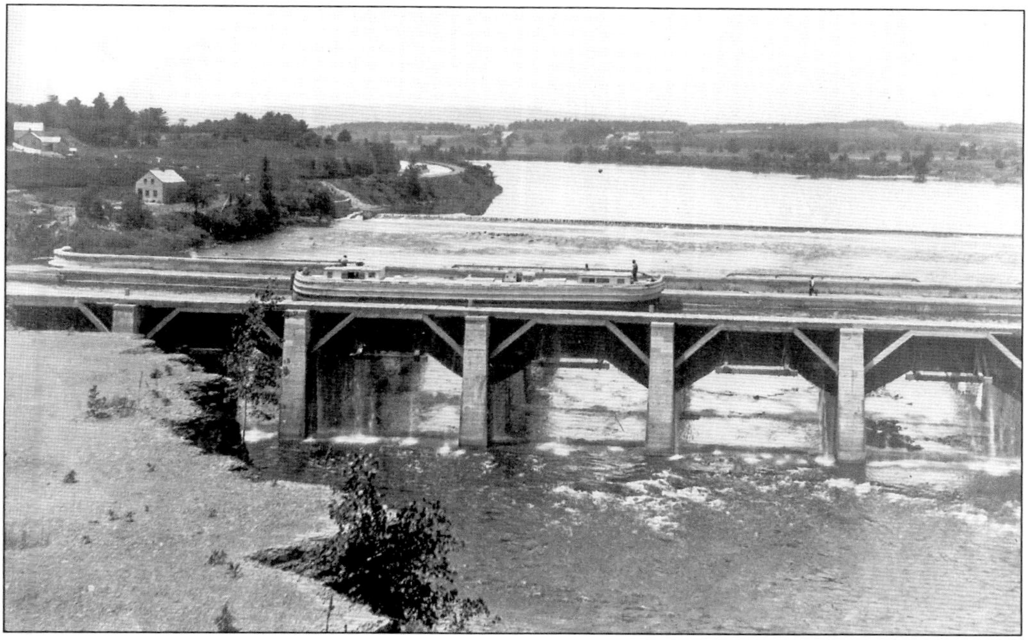

This photograph was taken from the top of the cliffs in Aqueduct looking west, prior to 1918. It shows a canal boat crossing the Mohawk River on the aqueduct. (SCHS, John Papp Collection.)

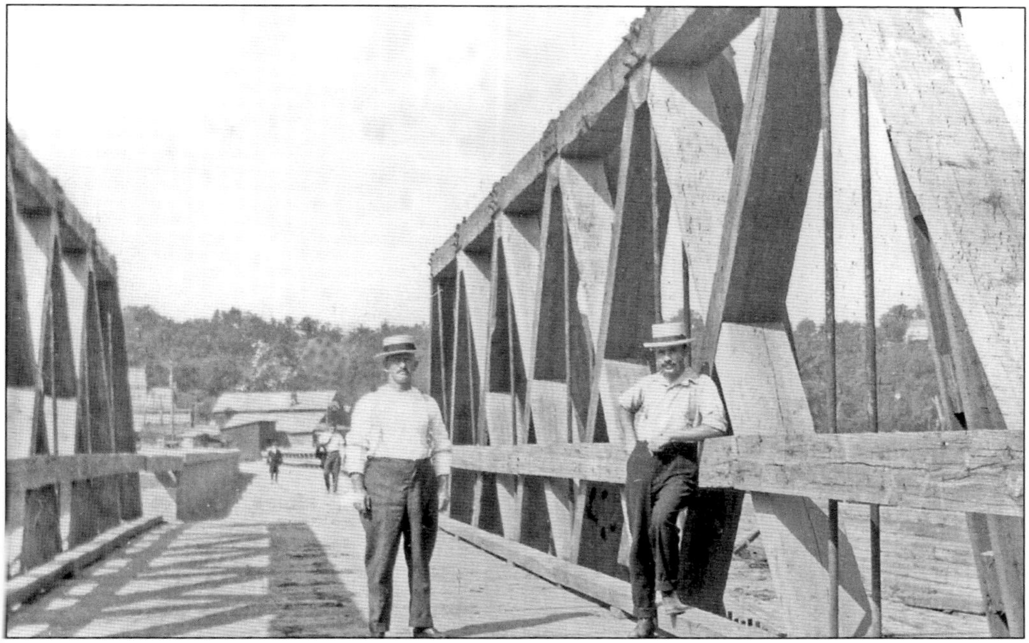

When the Erie Canal was replaced by the New York State Barge Canal, which followed the course of the Mohawk River, a temporary wooden bridge was built on the supports of the abandoned aqueduct. The men on the bridge are Mike Travis (left) and Charles George, residents of Rexford. (SCHS.)

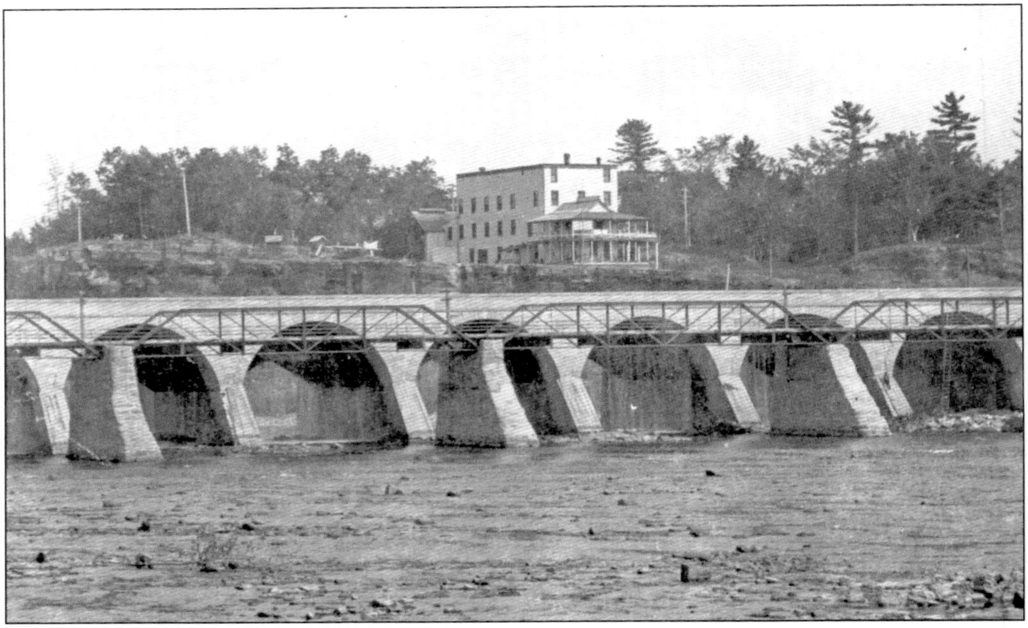

Here is the Williams Hotel as viewed from the north shore of the Mohawk River. In the foreground are a highway bridge to Rexford on its own substantial piers and the canal aqueduct behind it. (SCHS.)

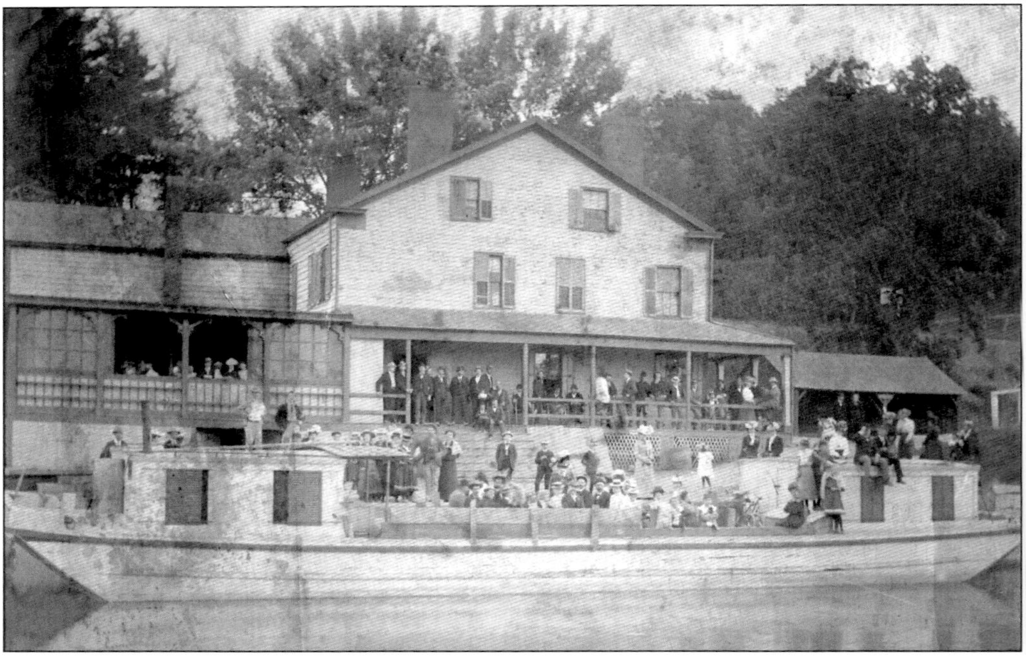

An Erie Canal excursion boat is docked at the Parker Hotel in 1895. For most of its existence, the hotel was known as the Craig Hotel except when Schenectadian John Nicholas Parker (1854–1907) bought and operated it under his name from 1891 to 1899. Parker lived at the hotel for the previous 11 years to help the proprietor, his uncle Hiram Parker. John is the same Parker who built the eight-story Parker building in Schenectady, the tallest in that city. (Karen Kast.)

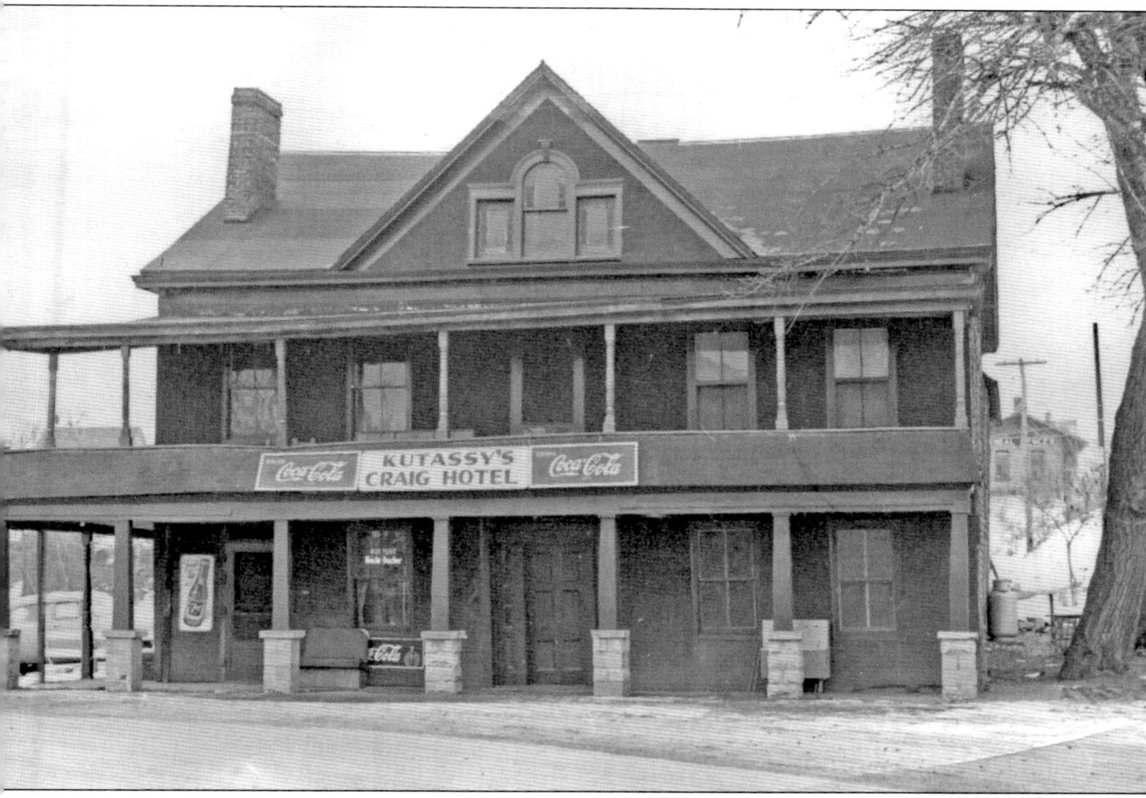

The Craig Hotel in Aqueduct was named for its first owners, Archibald and Margaret Craig. Archibald Craig (1775–1846) graduated from Princeton University at an early age, was accredited as a physician at age 19, and served as mayor of Schenectady from 1831 to 1832. The Craigs built the hotel around 1835 and operated it until it sold in 1852. Margaret and her son James bought it back in 1855 but sold it again in 1858. The hotel was operated by the McPherson family from 1911 to 1949, the longest tenure of any of the building's 23 owners. This picture was taken in 1951, shortly after the hotel was purchased by Roxy Kutassy-Mott. In 1972, she sold the hotel to Douglas Allen, who added a brick extension for use as a dining room and reopened it as the Olde Craig Hotel. In 1977, the older part of the building was severely damaged by fire. Allen removed the debris and opened just the surviving brick extension as a popular nightspot. In 1980, Schenectady County acquired and later demolished it to widen the Aqueduct Road approach to the Rexford Bridge. (Efner City History Center.)

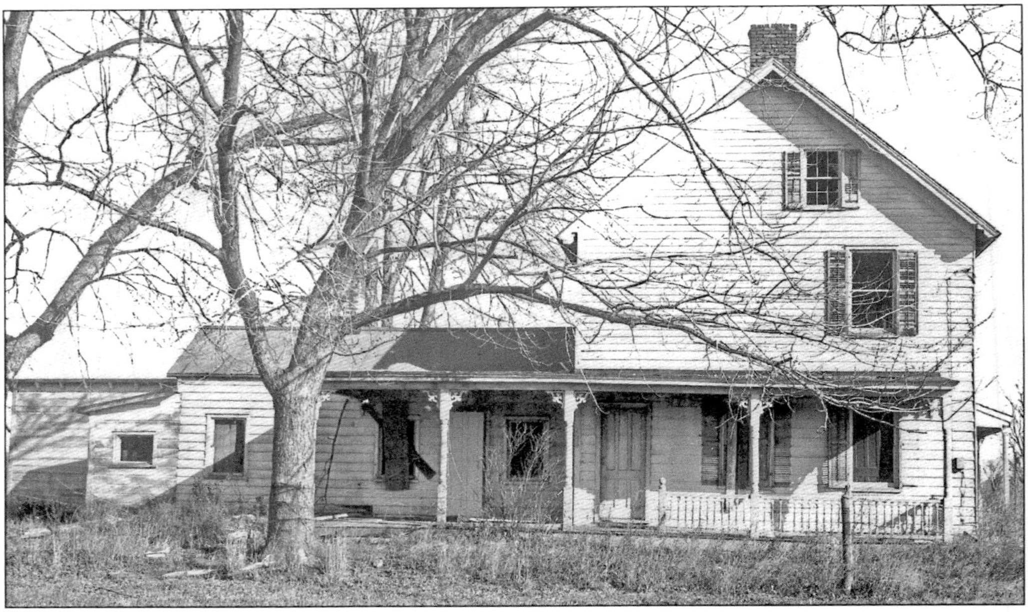

This house near the Aqueduct train station was the summer home of banker James R. Craig (1813–1877), the son of the first owners of the Craig Hotel. His primary residence was at 7 Church Street in Schenectady. He served as supervisor of Niskayuna in 1845, supervisor of the First Ward in Schenectady in 1855, and president of that city's board of education in 1857. He was the only person ever elected to office in both municipalities. (Efner City History Center.)

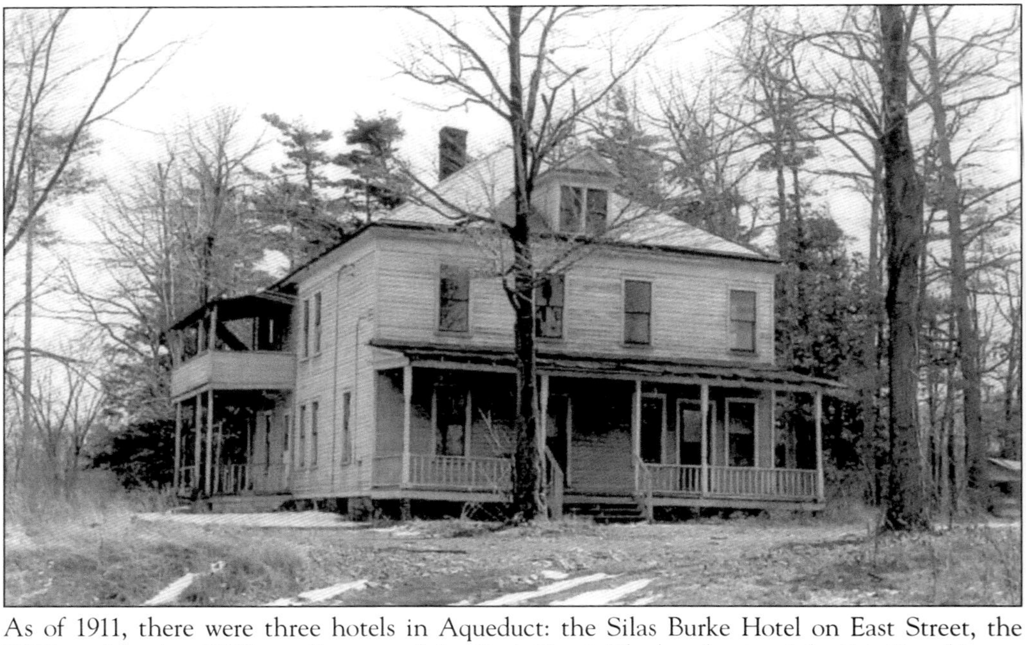

As of 1911, there were three hotels in Aqueduct: the Silas Burke Hotel on East Street, the Williams Hotel on Williams Street, and the Craig Hotel. The hotels served the Erie Canal boats, especially the popular *Kitty West*, and the trolleys going to Luna Amusement Park and the picnic groves in Rexford. After a fire damaged the Silas Burke Hotel, it was reconstructed to appear as shown. The building has been replaced by a private residence. (Richard Flanders.)

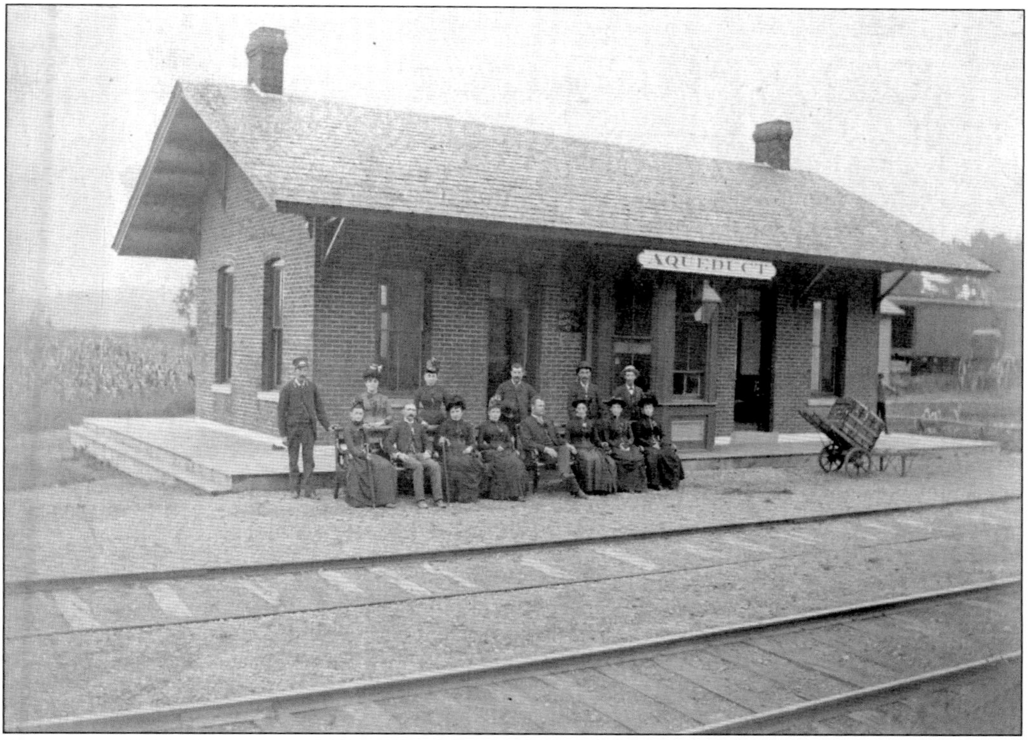

Here is an 1890 photograph of the Aqueduct railroad station, which was located on the north side of the Troy and Schenectady Railroad on what is now East Street. (SCHS.)

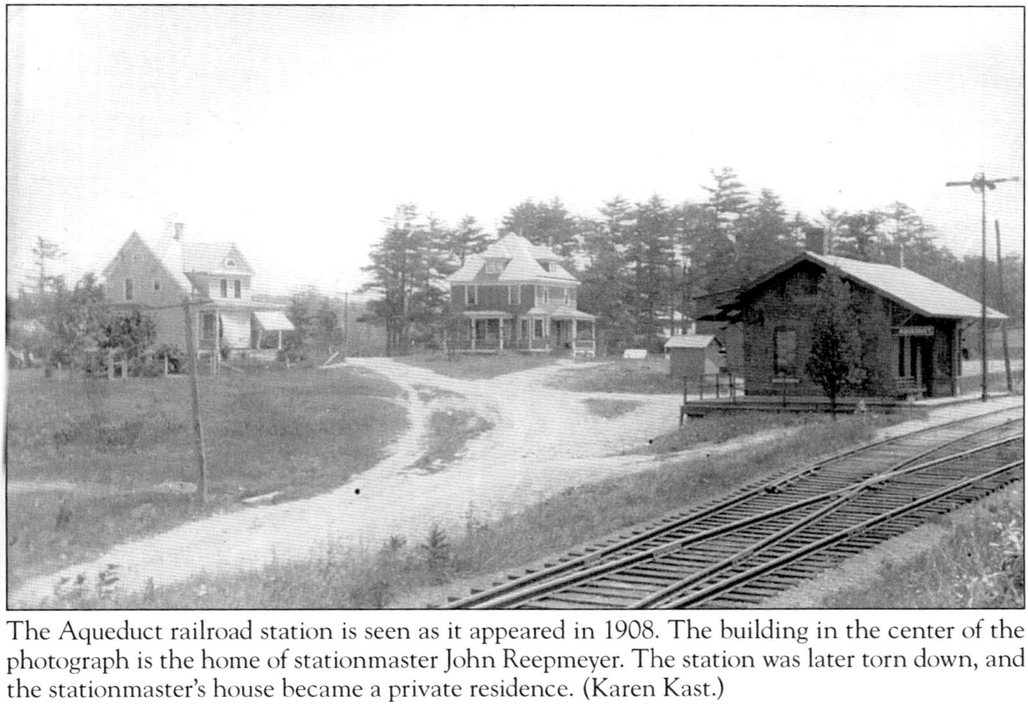

The Aqueduct railroad station is seen as it appeared in 1908. The building in the center of the photograph is the home of stationmaster John Reepmeyer. The station was later torn down, and the stationmaster's house became a private residence. (Karen Kast.)

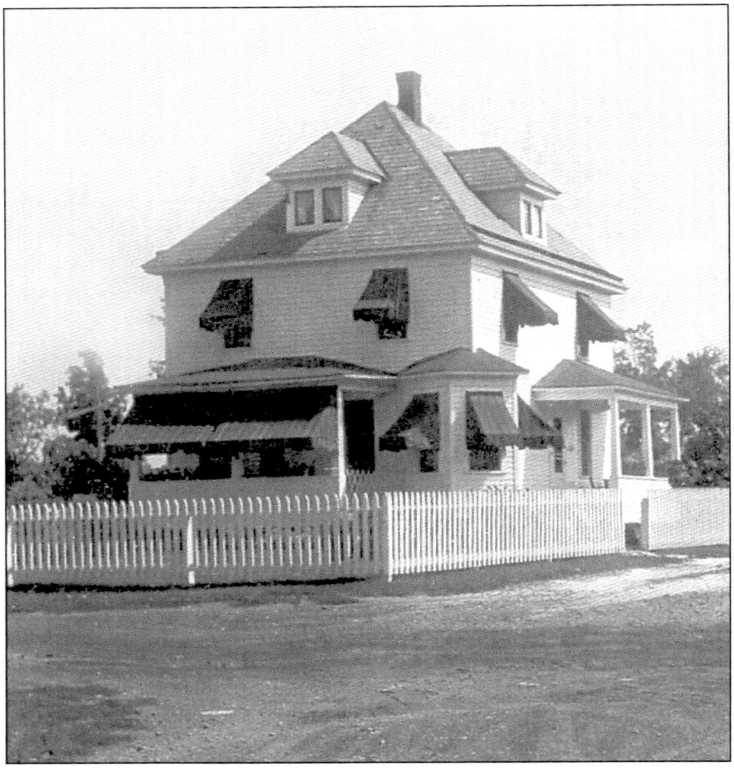

This is a 1942 view of the stationmaster's house for the Aqueduct station on the Troy and Schenectady Railroad. The photograph originally belonged to Carol Reepmeyer Kurowski, the stationmaster's daughter. (Karen Kast.)

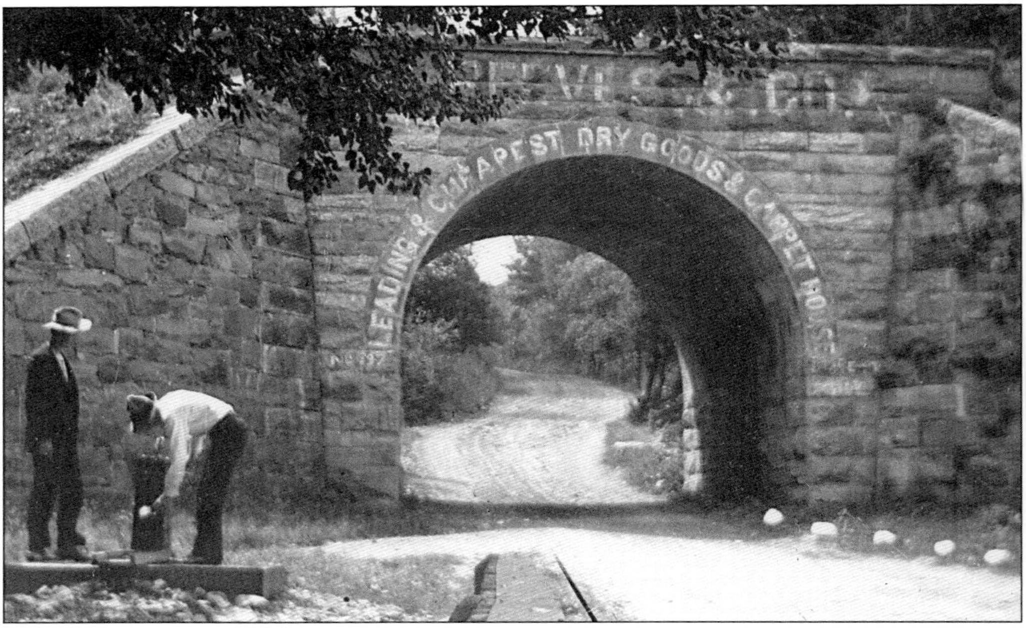

This overpass was built for the Troy and Schenectady Railroad around 1862. It passed over the old Balltown Road. It was later replaced by a newer underpass in 1910 when Balltown Road was rerouted. The men on the left are getting water from a pump. This photograph was taken in the early 1900s from the rear porch of the Craig Hotel. (SCHS.)

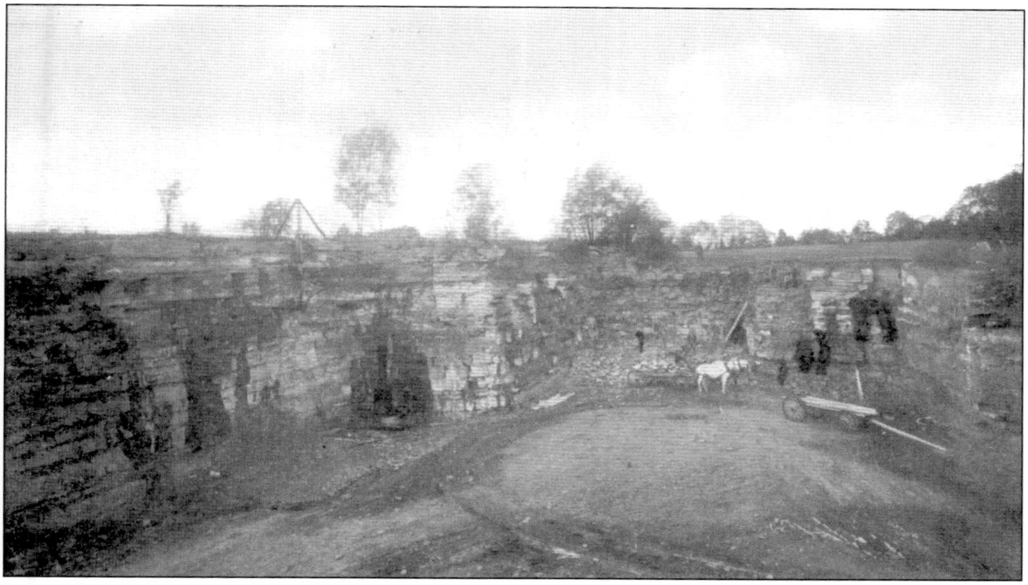

From the early 1900s through at least 1930, this stone quarry was operating east of Aqueduct on the Mohawk River. Known informally as Kellam's Quarry, it was owned by the Kellam and Shaffer Company. In the 1910 Schenectady city directory, the company listed its office as being at 314 State Street with its works on Maxon Road. Owner Newton J. Kellam of 332 State Street was born in 1862 and died in California in 1926. (SCHS.)

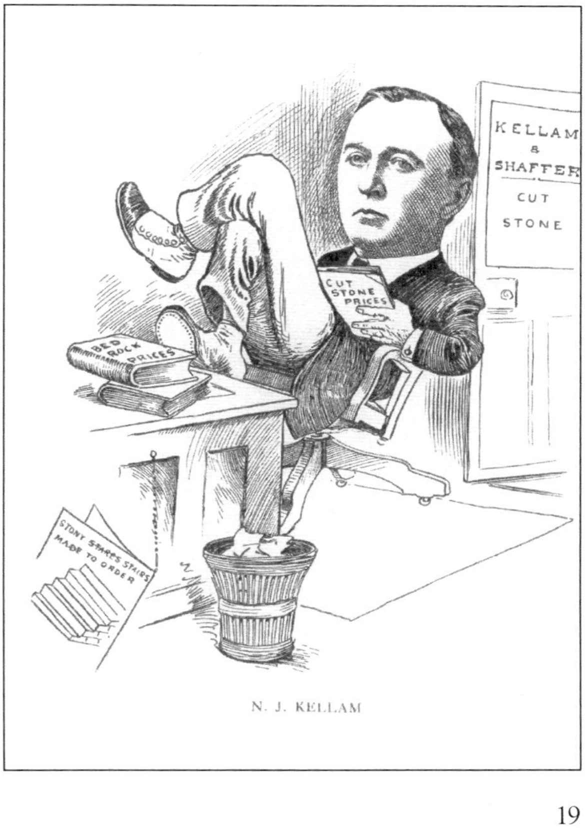

This is a caricature of quarry operator Newton J. Kellam, one of several that appeared in the Schenectady *Union Star* in 1910 and reprinted in 1953. The itinerant artist preferred anonymity. The series was collected and printed as a book called *Just for Fun*. To be chosen as the subject of one of these drawings was considered quite an honor. The second name on the door was that of Kellam's partner, Adam F. Shaffer (1869–1949). (Efner City History Center.)

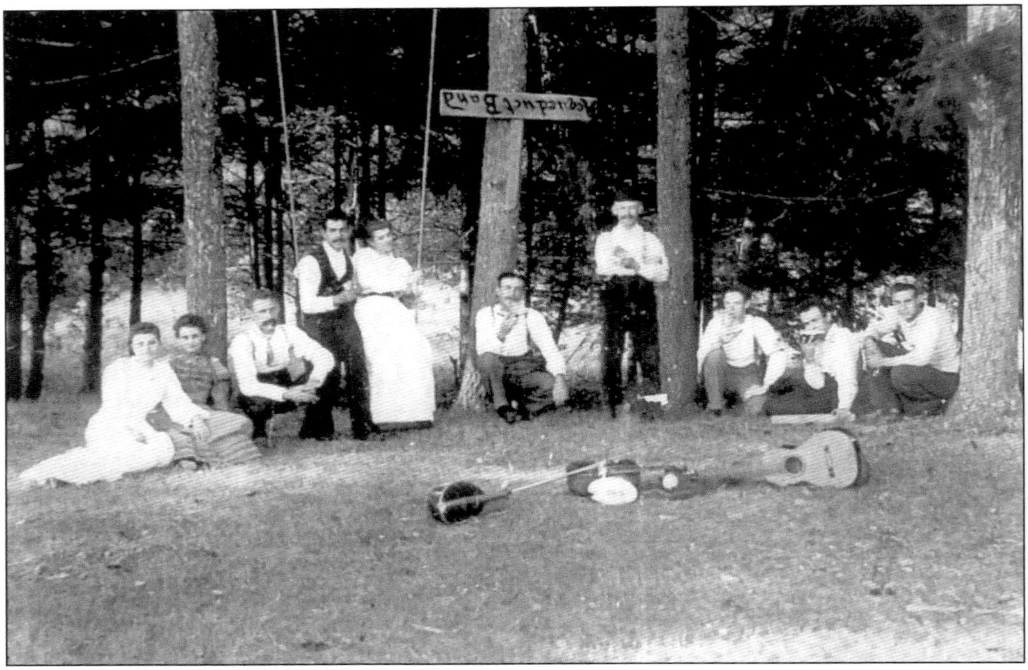

The Aqueduct Band was one of many community bands popular in the early 20th century. Here members perform in a picnic and ballpark area southeast of the Silas Burke Hotel. (Karen Kast.)

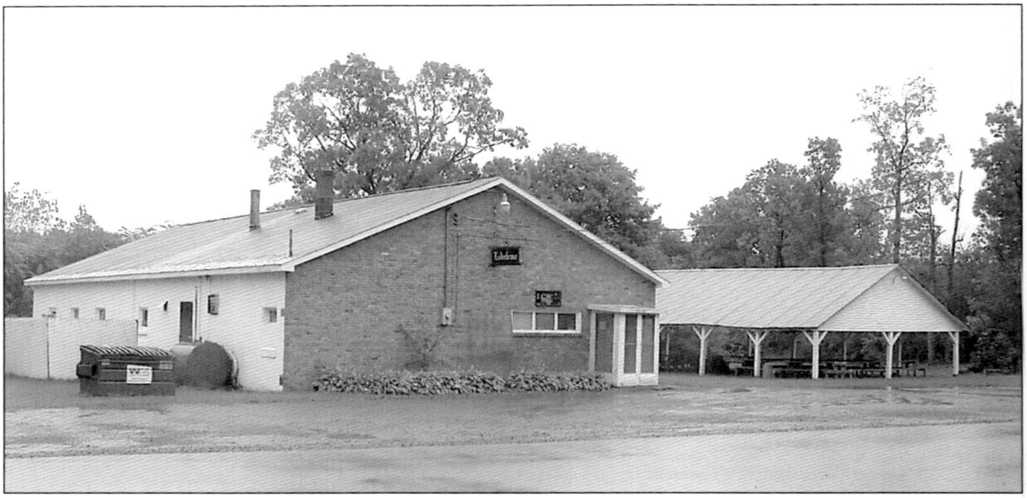

The Schenectady Liederkranz Club was organized as a choral society in 1871. In 1978, the club moved from its previous location in Schenectady to this building at 850 Middle Street in Niskayuna. The building, dating to 1929, was originally the headquarters of the Aqueduct Rod and Gun Club. The Schenectady Liederkranz Club disbanded in 2005, and the building is now a private home. (Francis Taormina.)

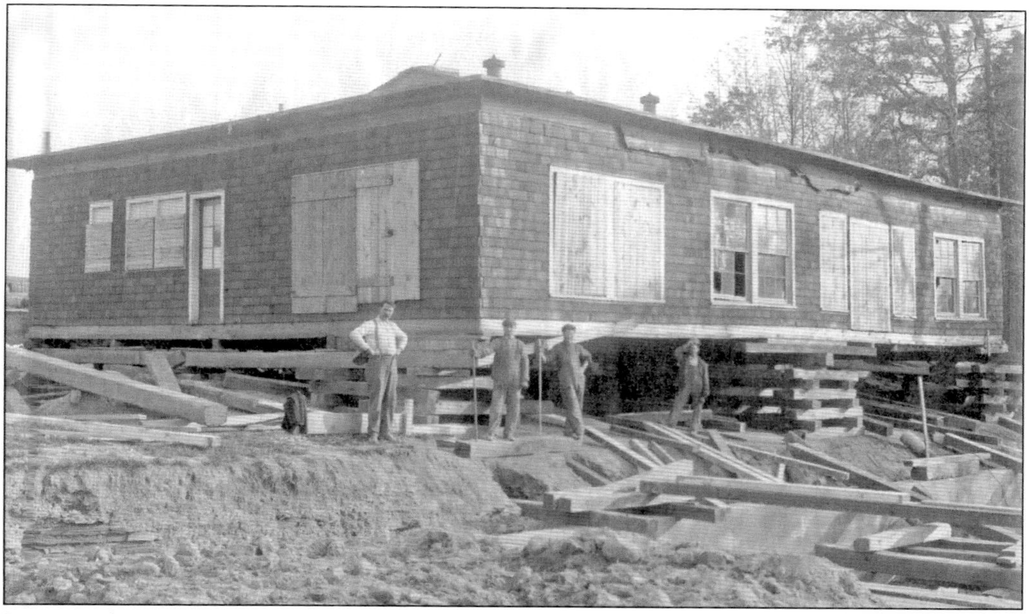

In 1908, this structure was moved from Hillside Avenue to an eight-acre site on Aqueduct Road to form the core of the American Locomotive Club. The American Locomotive Company (ALCO) established the club for use as a social organization for its employees. When ALCO withdrew financial support in 1959, disappointed members acquired the property and began to operate it as the Niskayuna Club, open to all willing to pay dues. (Richard Masse.)

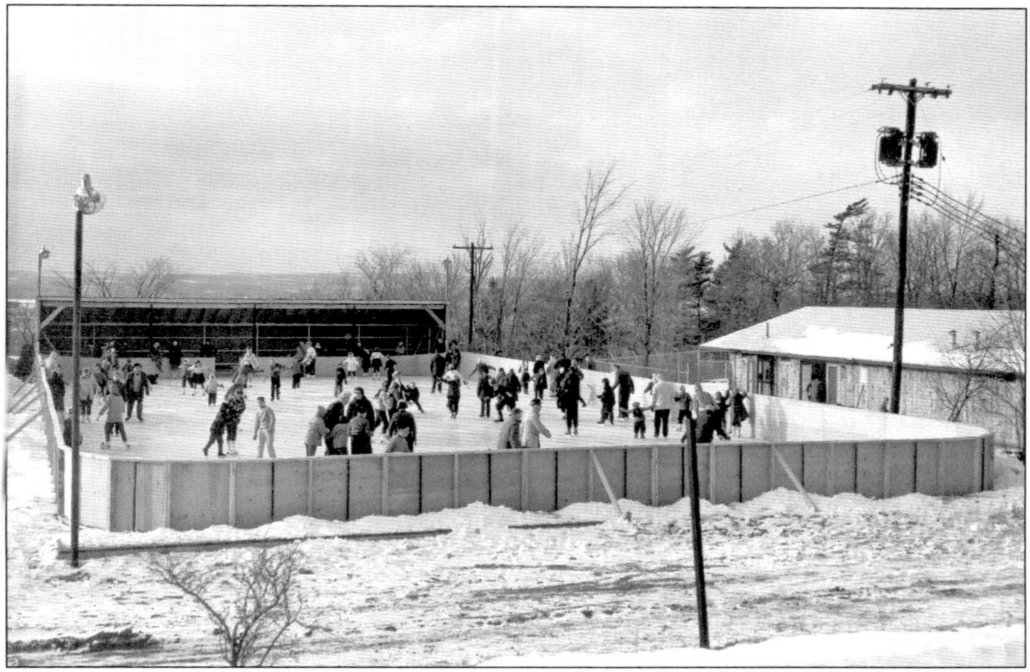

In 1961, the Niskayuna Club built a swimming pool and an outdoor skating rink. The photograph shows many good skates enjoying the rink on opening day in 1962. (Richard Masse.)

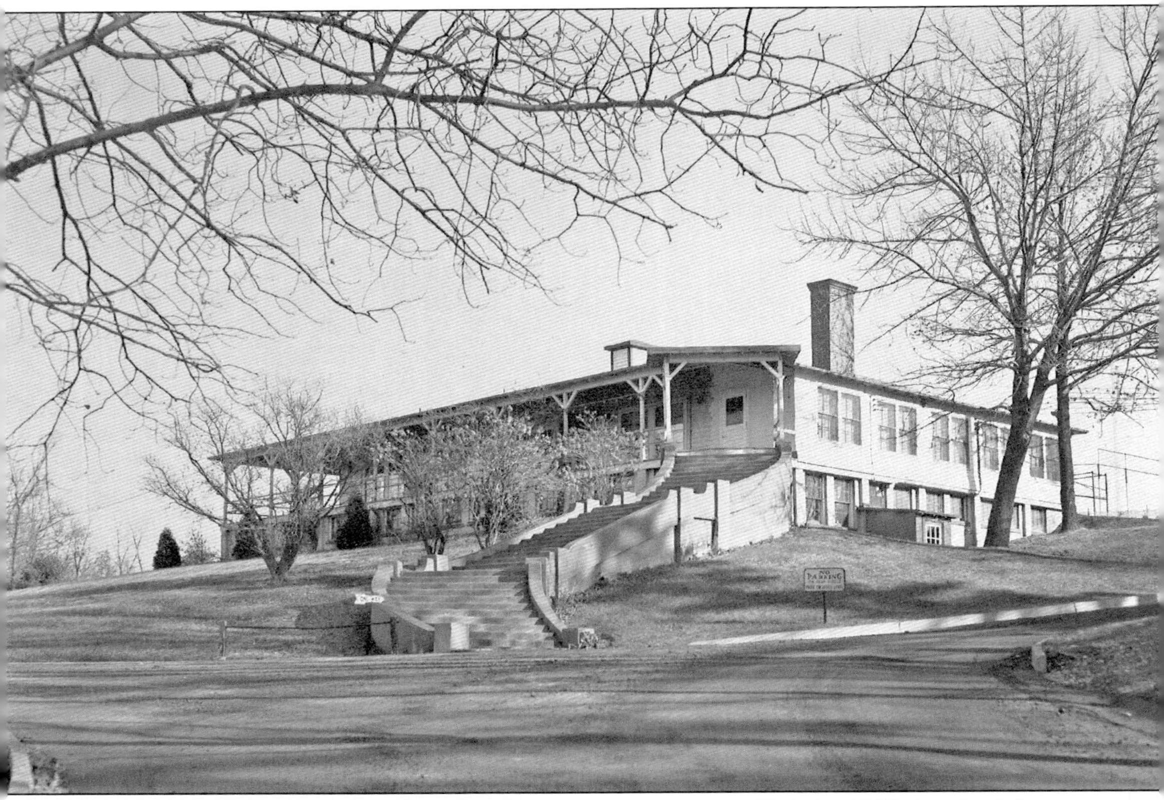

This building, constructed as the American Locomotive Club in 1908, has had five owners, each with interesting stories to tell but not all happy ones. This photograph shows the building as the Niskayuna Club in 1968, about two years before its nine-year run ended in bankruptcy. In 1970, Union College bought the club and 42 adjoining acres with a gift from Union trustee and alumnus W. S. Girling, class of 1917. Union College named it the Wallace S. Girling Center in his honor. He died in peace five months later. In 1990, Union Collge sold the now 50-acre parcel to the Lawrence Insurance Group, which removed the grand outdoor staircase, converted the interior to office space, and leased the outdoor pool to the Town of Niskayuna. Owner Albert Lawrence considered the site to be his company's world headquarters, but business turned sour, and he sold the premises to the town in 1998 for $400,000. The outdoor skating rink is gone, but the pool survived, and the building has become a very active community center. (Richard Masse.)

Two

TRANSPORTATION

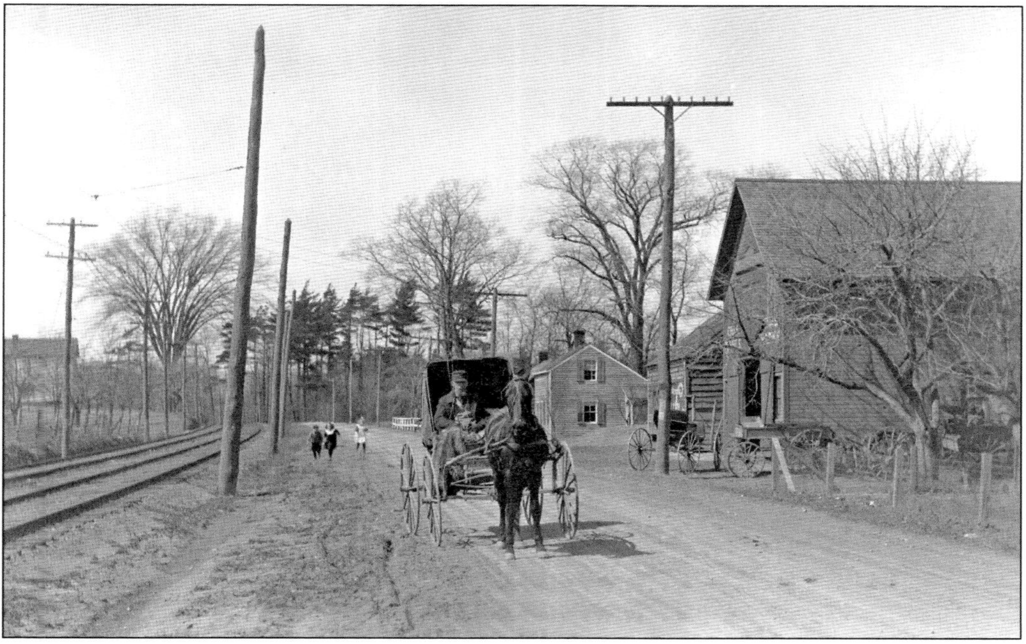

Looking west along the Troy–Schenectady Road in the 1890s, the King home is on the left. Charlie Marks's blacksmith shop and house are to the right. The person in the buggy may well be Nick Van Vranken, who had been town supervisor from 1869 to 1870. Later the development of paved roads and automobiles made it possible for Niskayuna residents to travel throughout the capital region to work and shop. (SCHS.)

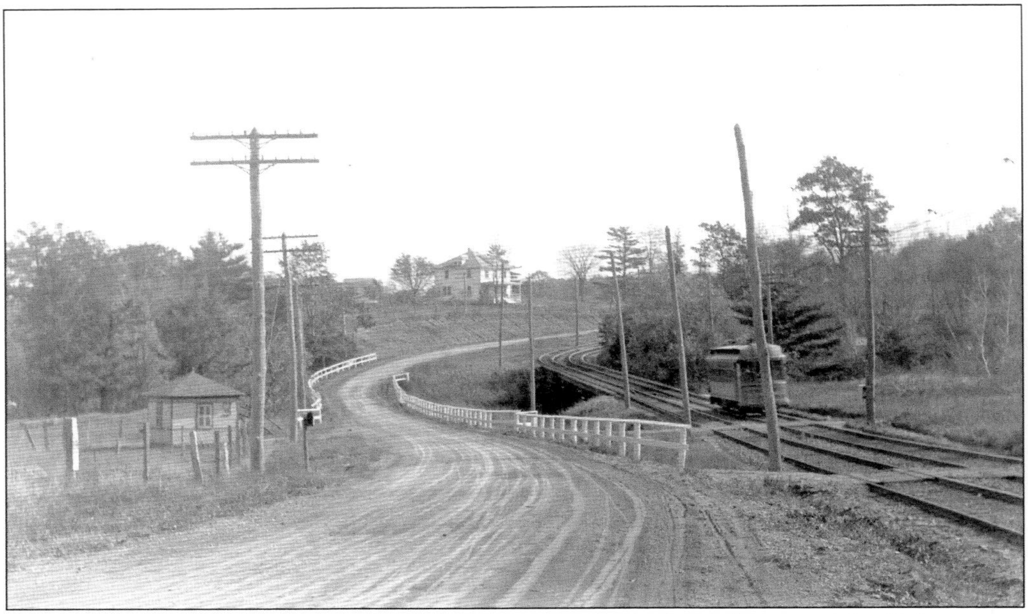

Trolleys became the primary form of public transportation in the early years of the 20th century. The Schenectady Railway Company, founded in 1895, developed the interurban lines from Schenectady to Albany, Troy, and Saratoga between 1902 and 1904. This picture from 1912 shows the area along Troy Road near the Niskayuna Reformed Church. (Efner City History Center.)

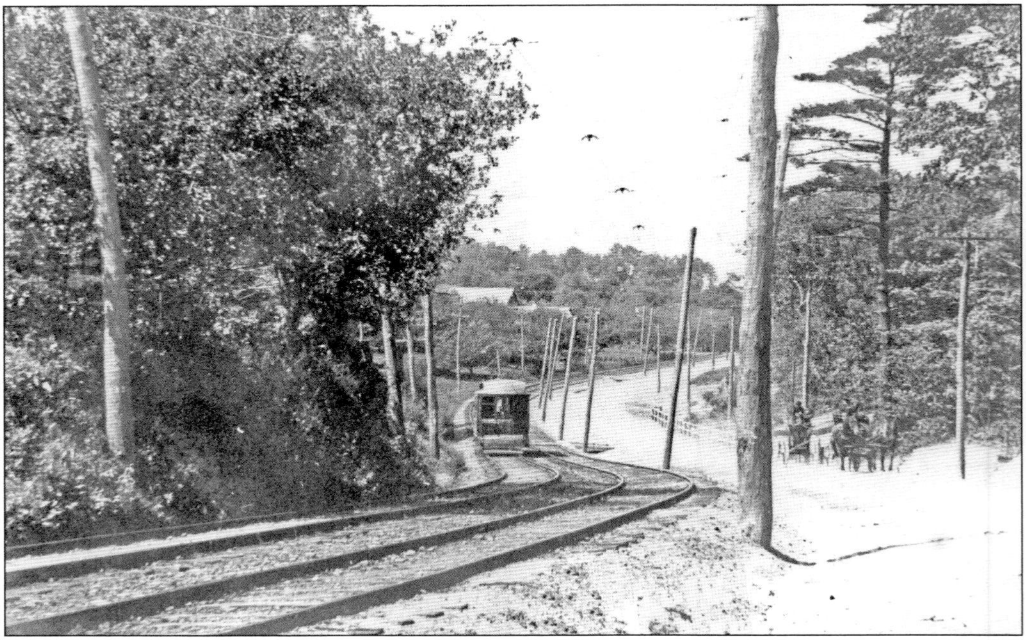

Pictured in 1912 is the same area as above but facing west, showing an eastbound trolley between Niskayuna Road and Vly Road heading toward Schenectady. The Rice farm building can be seen in the left background. Note the two horse-drawn wagons on the right. Starting with two miles of track and four cars in 1895 and expanding to 124 miles and 160 cars by 1904, the trolley was instrumental in the development of Niskayuna. (Efner City History Center.)

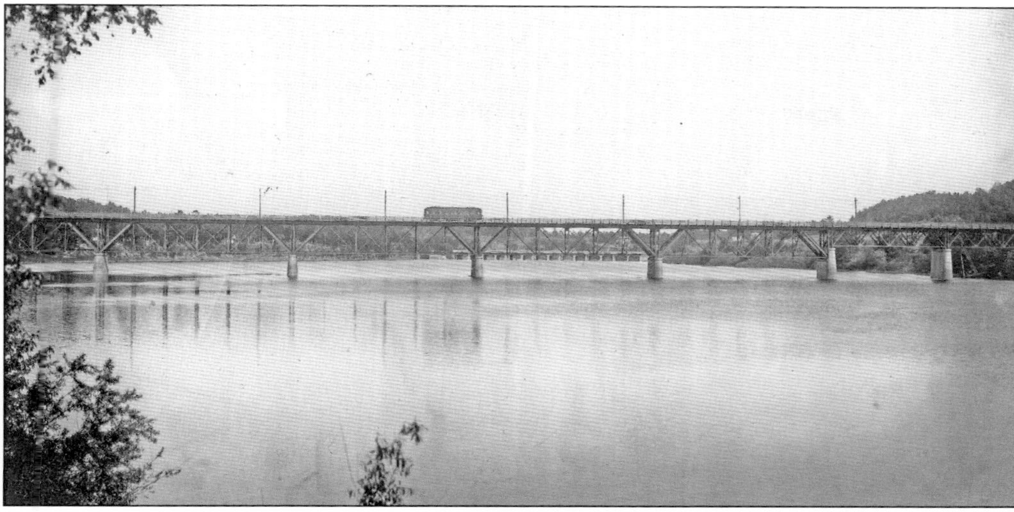

Spanning the Mohawk River between Aqueduct Road in Niskayuna and Alplaus Avenue in Glenville, this bridge was known simply as the trolley bridge and billed as "the longest trolley bridge in the world." When the Schenectady Railway Company expanded its lines between 1902 and 1904, it included the run to Saratoga with a stop at Luna Park (later Dolle's Park) in Rexford. This photograph was taken in about 1904. (SCHS.)

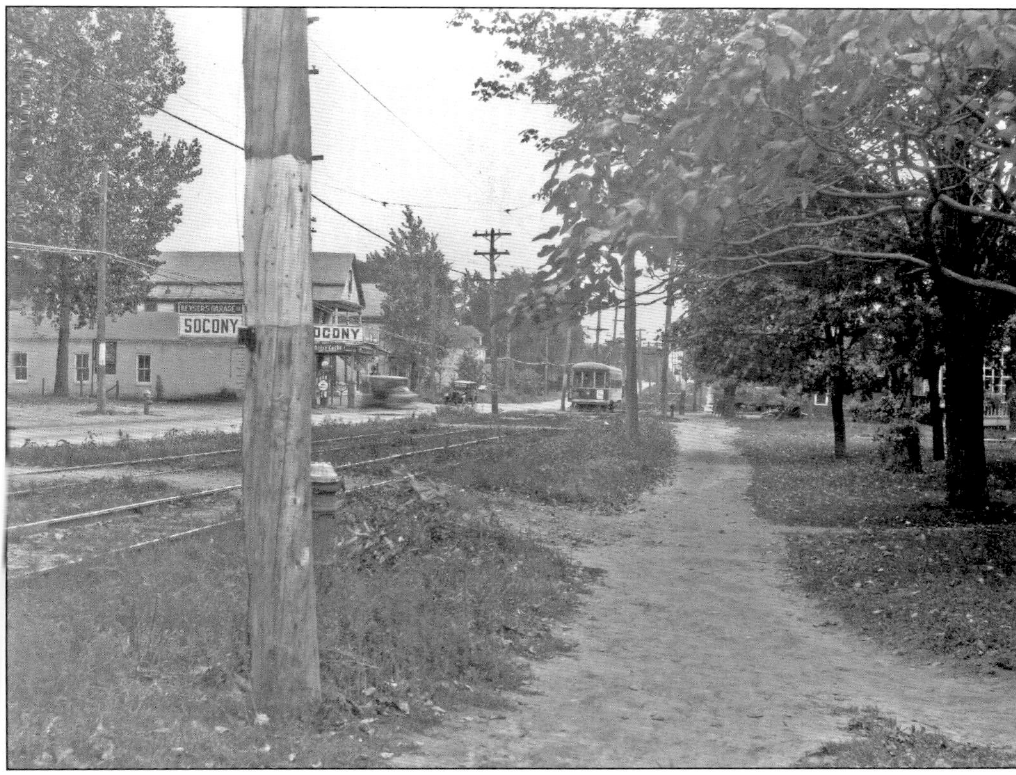

The photograph shows the Schenectady Railway Company's trolley on upper State Street near Barringer Street. Note the Socony gasoline station on the left. The photograph is undated. (SCHS, John Papp Collection.)

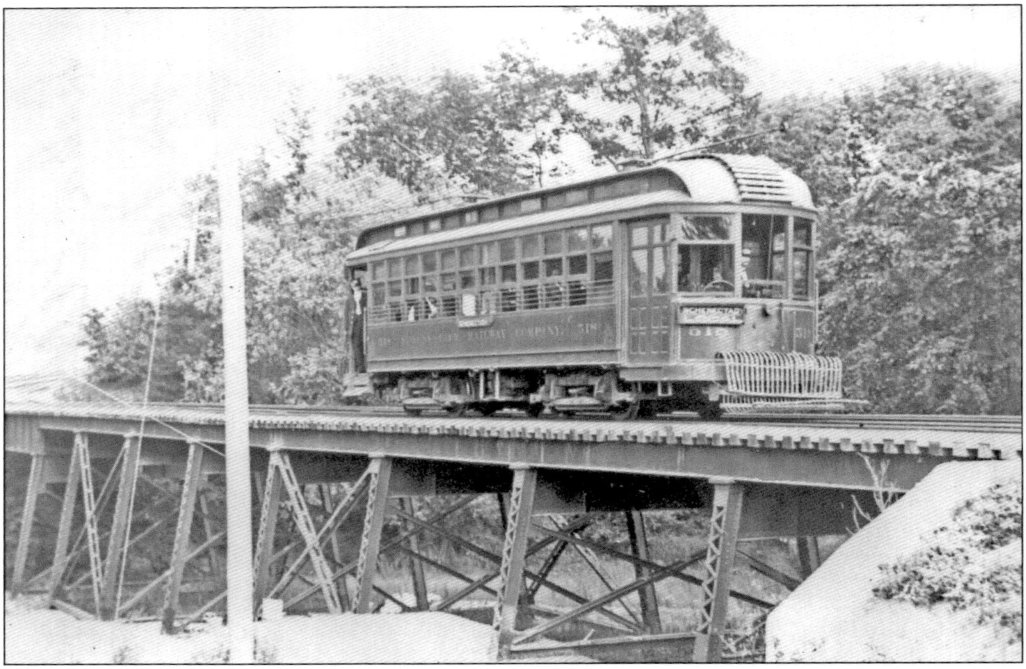

Here is a trolley car crossing the steel bridge over the Lisha Kill Creek in about 1920. Note that there are both a driver and conductor on this crowded car. Fares on the Troy–Schenectady line at the time were 7¢ per zone, with about 12 stops. (Efner City History Center.)

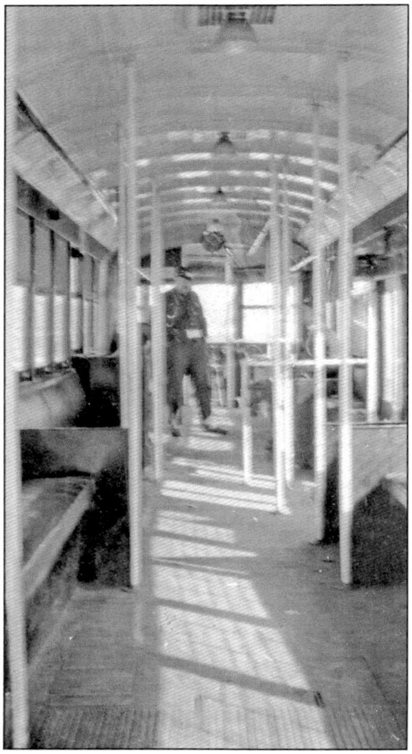

This view of the interior of a trolley shows conductor Joseph Cerveny on a car going from Schenectady to Rosendale Road. The Schenectady Railway Company provided employment to a large number of local residents for many years. By the early 1930s, buses had replaced the trolleys, and the tracks were removed. Uninterrupted public transit from Troy through Schenectady and continuing north to Saratoga would never again be anywhere near as rapid, effective, and inexpensive. (Paul Pakan.)

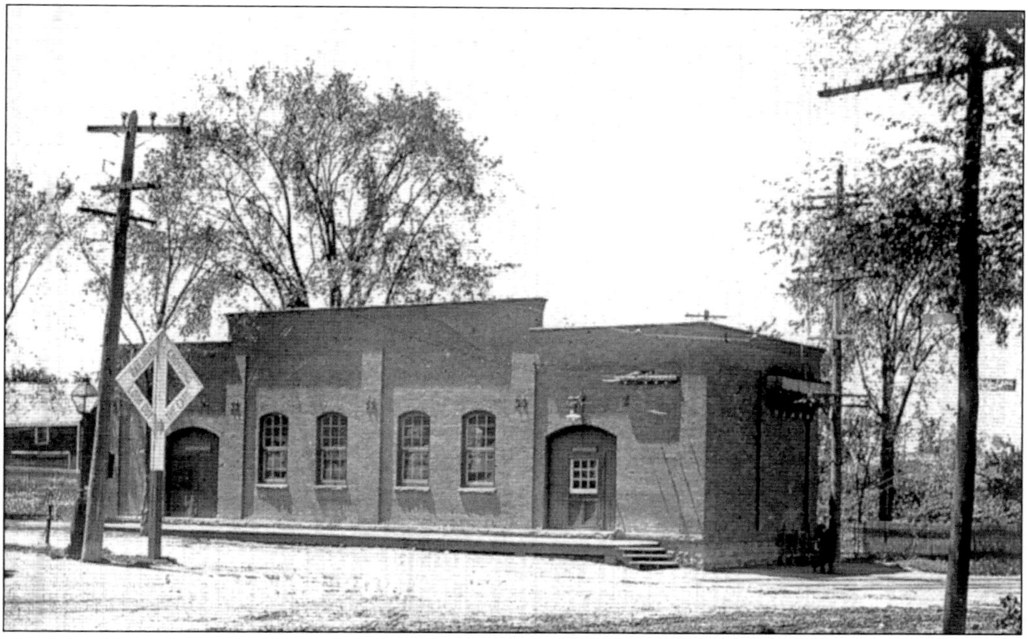

This Latham generating station in Colonie provided power for the Schenectady Railway Company. It controlled the electrical power for the trolleys running through Niskayuna along the Troy–Schenectady Road. (Kevin Franklin.)

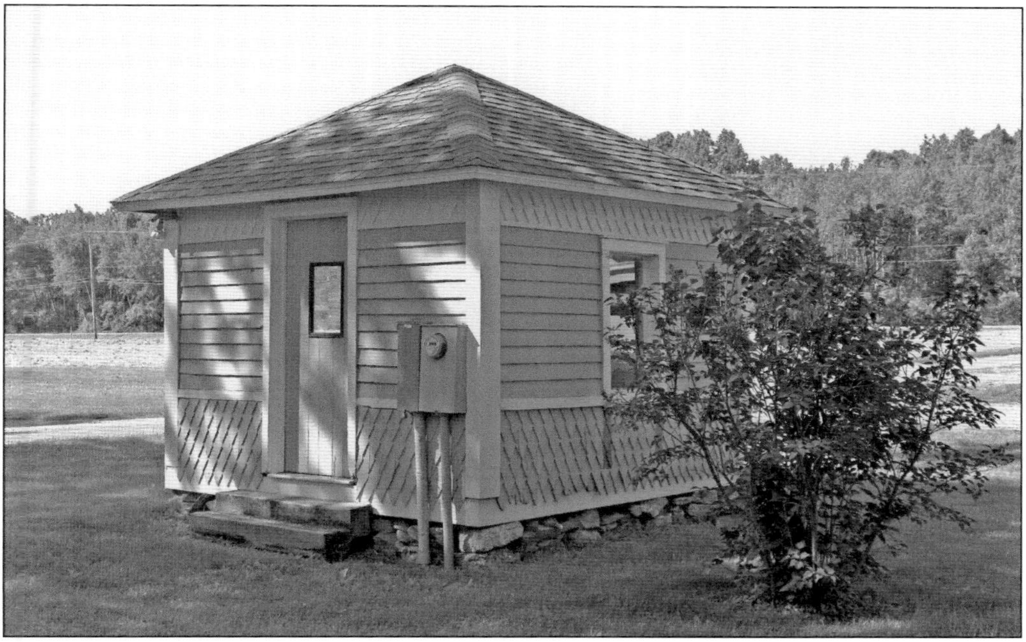

This trolley stop building, used from 1903 until 1936, was located at stop No. 14, just east of what is now the Holy Redeemer Cemetery on the Troy–Schenectady Road. It was originally located on part of the extensive property of Union College biology professor William T. Winne (1913–1998) that is now part of the cemetery. The shelter was donated to the SCHS by Nancy Holsberger and is currently displayed at its Mabee Farm Historic Site. (SCHS.)

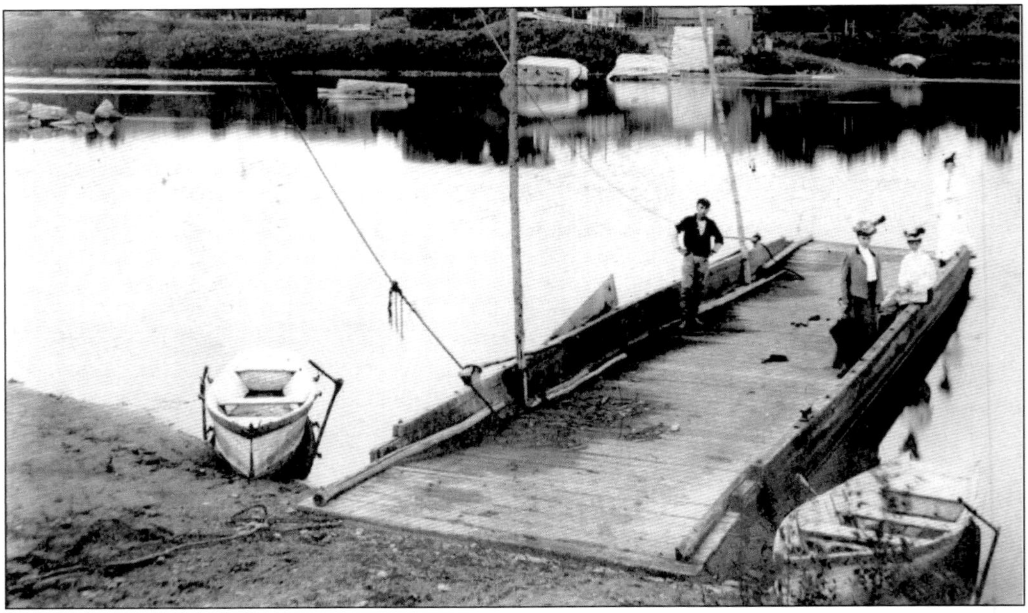

The ferry scow at the southern landing of Vischer's Ferry is pictured here in 1908. The ferry was used to cross the Mohawk River and the adjacent Erie Canal on the northern side to connect the Rosendale hamlet to Saratoga County. The ferry, initiated by Eldert Vischer in 1790, operated until 1923. The abutments for a nearby short-lived bridge that was destroyed by ice floes are visible in the picture. (Office of the Clifton Park Town Historian.)

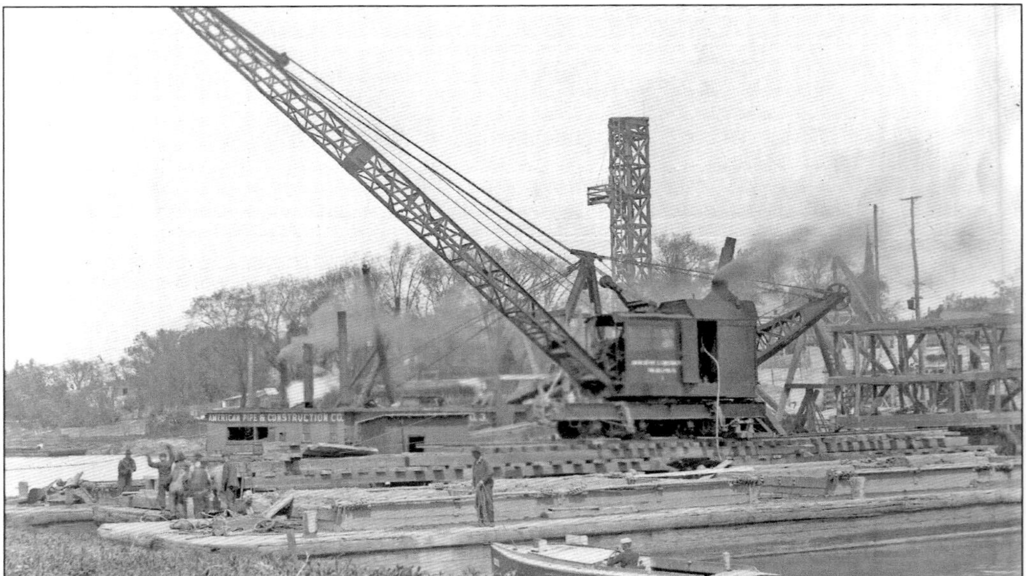

The Erie Canal and later the New York State Barge Canal played an important role in Niskayuna's early development. This 1914 photograph shows the construction of Lock 7 using steam-driven equipment. The original building and lock were located in Saratoga County on the north side of the Mohawk River. When the barge canal was created, the present Lock 7 and control building were built on the Schenectady County side of the canal in Niskayuna. (SCHS.)

This is the powerhouse at Lock 7 in Niskayuna. The New York State Barge Canal, still often referred to as the Erie Canal, was built between 1915 and 1918 to replace the original Erie Canal. (SCHS.)

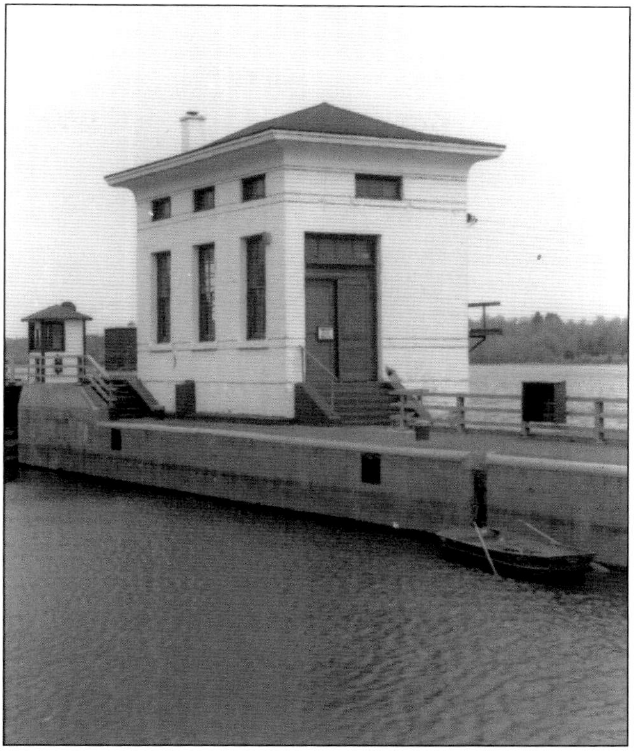

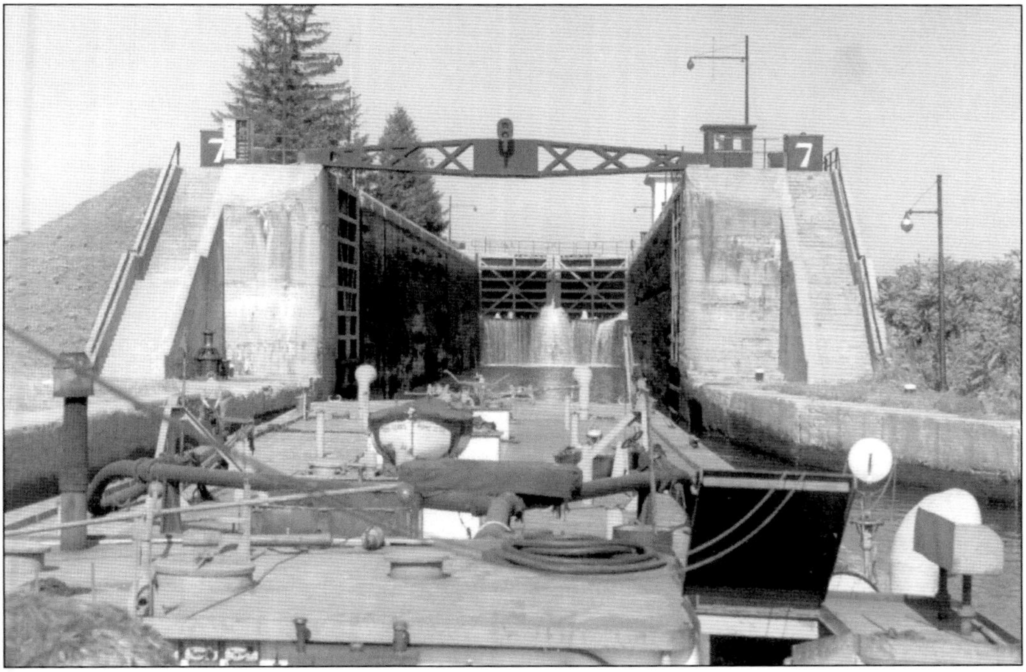

A tugboat makes its way into Lock 7 of the Erie Canal at Niskayuna. Although pleasure craft are the most common users of the canal, the New York State Canal Corporation is trying to encourage more commercial traffic to use it. (SCHS.)

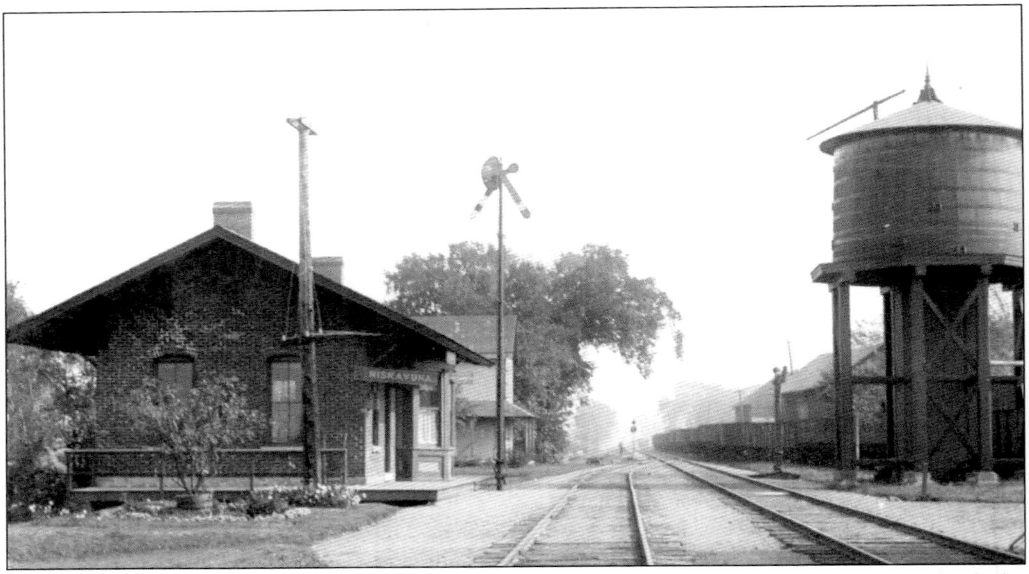

The railroad station near the eastern end of Rosendale Road in Niskayuna was built by the Troy and Schenectady Railroad in 1843. It later became part of the New York Central Railroad. The station was constructed using local lumber and bricks made in Niskayuna. The water tank was removed in 1925 as was the privy behind the station. (Office of the Town of Colonie Historian.)

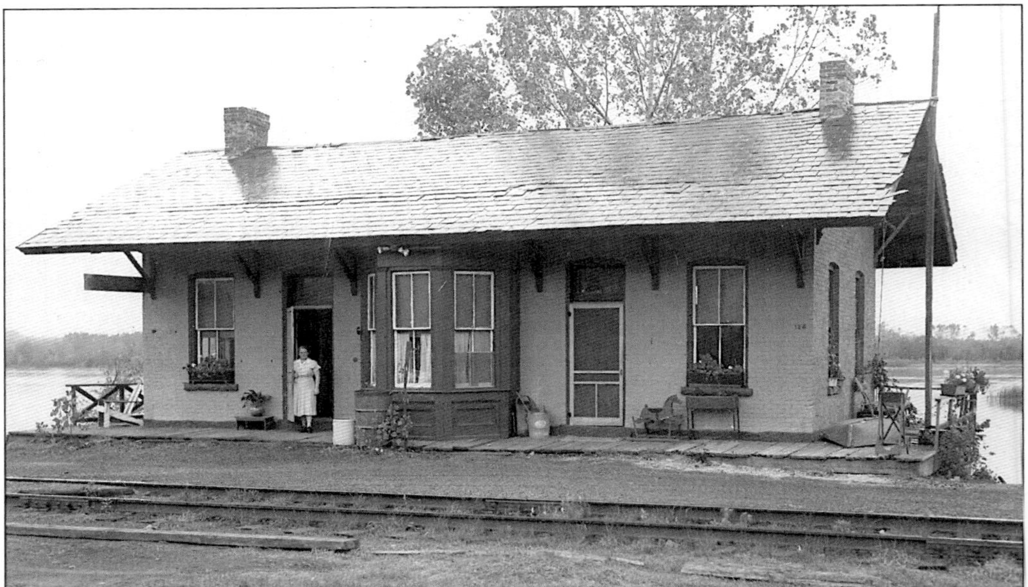

When passenger traffic on the Troy and Schenectady Railroad ceased in 1923, the Niskayuna station was rented for private use. During the 1950s, the railroad station was converted to a private residence. (Efner City History Center.)

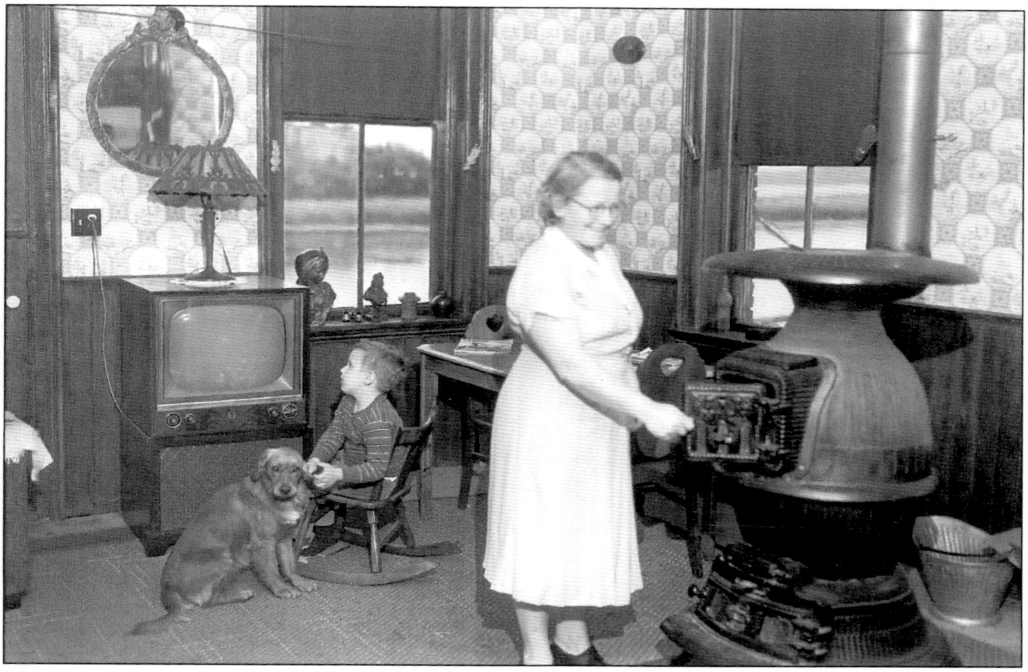

This interior photograph of the railroad station shows its transformation into a home. Note the stark contrast between the old stove and the 1950s-era television. The stationmaster's office was converted for use as a kitchen. (Efner City History Center.)

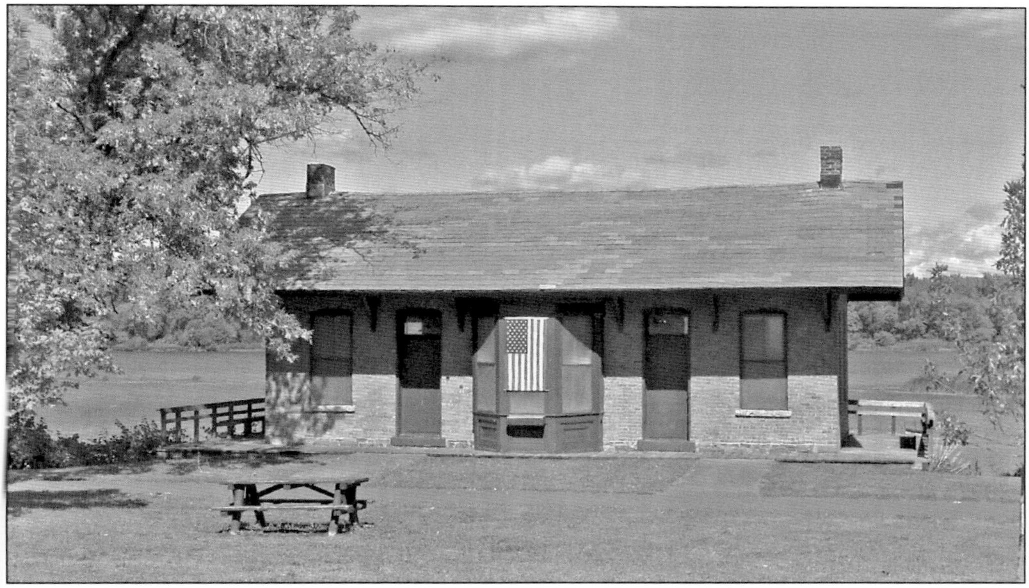

Today the station, which was restored as a 1976 bicentennial project, is a popular stop on the hike-and-bike trail that follows the old railroad tracks. A picnic area extends farther to the left beyond the range of the picture. Extensive parking and newly added restrooms between the station and Rosendale Road make this a very busy spot on weekends all year long, especially spring through fall. (SCHS.)

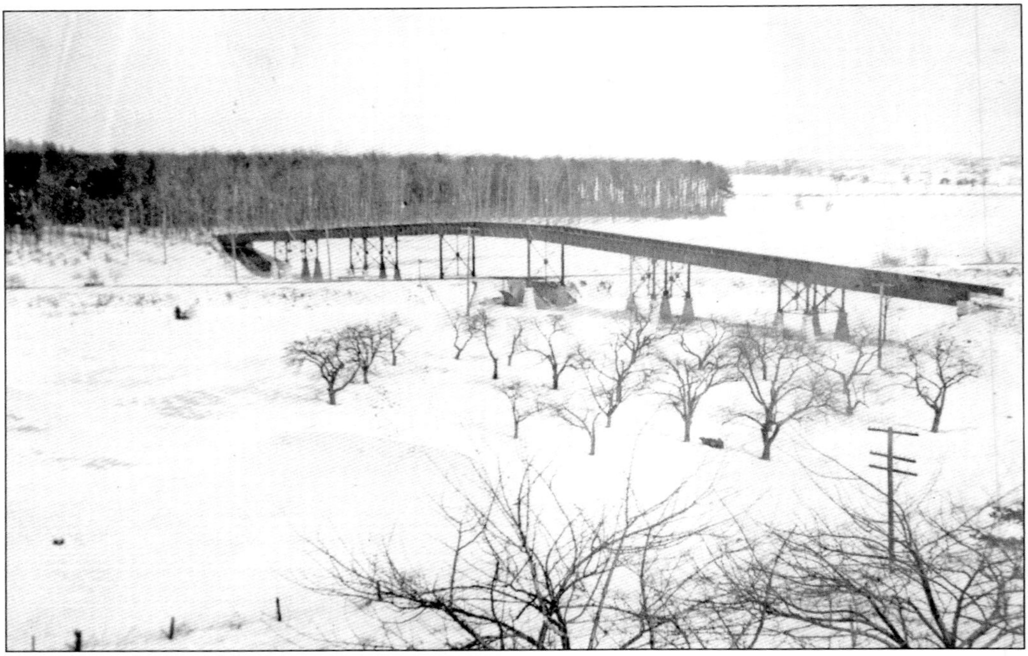

This early picture shows the Niska Isle Bridge in winter. Driving over this bridge is not for the faint of heart, although it is done regularly by residents of the "isle," which is actually a peninsula almost as wide as it is long. (Efner City History Center.)

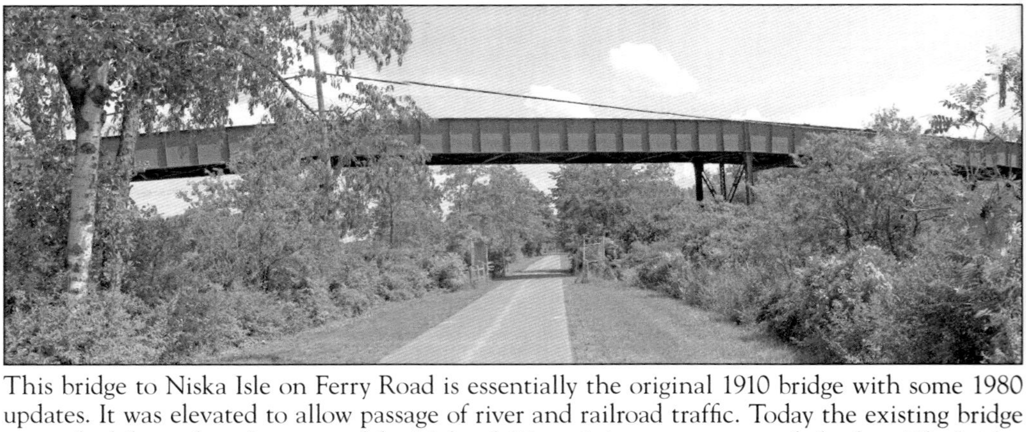

This bridge to Niska Isle on Ferry Road is essentially the original 1910 bridge with some 1980 updates. It was elevated to allow passage of river and railroad traffic. Today the existing bridge spans the bike path and an arm of the Mohawk River. It is very narrow and obsolete. The bridge is scheduled for replacement in the near future. (SCHS.)

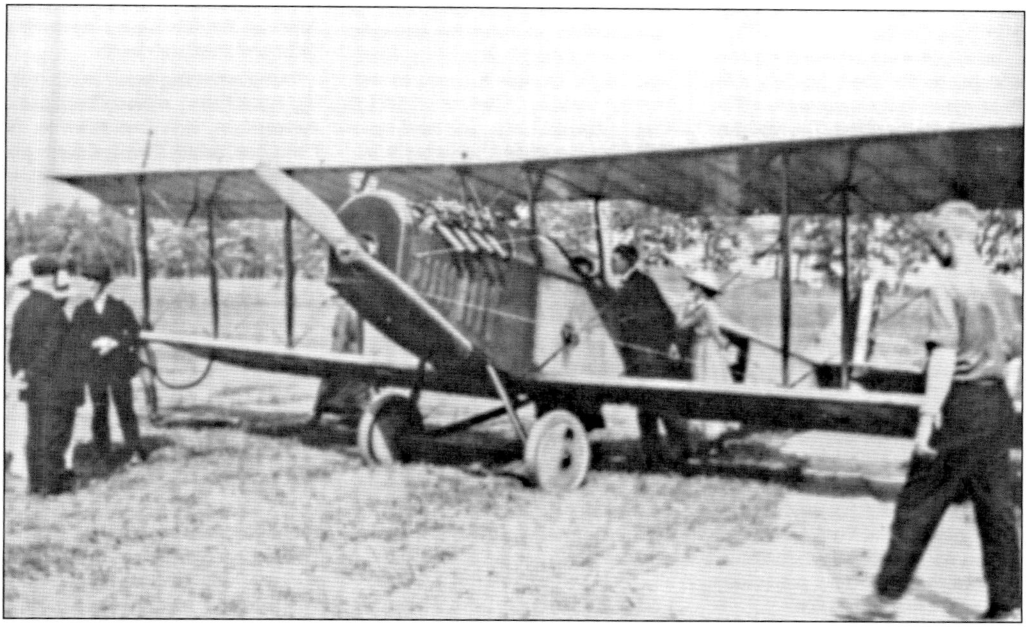

Onlookers gather excitedly around a biplane that has just landed on a grass airfield off Eastholm Road in 1914. Niskayuna once extended farther to the southwest, including what is now the Woodlawn section of Schenectady. (Photograph reprinted with permission from *The Best of Old Dorp* by Larry Hart.)

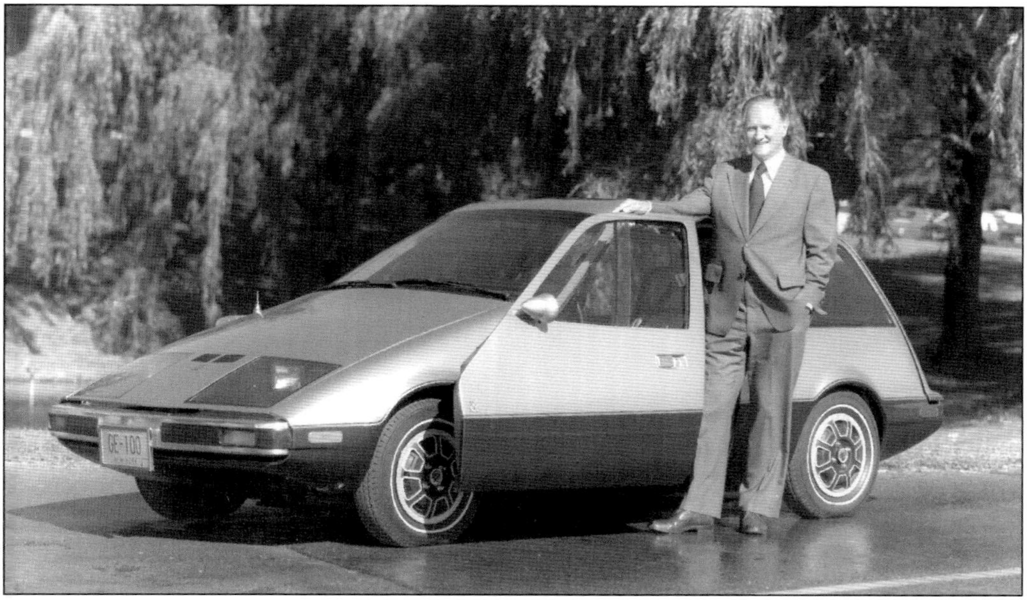

Niskayuna resident Jim Lafferty of the General Electric Research and Development Center poses with the GE-100 electric car. For its 1978 centennial, General Electric showcased it to demonstrate how well an electric car could perform. The engineers who designed the vehicle estimated that if 100,0000 were mass-produced, the car could be sold for $6,000. That never happened, but the project foreshadowed the hybrid and electric vehicles that are beginning to take hold 30 years later. (Schenectady Museum.)

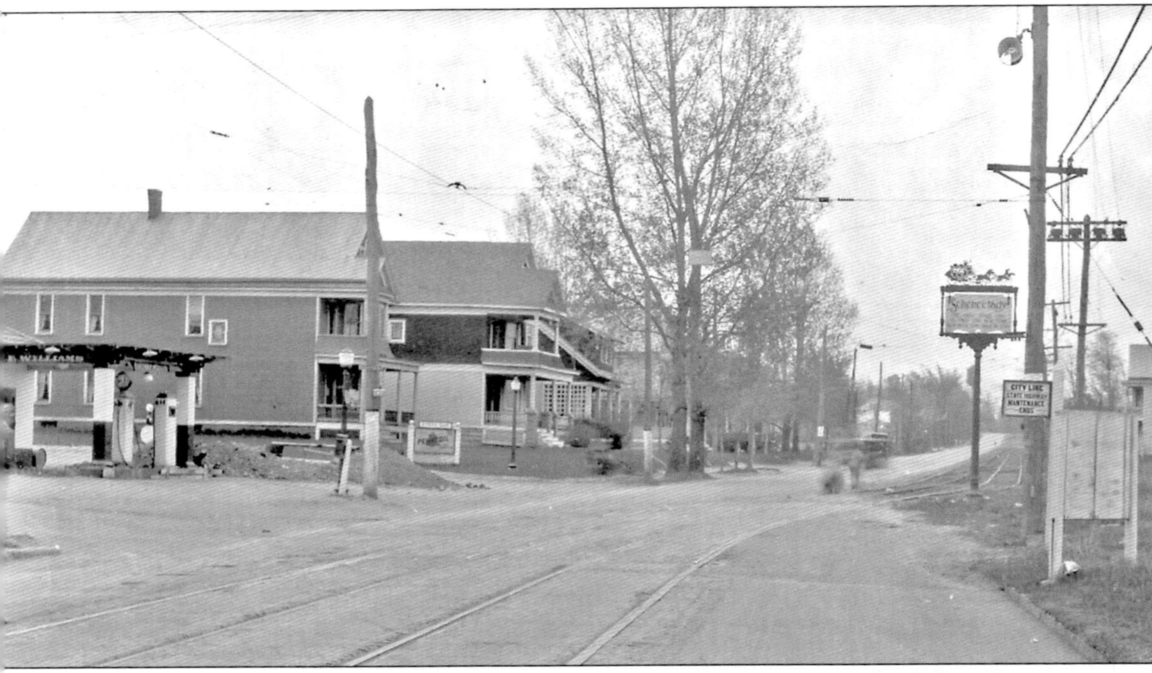

Here is Union Street looking east toward Troy Road in 1928. On the left is Van Antwerp Road. The double trolley tracks of the Schenectady Railway Company that connected with the interurban lines to Troy were removed in the mid-1930s. The historic marker at the city line, one of three, commemorates the first stage route to Albany in 1795. The marker was removed when the tracks were torn up. (SCHS.)

Three

BUSINESS AND INDUSTRY

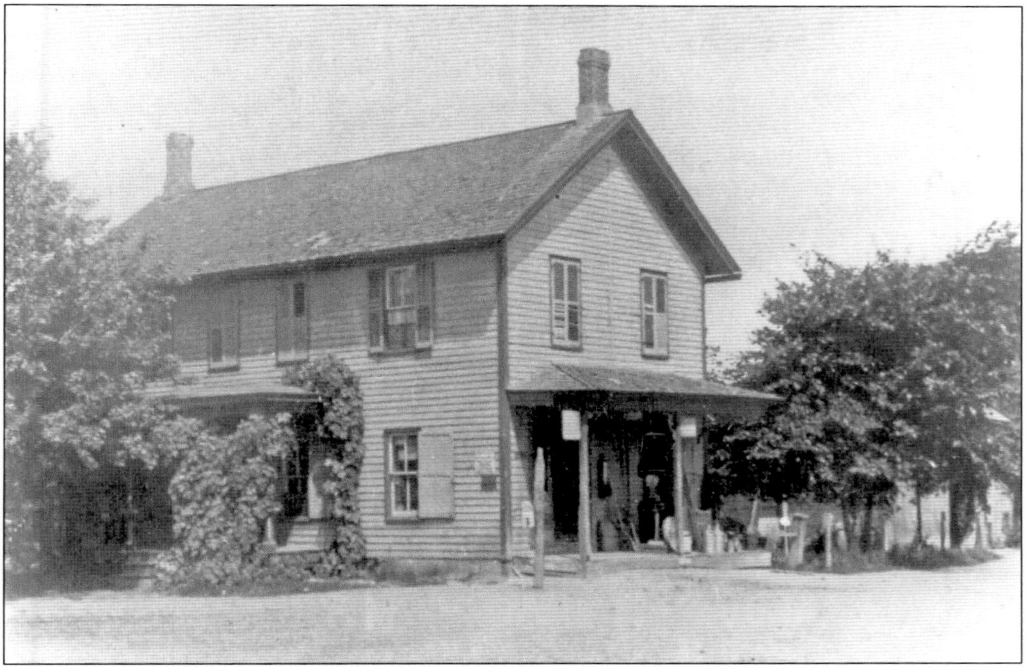

This building on the corner of Rosendale and Troy Roads opposite Vly Road was built in 1844. John P. Miller was the first to operate a general store there from 1877 to 1896. Charles Marks then bought the store and operated it until the Marks' family sold it to Charles Denison in 1930. When Charles Denison died in 1961, his son Charles Jr. and his wife Margaret operated the business as a general store and contract post office until 1970. When they retired that year, their longtime clerks Mildred Felpel and Joseph Chernichek did so too. The loss of the operating store and post office that the whole community loved was a sad event, and when the new owner demolished it and replaced it with a gasoline station, the wound deepened further. The station did not prosper and is itself gone, leaving only its vestige in the form of steel canopies that no longer have gas pumps to protect. (Efner City History Center.)

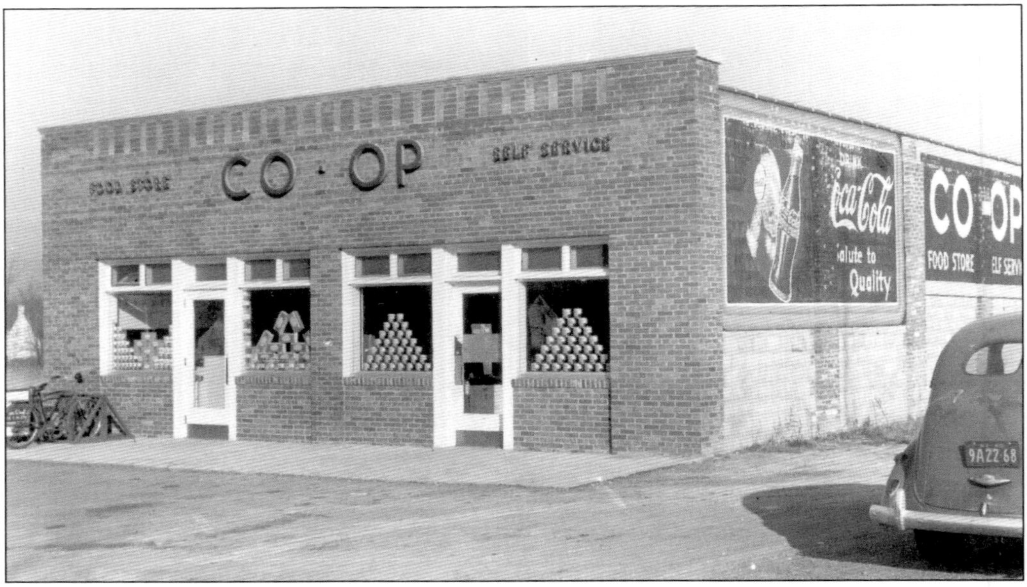

The Niskayuna Consumer's Co-operative (CO-OP) on Nott Street near Balltown Road was organized in 1943 by 300 area residents, led by Abraham Lincoln Marshall (1896–1974), manager of the General Electric Chemical Research Department. Shares were sold, and the building was constructed of donated bricks for $12,000. For over 60 years, it has been a Niskayuna institution, a relatively small neighborhood market whose shoppers know one another and who consider it an unofficial community center. (Niskayuna Consumer's Co-operative.)

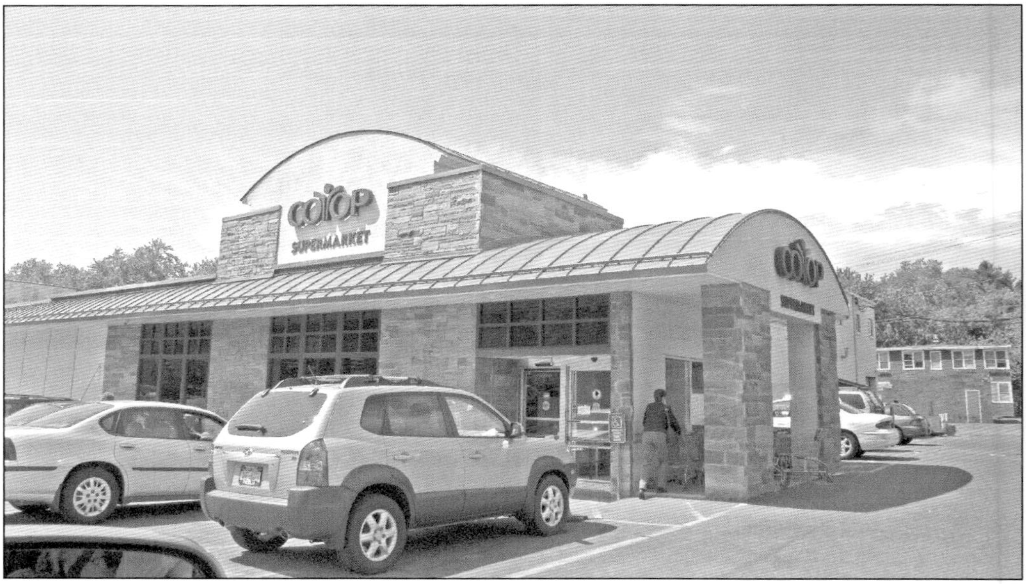

Renovated in 2003, the Niskayuna Consumer's Co-operative still thrives. The building at the rear right is the back of one of the units of the Crescent Road Apartments. The complex was built in 1940 with bricks salvaged from the demolition of the home of General Electric wizard Charles Proteus Steinmetz on Wendell Avenue in Schenectady, despite the efforts of former president Herbert Hoover to save it. Leftover bricks were used to build part of one interior wall of the CO-OP. (SCHS.)

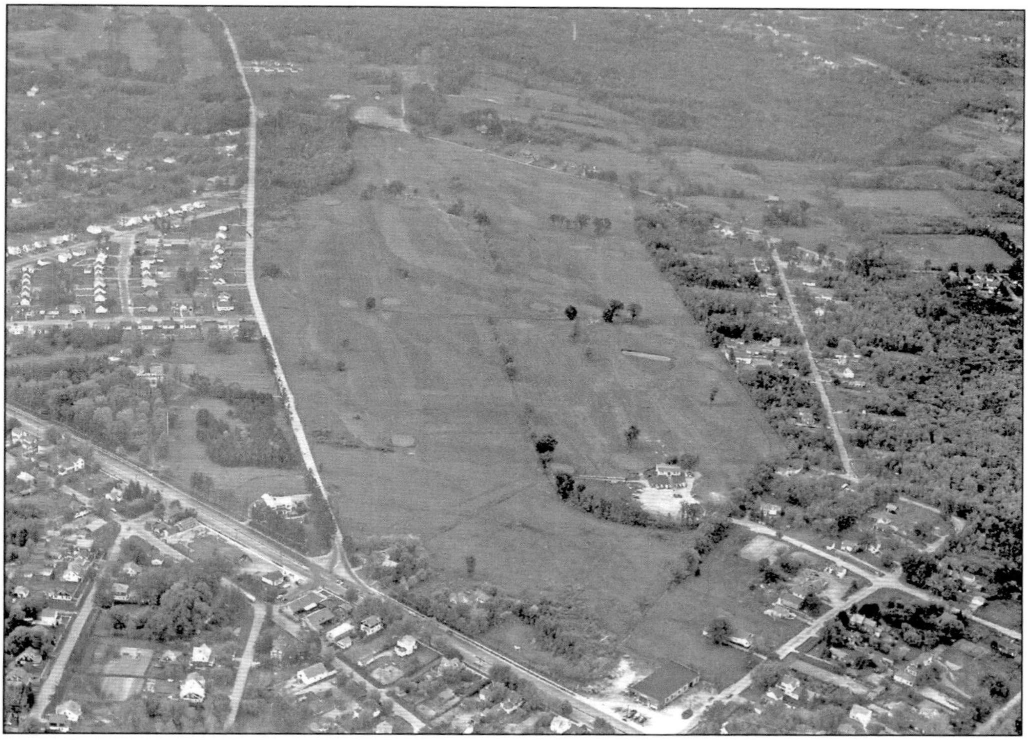

Bounded by Consaul and Balltown Roads and extending nearly to Route 5, the Stanford Golf Club was begun on land that was once a racehorse farm belonging to the Stanford family. James W. Veeder and Edward (Ned) Vrooman of Schenectady were the founders. Here the course is shown as it appeared in 1962. (SCHS, Larry Hart Collection.)

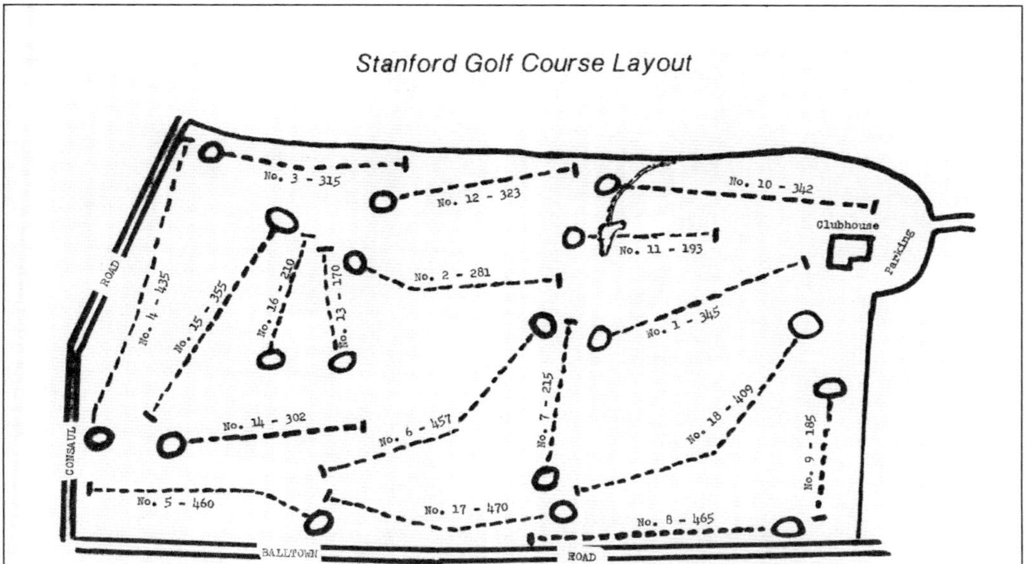

This diagram of the Stanford Golf Course shows the layout of the greens and the playing length of each leg in yards. (SCHS.)

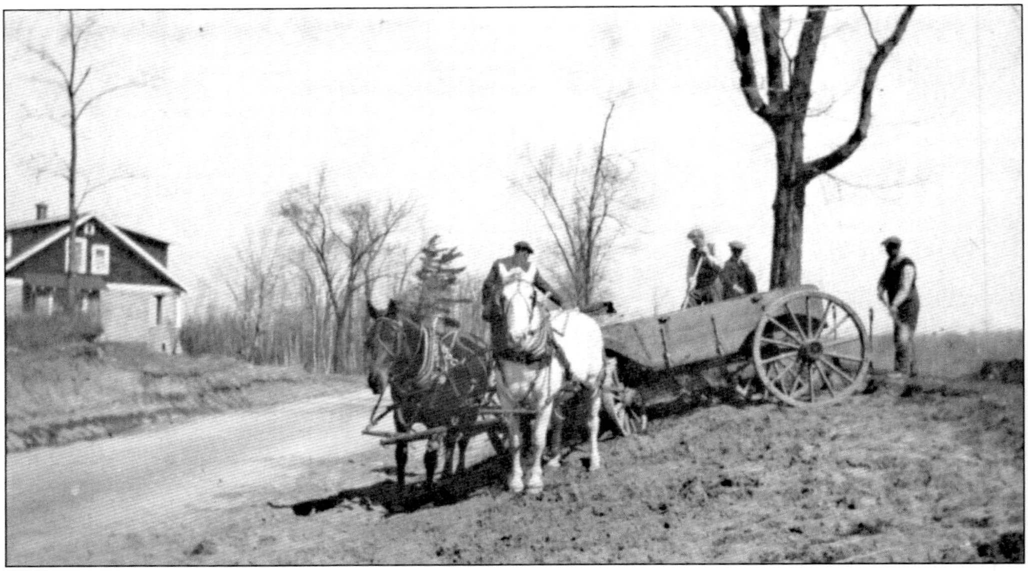

Workmen load up a wagon with sand at a sandbank along Balltown Road. The sand was used in the traps on the Stanford links in May 1925. Construction began in 1924. (SCHS.)

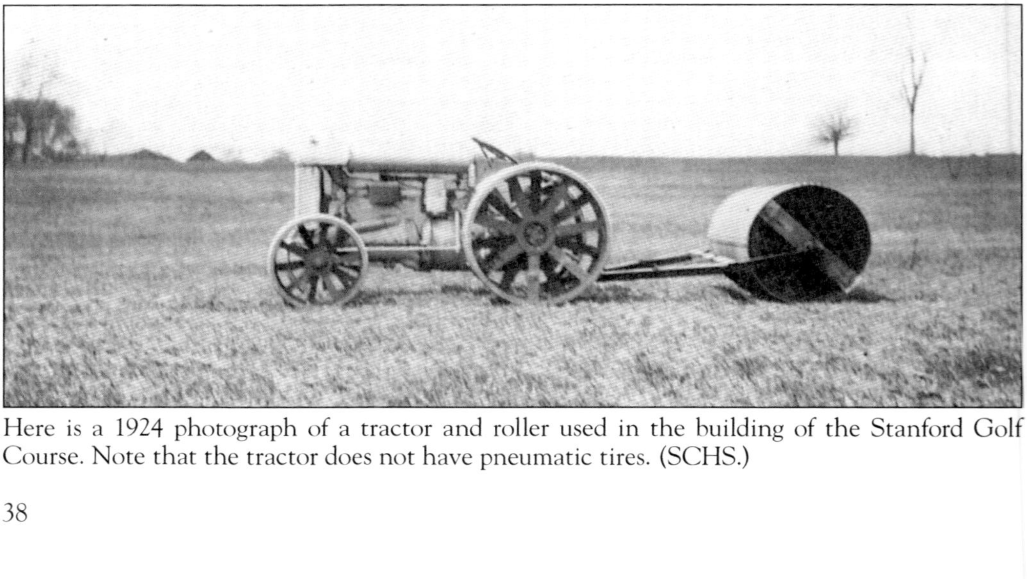

Here is a 1924 photograph of a tractor and roller used in the building of the Stanford Golf Course. Note that the tractor does not have pneumatic tires. (SCHS.)

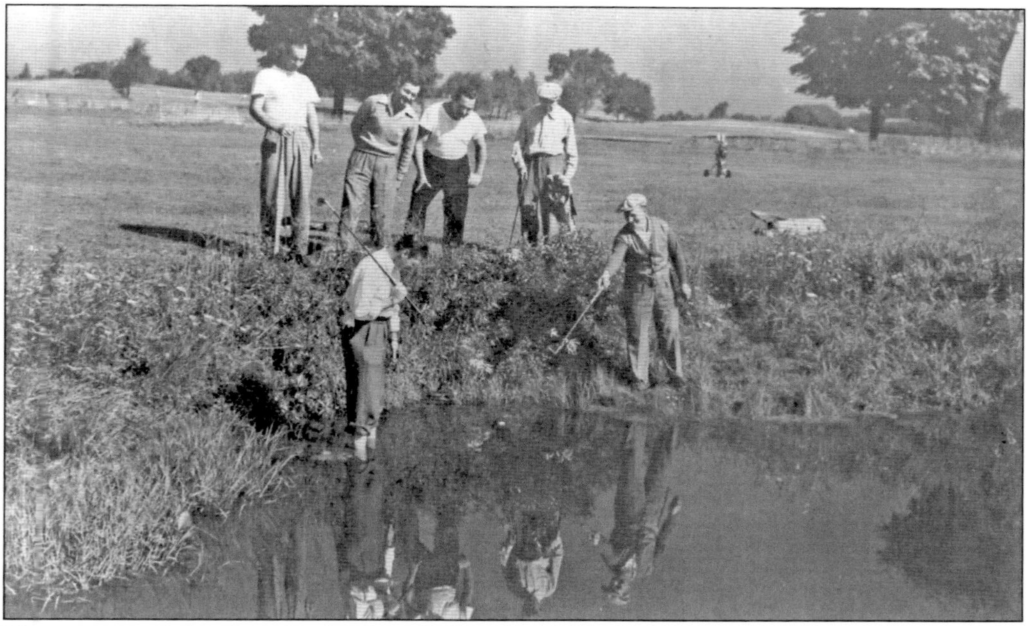

This is a familiar scene at the Stanford Golf Course's "ole watering hole" in front of the 11th green. A helpful golfer points out where his partner's ball has landed in a rather difficult lie while kibitzers look on. Across the gently rolling hills in the far background is Consaul Road. The entire area is now occupied by the Mohawk Commons, Oswald D. Heck Developmental Center, Hannaford supermarket, and other businesses and parking lots. (SCHS.)

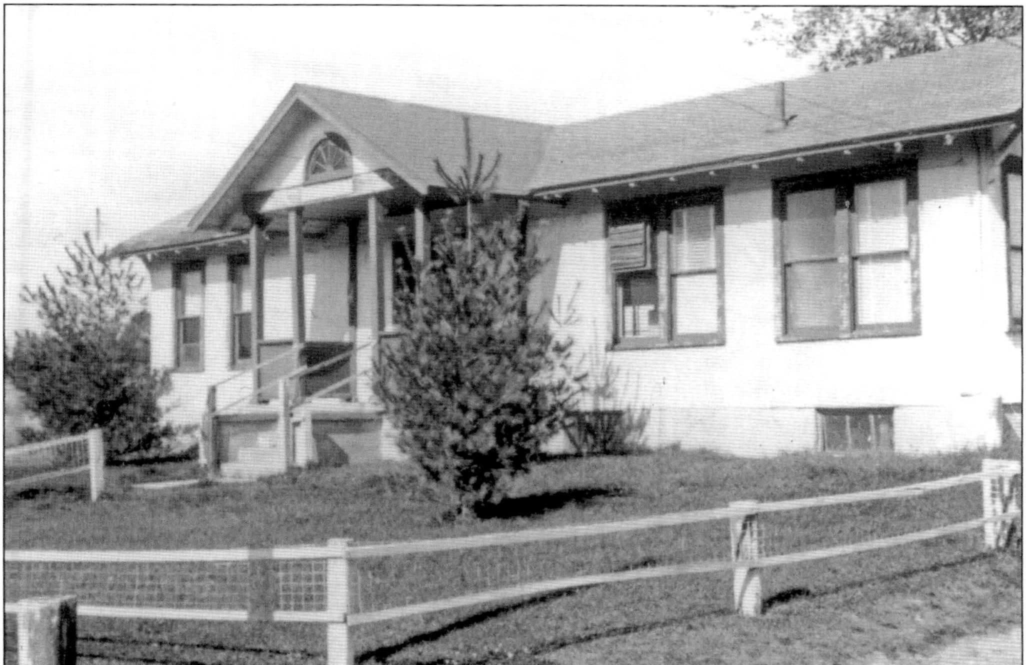

This is the Stanford Golf Course clubhouse in 1968. A year later, ground was broken for the Mohawk Mall, marking the end of the 45-year history of the club and its golf course. (SCHS.)

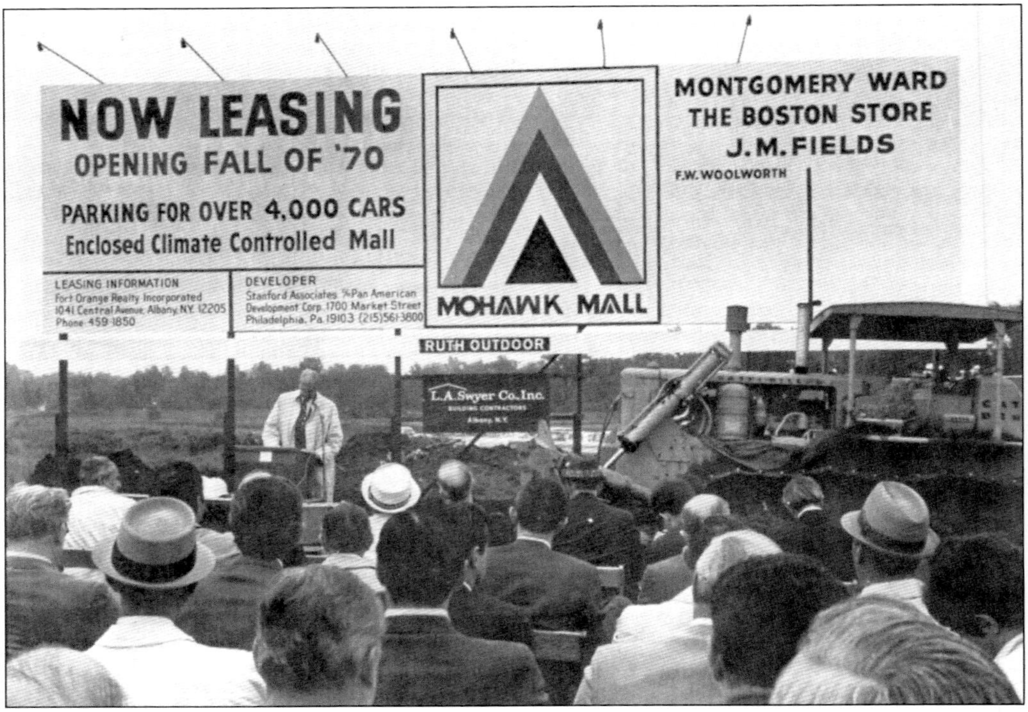

Balltown Road was the location of the groundbreaking ceremony for the Mohawk Mall, a 630,000-square-foot enclosed mall. The parking lot was designed to handle 4,000 cars. The mall opened on October 5, 1970. (SCHS.)

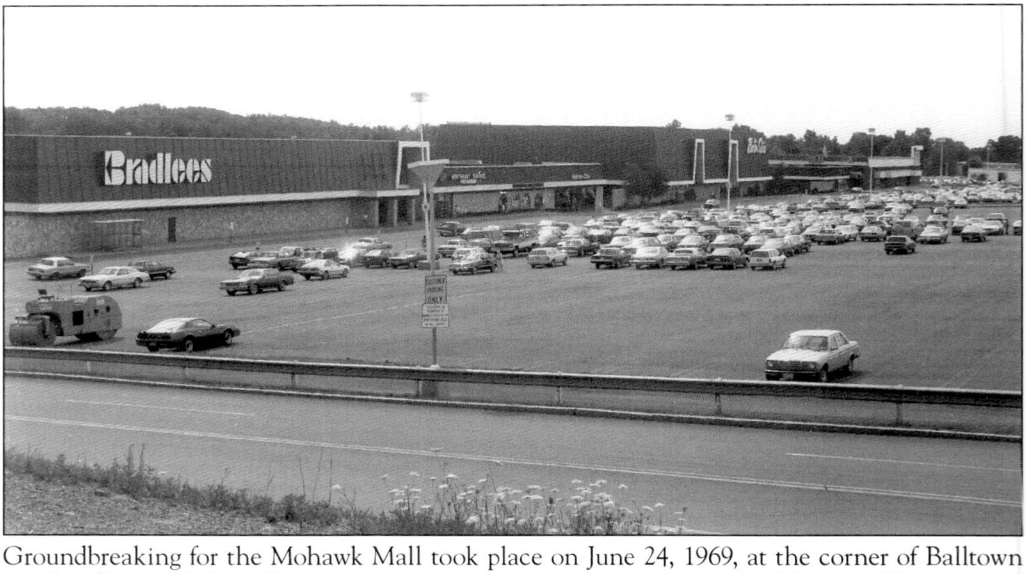

Groundbreaking for the Mohawk Mall took place on June 24, 1969, at the corner of Balltown Road and Route 5 (State Street). It was the site of the former Stanford Golf Course. When opened in the fall of 1970, the original anchor stores were Montgomery Ward, the Boston Store, and J. M. Fields. Bradlees and Price Chopper were later tenants. The Mohawk Mall was demolished in 2000 and replaced by Mohawk Commons. (Efner City History Center.)

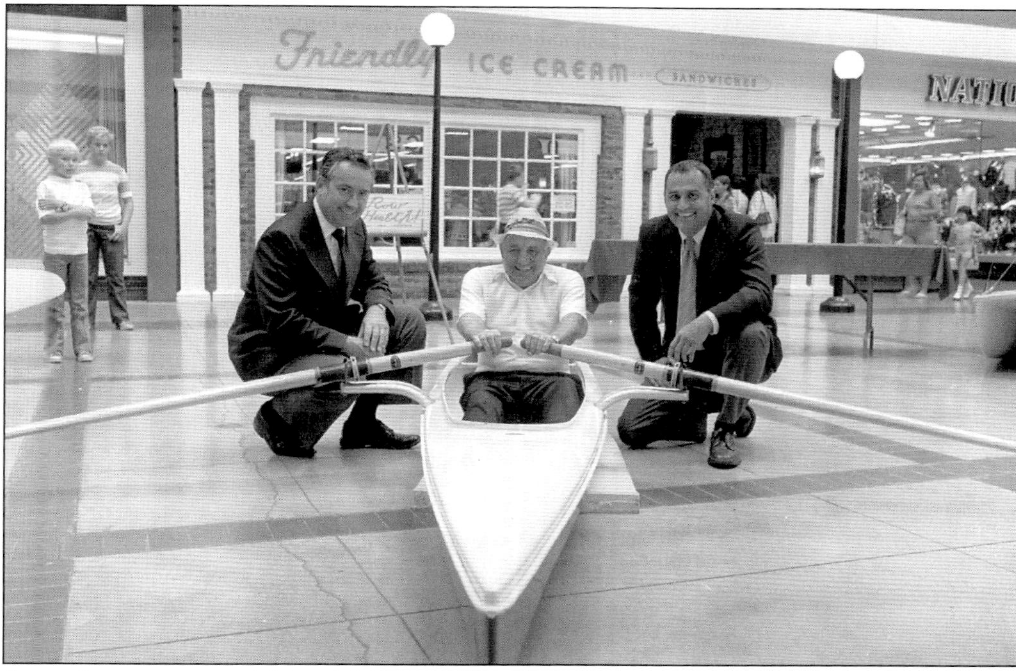

An early promotion at Mohawk Mall in 1973 was for the annual Mohawk Regatta. Pictured in front of the popular Friendly's ice-cream store are television personality Ernie Tetrault, Dick Weber Sr., and Paul Lazier. (SCHS.)

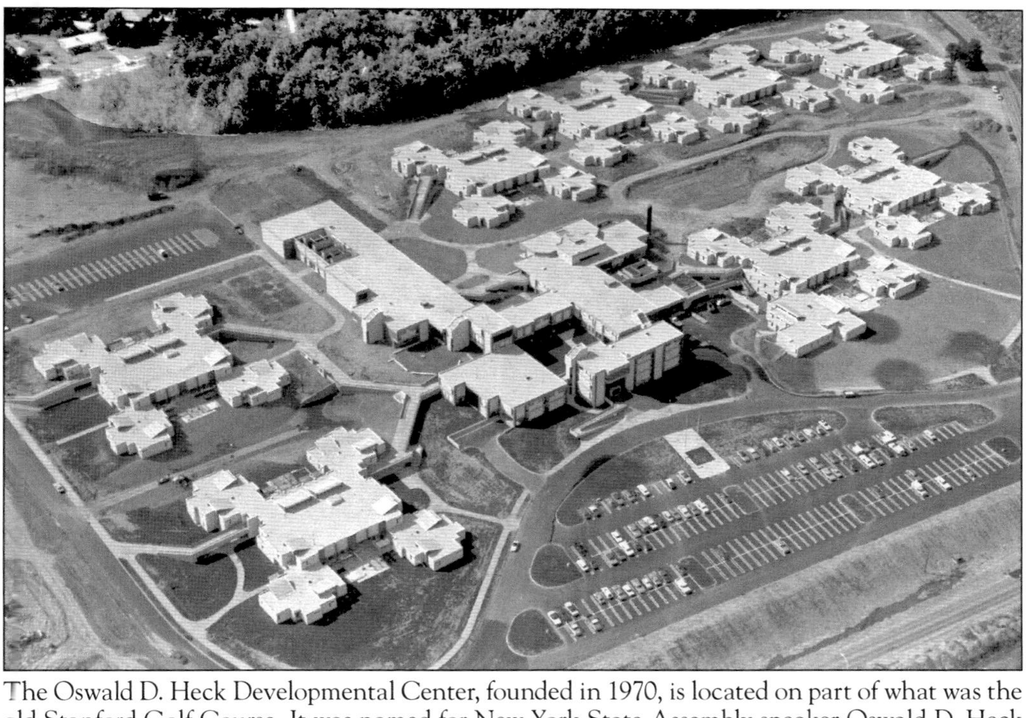

The Oswald D. Heck Developmental Center, founded in 1970, is located on part of what was the old Stanford Golf Course. It was named for New York State Assembly speaker Oswald D. Heck of Schenectady. It is used currently as a center for developmental disabilities services. (SCHS.)

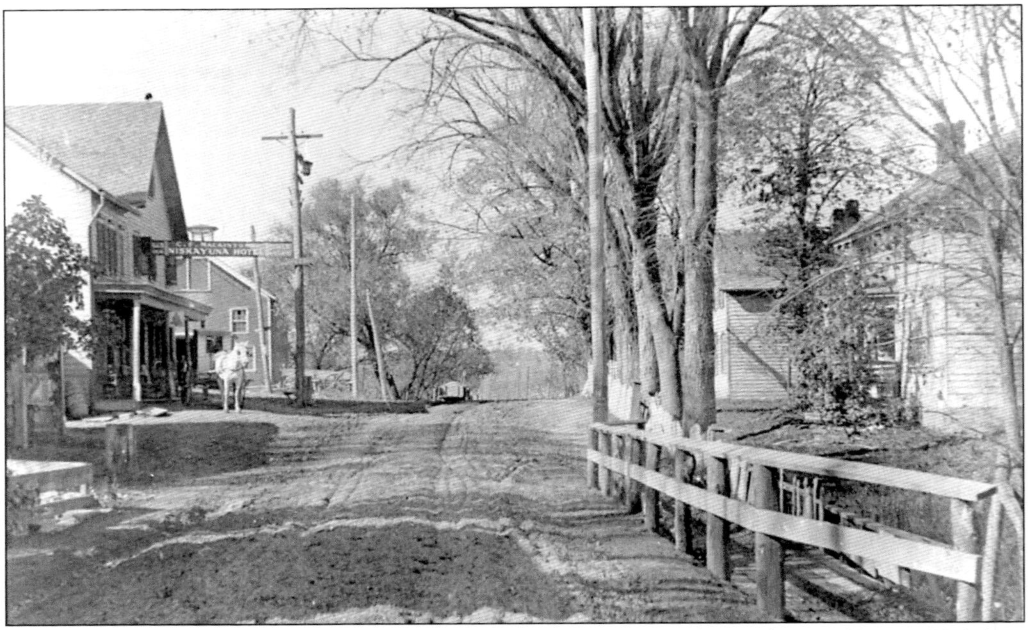

The Niskayuna Hotel, shown on the left, was purchased in 1886 by Bridget and Pierce Holohan from the Niskayuna Shaker community. It was located at the corner of River Road and Niskayuna Road. Earlier it was Miller's Hotel. The Millers rented it from the Shakers. The hotel was sold to Bridget's sister and brother-in-law, Mary and Cornelius Macintosh, in 1910. It was destroyed by fire in 1930. The picture below shows the location today. (Carolyn Veeder.)

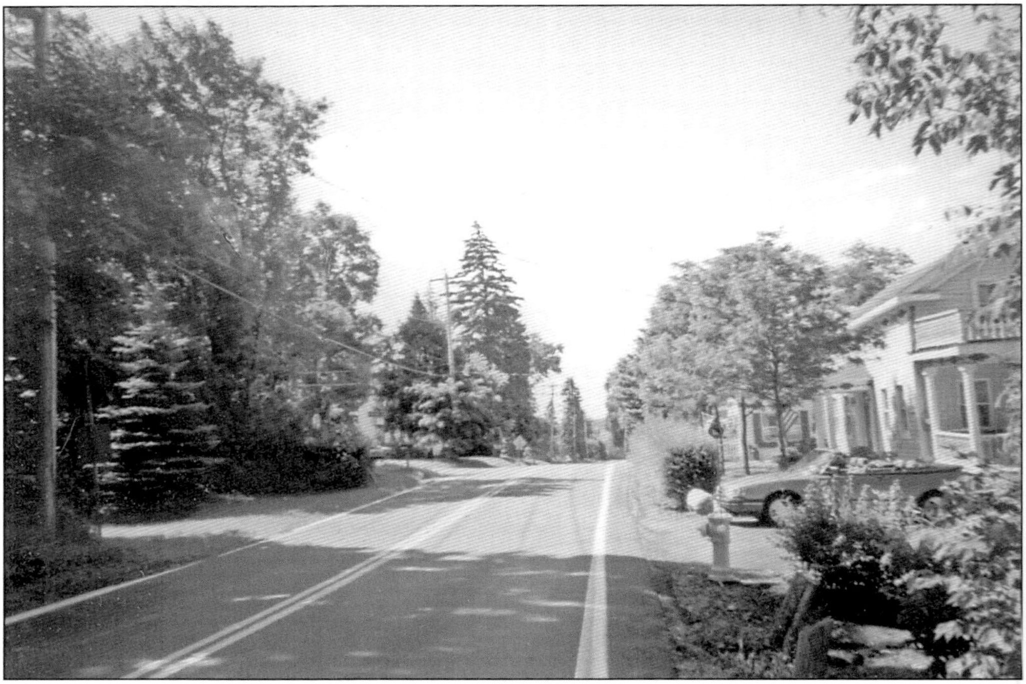

This current photograph is taken from the same vantage point as the preceding photograph. (Carolyn Veeder.)

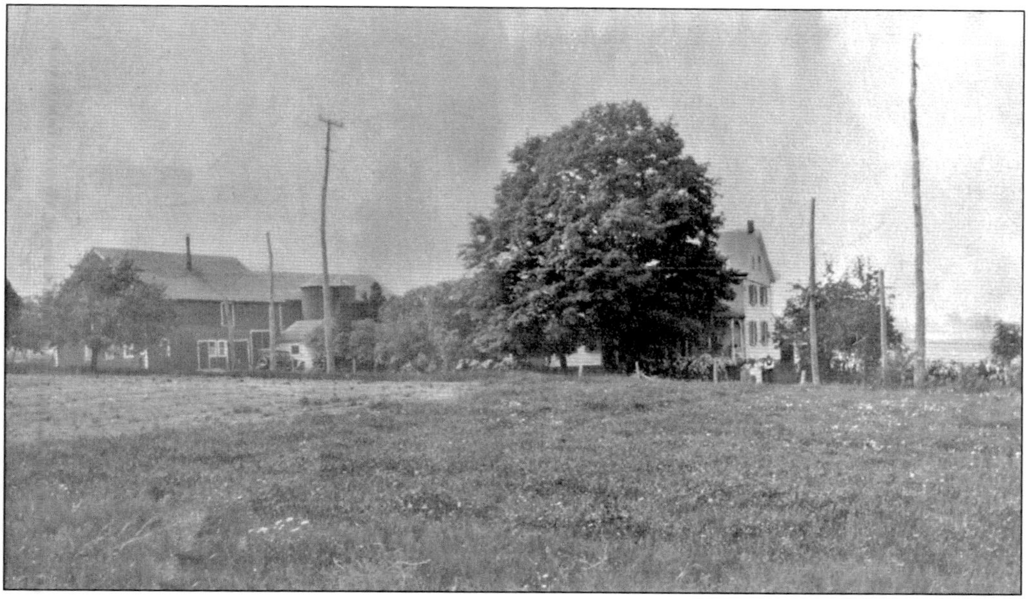

The Orchard Farm Dairy on River Road, purchased by Henry C. Finke in 1889, was a combination dairy and fruit farm. Finke's youngest son, George Albert, became the owner upon Henry's death in 1915. During this time, many improvements were made, including the bottling and pasteurization of milk for home delivery. (Al Finke Jr.)

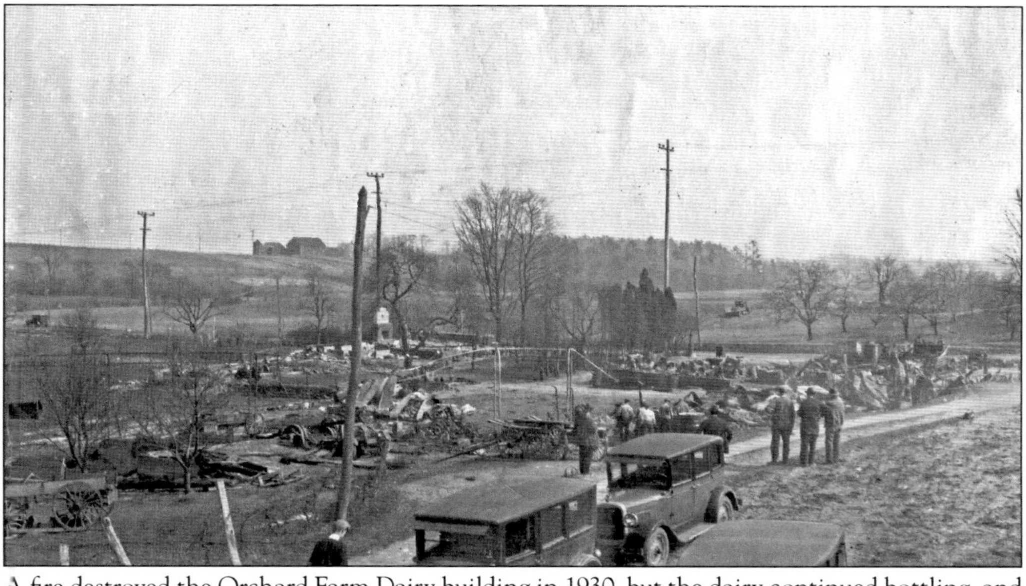

A fire destroyed the Orchard Farm Dairy building in 1930, but the dairy continued bottling, and home delivery remained in place until the farm was sold in 1966. (Al Finke Jr.)

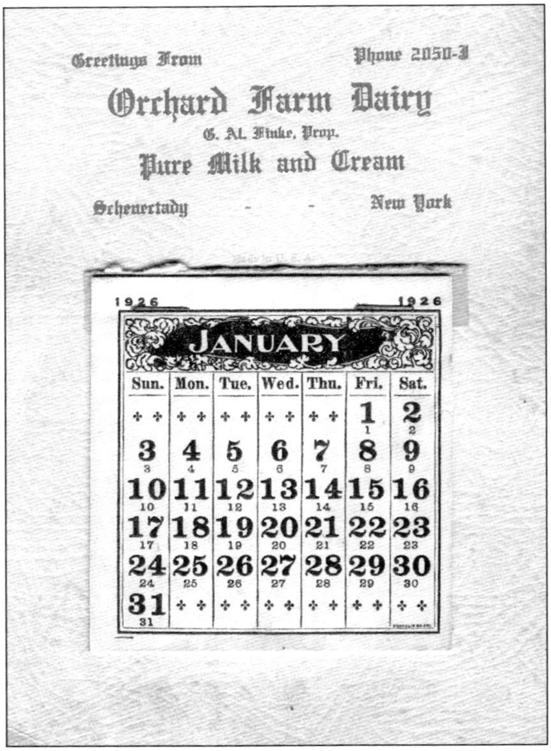

Promotional materials such as this 1926 calendar were distributed throughout the area served by the Orchard Farm Dairy. (Al Finke Jr.)

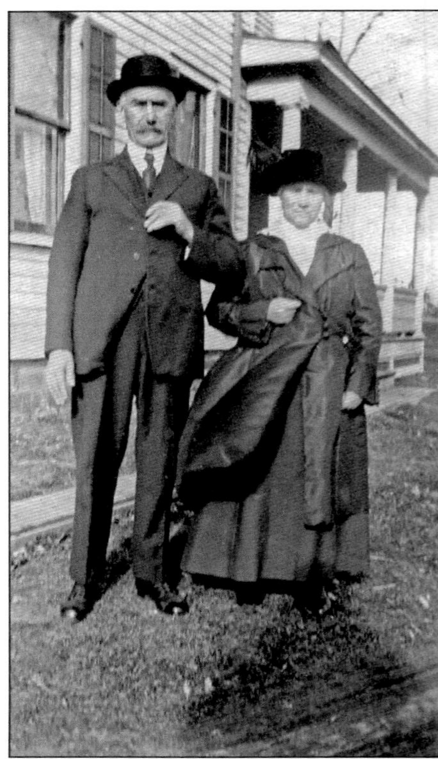

William and Josephine Giniecki, dressed in their finest, pose for this 1921 photograph. Immigrants from Poland in 1889, they raised eight children. Their third child was Mary Julia, who married Joseph F. Tys. Vincent, the youngest, started Country Gardens Nursery on Consaul Road. (Carole McCarthy.)

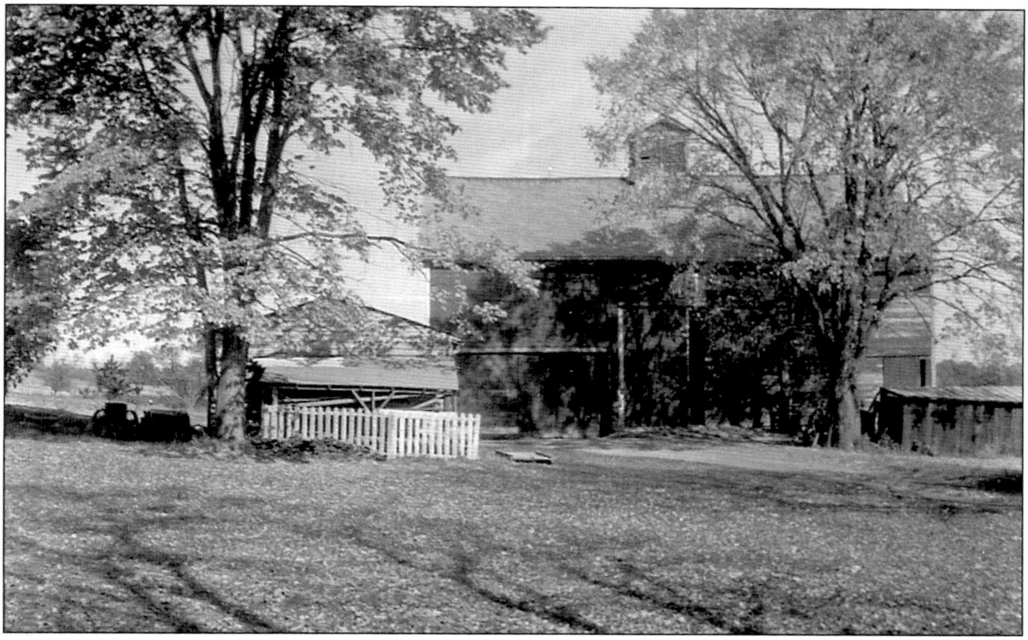

The 50-acre Tys family farm was purchased in 1925 by Joseph F. and Mary Julia (Giniecki) Tys from Christopher and Angie Shopmeier. It was located at the corner of Consaul Road and St. David's Lane across the street from the farm owned by her parents, William and Josephine Giniecki. Most of what was farm acreage is now the site of the Glen Eddy retirement home that was built in the 1990s. (Carole McCarthy.)

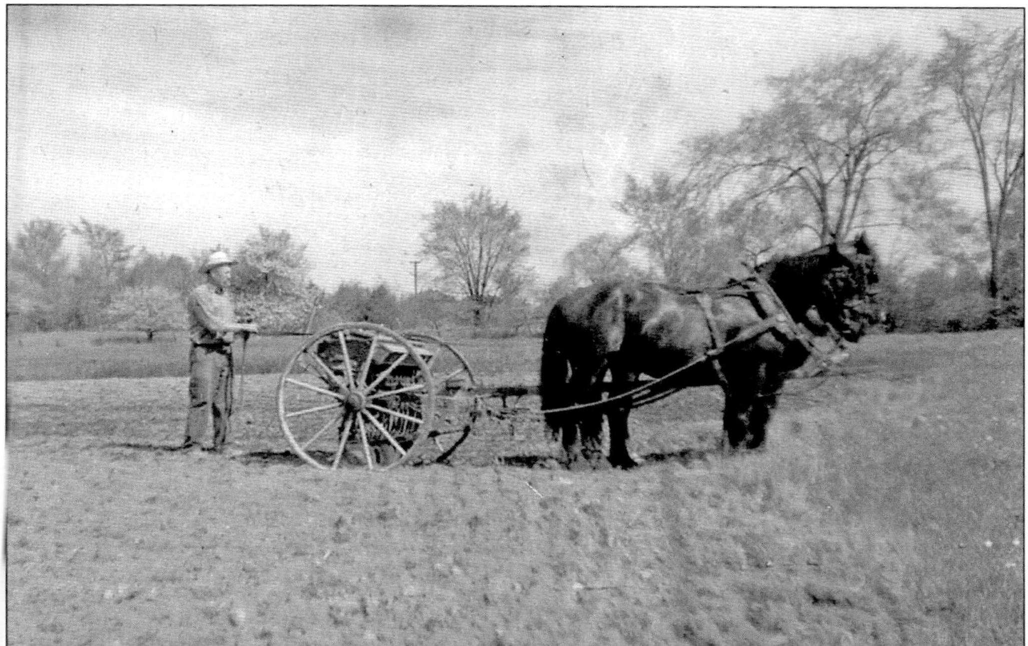

Horses were still being used to pull the planter in this 1953 photograph. Pictured is Joseph F. Tys driving Jimmy and Jerry. Many farms used workhorses well into the 1950s. (Carole McCarthy.)

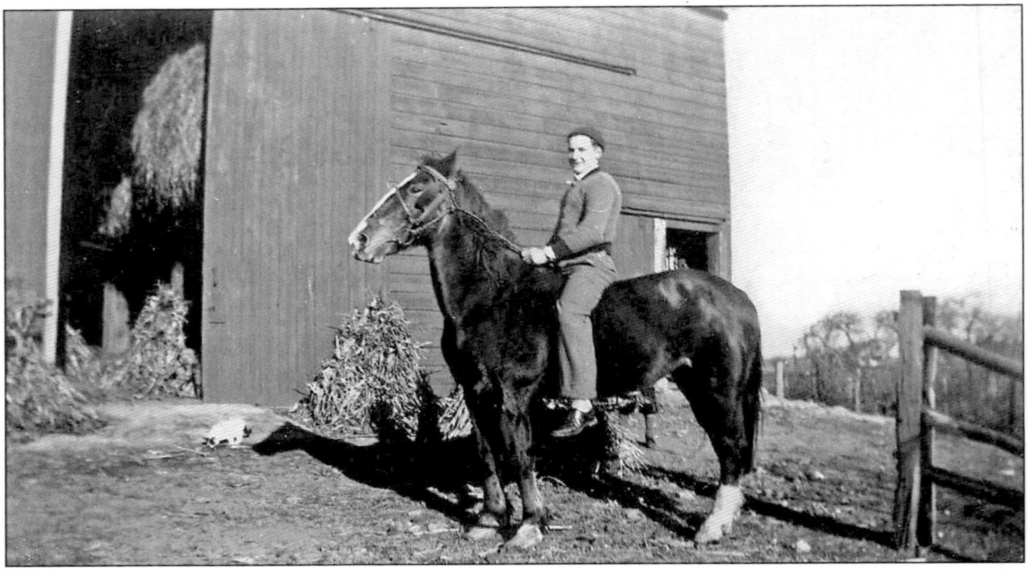

Jerry appears again in this 1938 picture, being ridden by Victor Tys, the brother of Joseph F. Tys. The barn just off Consaul Road was spared when the Glen Eddy facility was built, and it is still standing. (Carole McCarthy.)

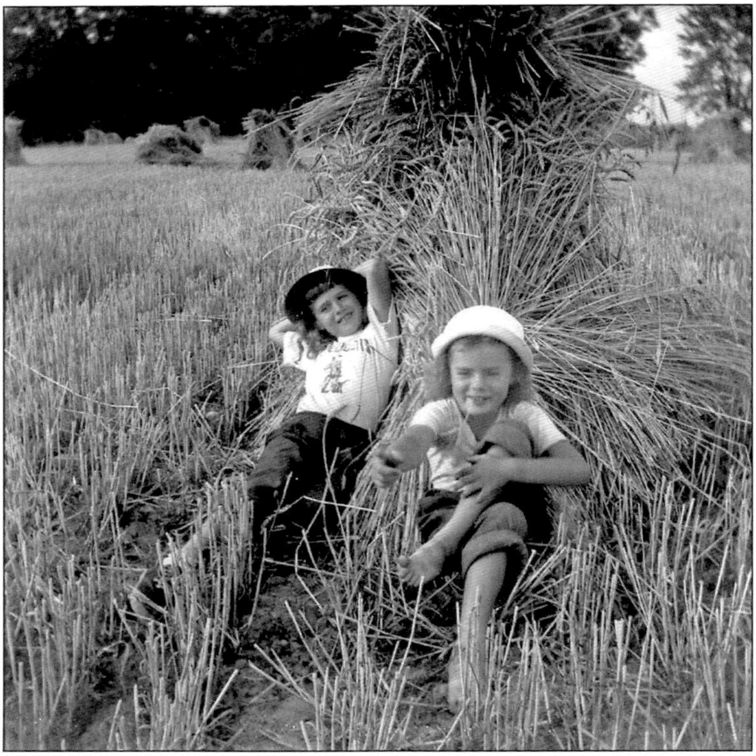

This picture, taken in the summer of 1950, shows Barbara Joan Groncki and Carole Lynn Groncki helping in the wheat fields. Wheat bundles were stacked in pyramids to protect the wheat from the elements. (Carole McCarthy.)

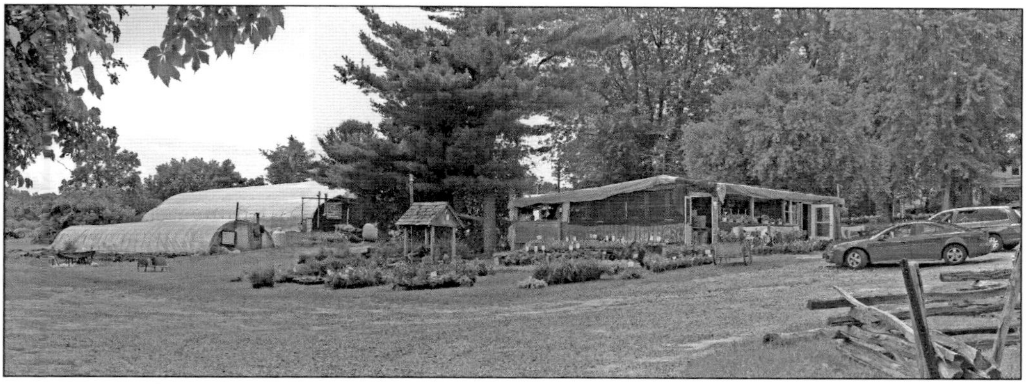

Country Gardens Nursery is located on the original Giniecki farm. Founded in the early 1940s by Vincent Giniecki, it was run by his son William until recently. The nursery and what remains of the farm was sold in 2008 and will be replaced by a residential development. (Carole McCarthy.)

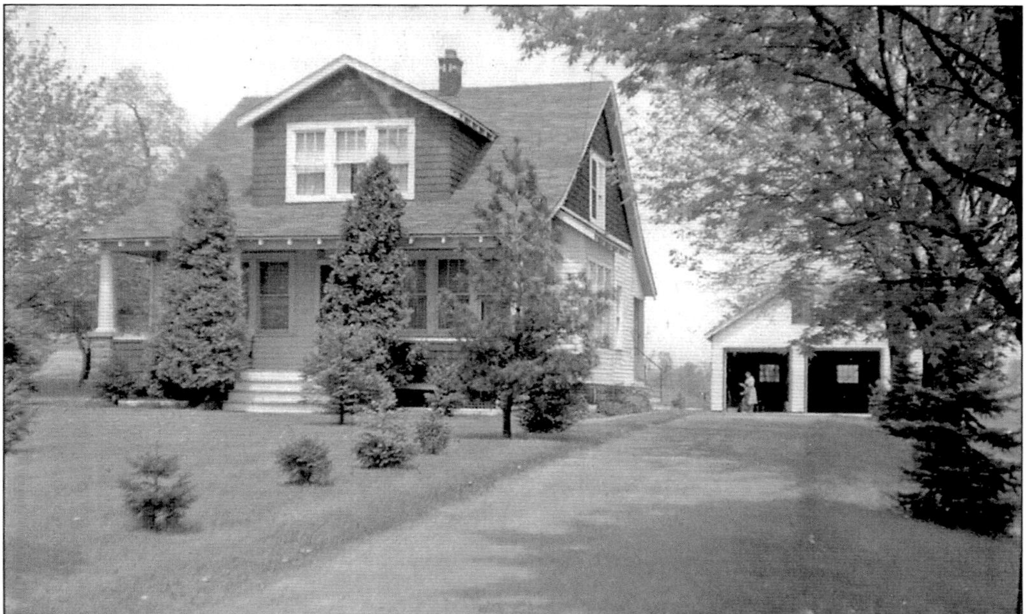

Here is the home of Joseph F. and Mary Julia Tys. This house was built in 1932. The garage was added in 1945 by Joseph and his son Victor. Mary stands in the doorway of the garage. (Carole McCarthy.)

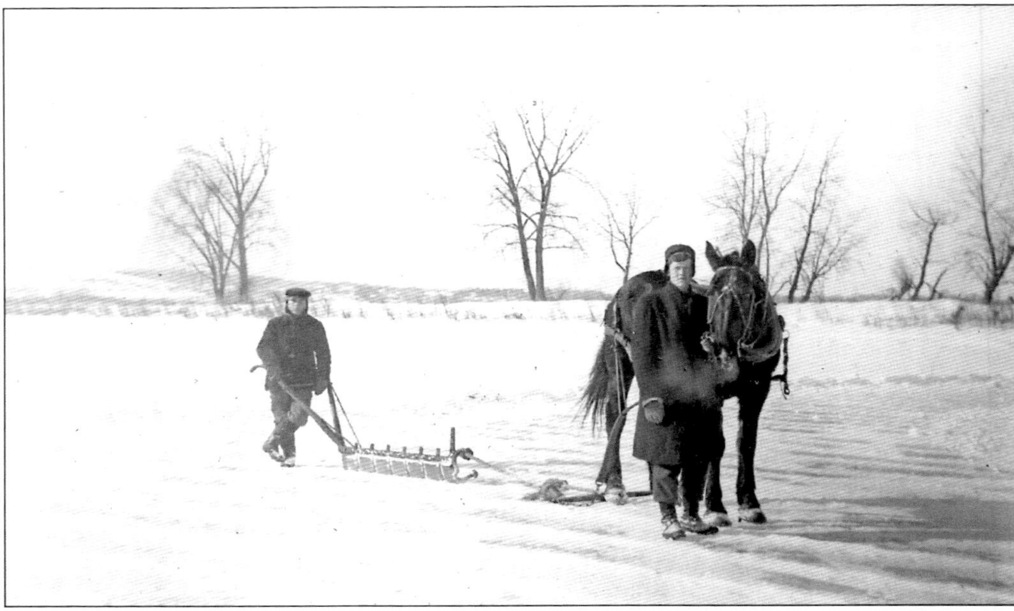

Prior to the early 1930s when manufactured ice began to come on the market, ice was harvested from local lakes, ponds, or rivers. This early-20th-century photograph shows ice cutting on the Mohawk River near Niskayuna. The horse used in the ice-cutting process seems just as pleased to pause for his photograph as the ice cutters. (Karen Kast.)

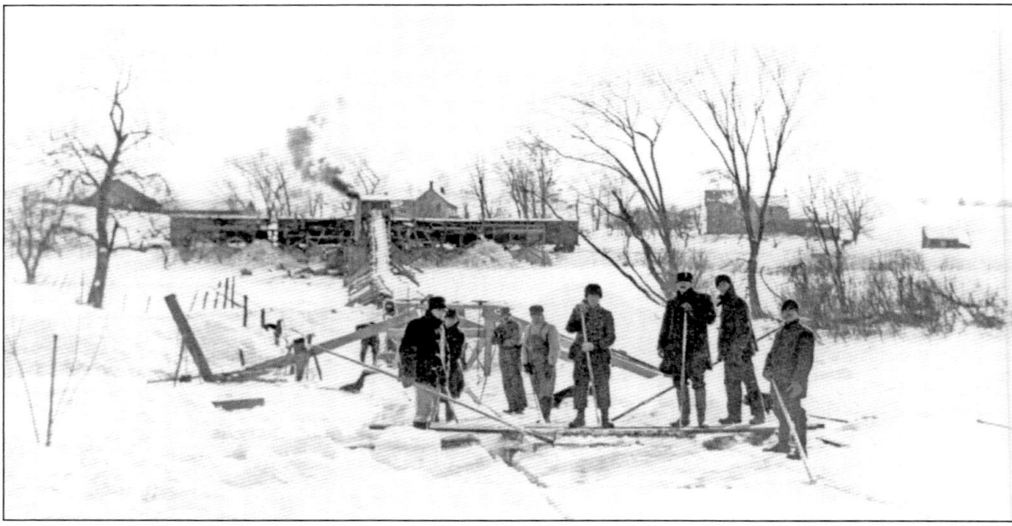

Pictured here are New York Central Railroad ice cutters working near Forts Ferry in Colonie. Ice from the Mohawk River is being run up a chute and loaded into a train. The ice was then taken to the Niskayuna train station and shipped out to purchasers. The place name *Forts Ferry*, originally Fort's Ferry, derives not from a fort but rather from the ferry established there in 1728 by Nicolas Fort. (Efner City History Center.)

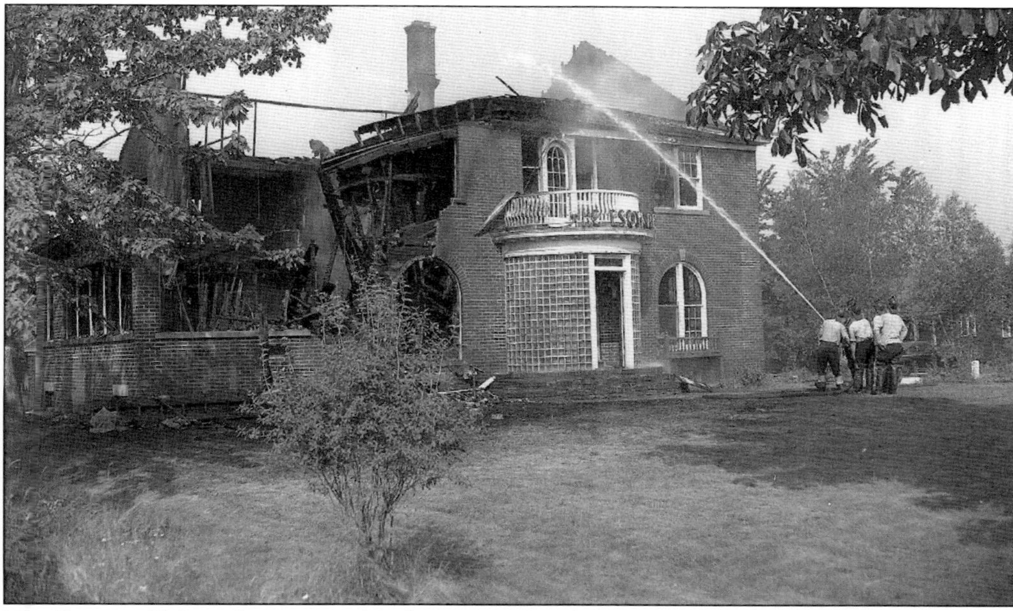

The Esquire Club at the corner of Balltown Road and Dewitt Avenue in Schenectady, just over the Niskayuna border, was severely damaged by fire on June 21, 1949. The Esquire Club, opened by Thomas Fitzgerald in 1930, and the Pine Point Inn, just up the street, were typical of the dance halls or roadhouses of the era. These two were strongly supported by the golfers from the Stanford Golf Course across the street. (SCHS.)

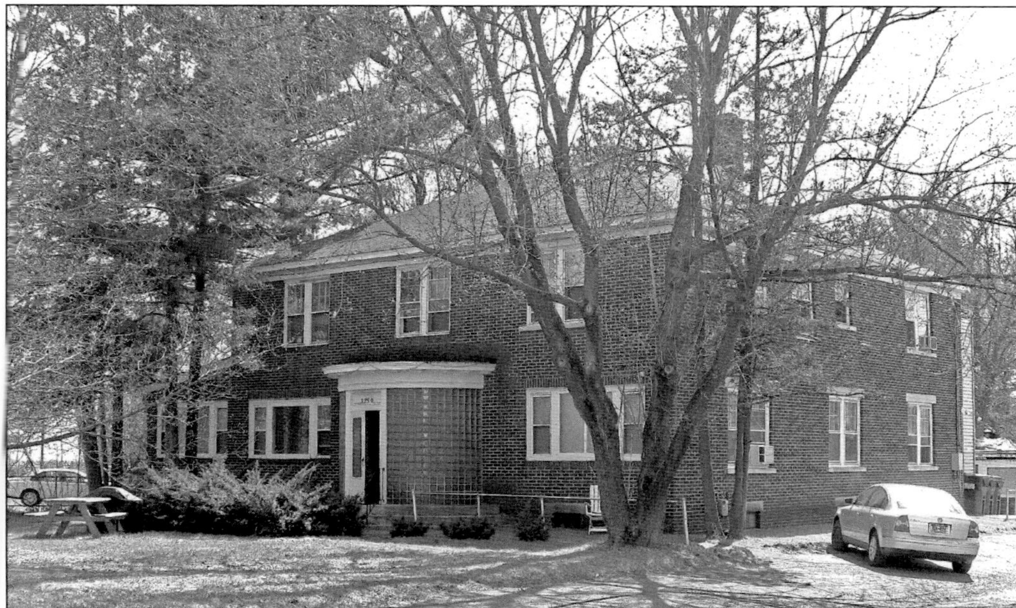

After the fire, the Esquire Club was rebuilt and converted for use as an apartment house. The Pine Point Inn is gone, replaced by a gasoline station and the Niskayuna branch of Trustco Bank, but the Esquire lives on. Note that the entrance to the building still has the same distinctive curved-glass highlight as when it was a nightclub. (SCHS.)

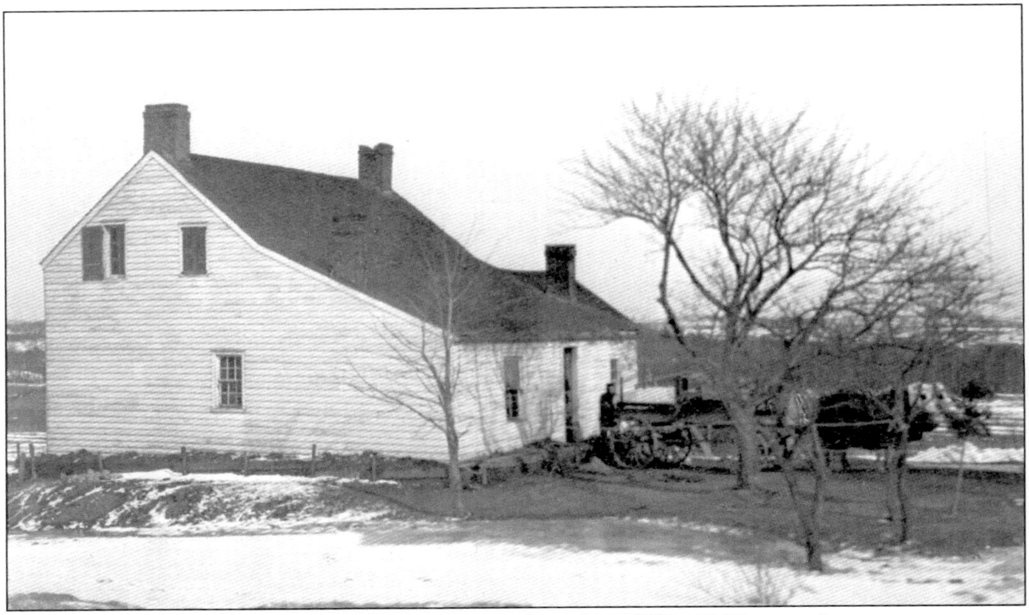

This house and 150 surrounding acres were purchased by Willis T. Hanson for use as a country estate in 1910. He purchased the property from John Zenner, a local farmer for whom the current Zenner Road is named. Zenner's original house and barn were preserved by the Hansons, but both buildings were demolished when the property was purchased by General Electric in 1945. (SCHS.)

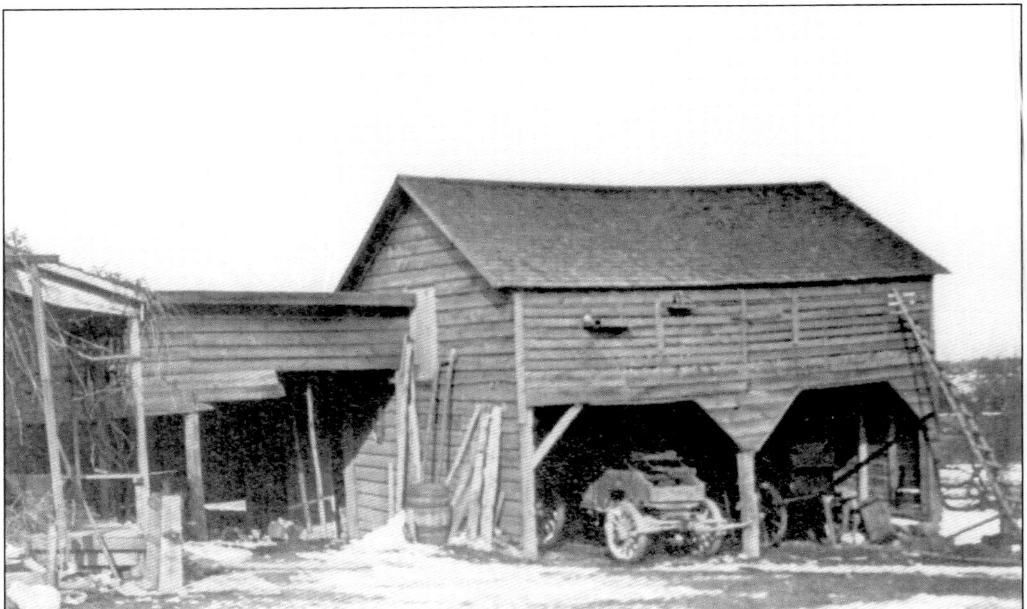

The Zenner farm was the first all-electric dairy farm in New York State, supplying much of the surrounding community with milk and other dairy products. But by the end of the farm's productive days, the Zenner family's largest barn had fallen into disrepair, which was one of the factors that made them receptive to Hanson's offer. (Efner City History Center.)

Bottles like this that carry the Zenner logo are highly prized by collectors. So are similar bottles from other Niskayuna dairy farms, such as the Orchard Farm Dairy on River Road and Green's Farm, for whom Green's Farm Road off Nott Street East is named. (Town of Niskayuna.)

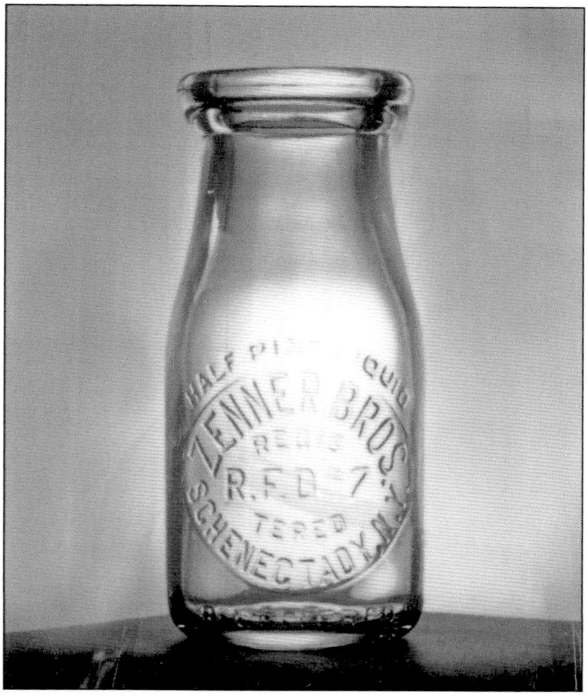

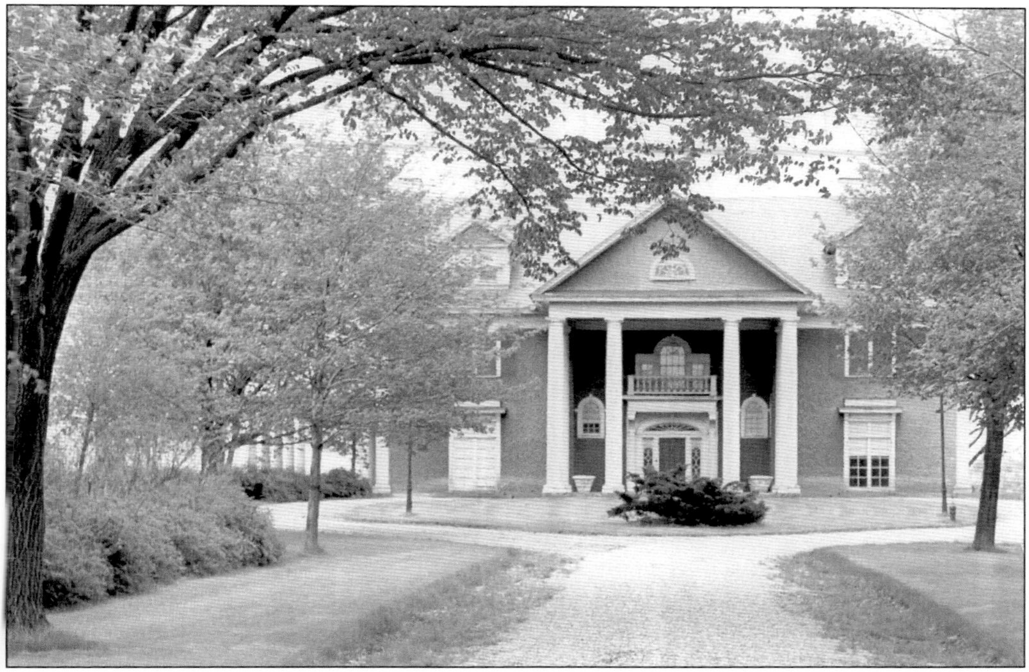

This is the elegant mansion that Hanson built after acquiring the Zenner farm in 1910. He called his new property the Knolls because it extended over five of them, one of which rose 200 feet over the Mohawk River. He chose the site as a summer home because neither automobiles nor roads were well developed, and the Knolls was considered to be well out in the country. (Efner City History Center.)

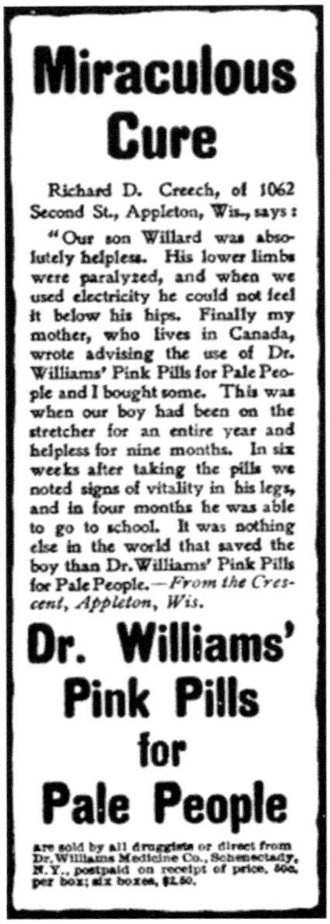

Willis T. Hanson was noted for his association with the Dr. Williams Medicine Company, which originated Pink Pills for Pale People. In the late 1800s, Hanson acquired the sole distribution rights for his patent medicine business, and it became a huge financial success. At this time, there were virtually no laws to control the contents of patent medicines or the sometimes-outrageous claims made by their manufacturers. The Pink Pills worked best after extensive sunbathing. (SCHS.)

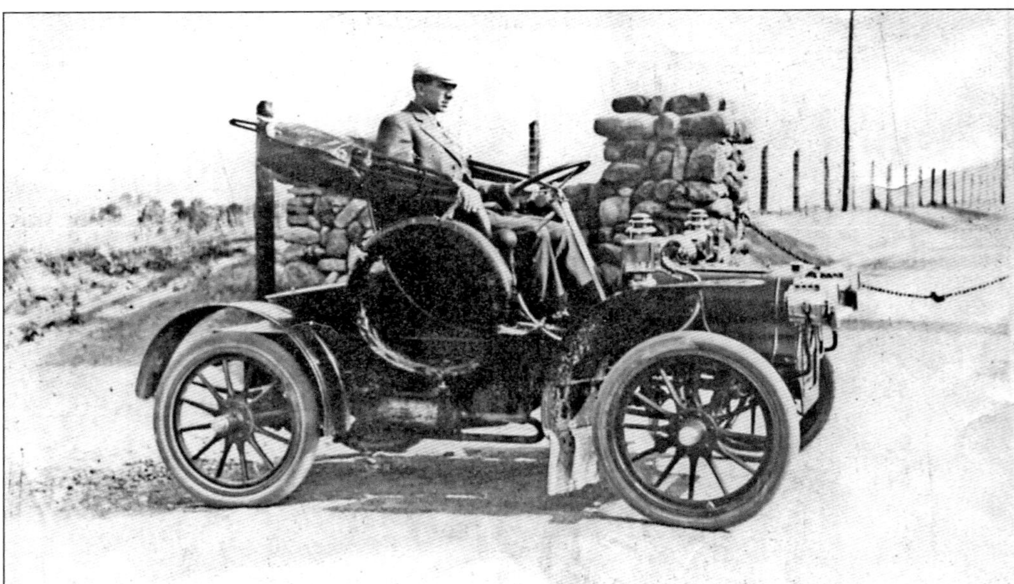

This 1906/1907 Cadillac Roadster is believed to have been owned by Hanson, an avid and early owner of luxury automobiles. The Roadster had a one-cylinder gasoline engine and what is known as a tulip body. Although this type of car was available only to the privileged few, it and other less-expensive cars marked the beginning of the age of automobiles and the rapid growth of suburban areas such as Niskayuna. (SCHS.)

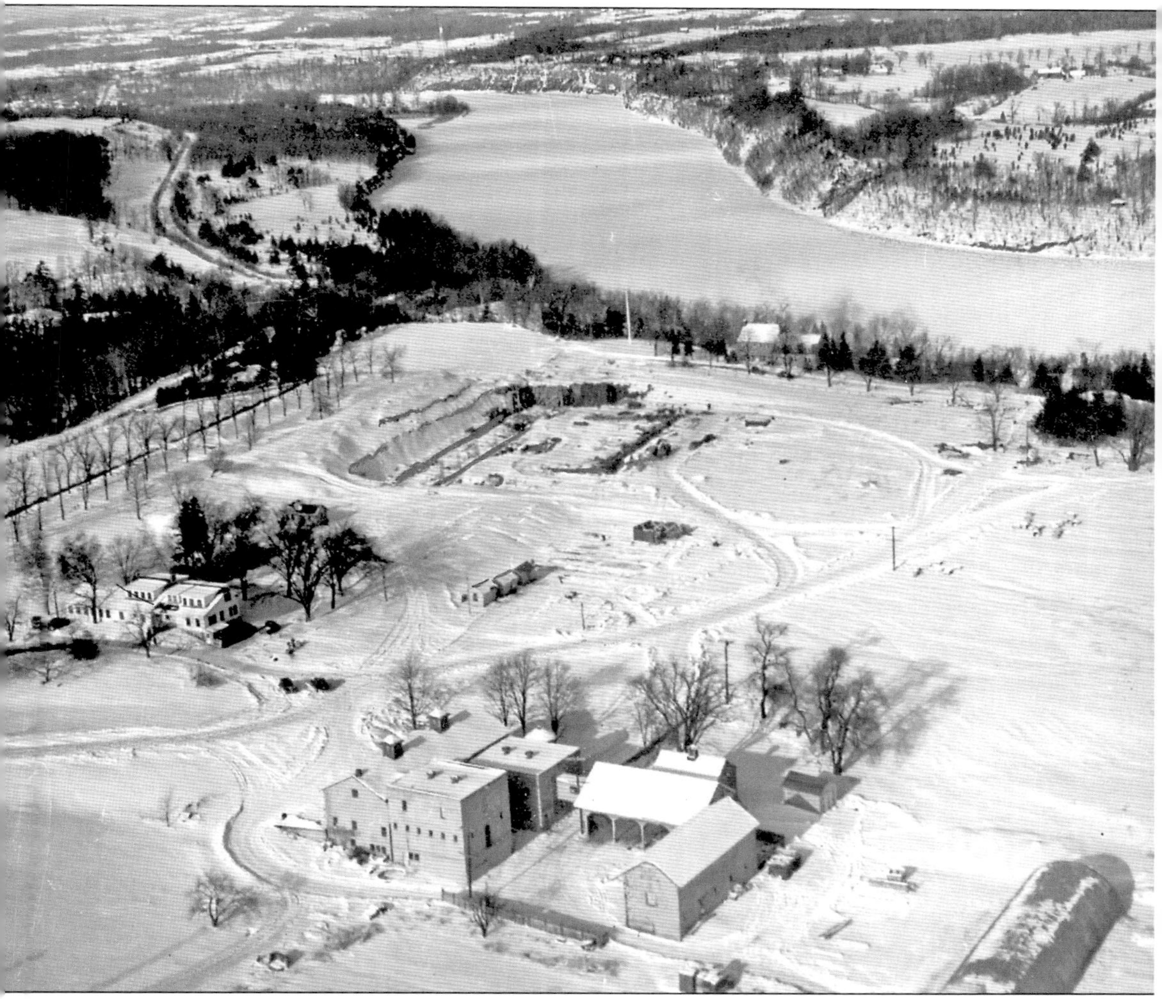

In 1945, General Electric purchased the Knolls estate, which had been closed since the 1930s. The picture above shows General Electric Research and Development Center under construction, a facility that opened in 1950. Next door, also on original Hanson property, is the Knolls Atomic Power Laboratory (KAPL), which was operated by General Electric for the Naval Reactors program of the U.S. Department of Energy from 1946 to 1993. Subsequently it was run by Lockheed Martin (originally called Martin Marietta) from 1994 to January 31, 2009, and by the Bechtel Corporation since the following day. (SCHS.)

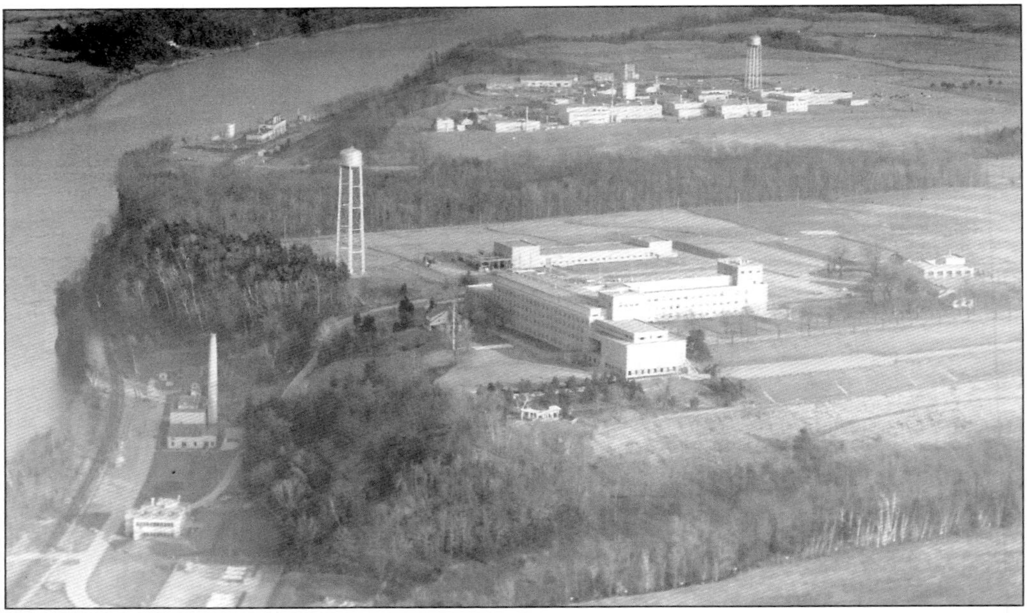

Facing east, this aerial view of the Knolls estate shows General Electric Global Research in the foreground and KAPL in the background. The Mohawk River borders the properties to the left and top in this photograph. The Knolls is part of the 1,000-acre land patent granted to Isaac Switts in 1707 in compensation for property in Schenectady that he lost after being captured and taken to Canada during the Stockade Massacre of 1690. (SCHS.)

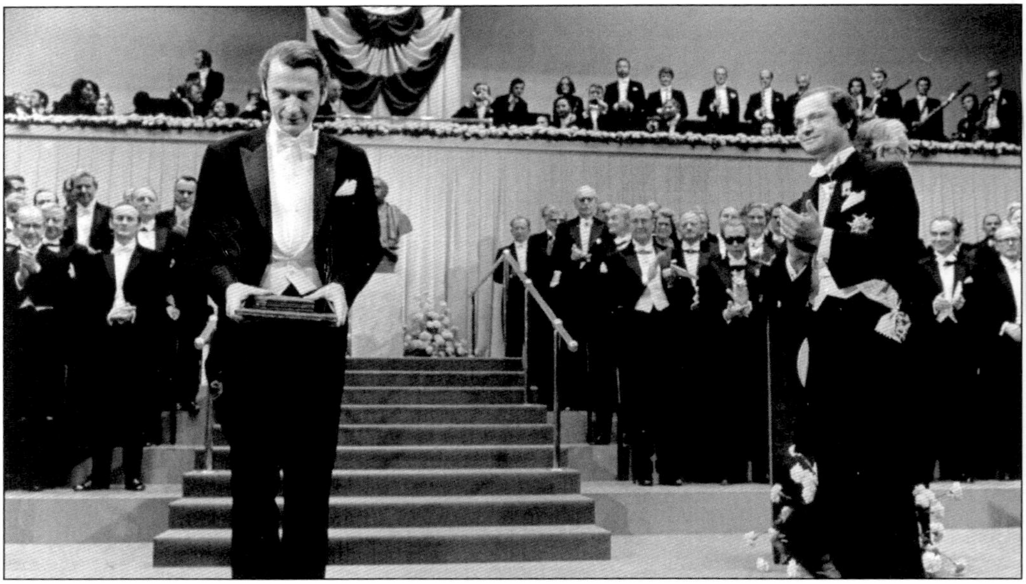

Pictured here, Niskayuna resident Dr. Ivar Giaever receives the Nobel Prize in Physics in 1973 in Stockholm, Sweden. Born in Norway, he emigrated in 1954 to work for General Electric of Canada. After his research at the General Electric Research and Development Center, which began in 1958, he left the job in 1988 to become professor emeritus at Rensselaer Polytechnic Institute in Troy, where he had earned his doctorate in physics in 1964. His current research is in biophysics. (Schenectady Museum.)

This is the medal bestowed on Giaever in Stockholm on December 12, 1973, in recognition of his 1973 Nobel Prize in Physics. The prize was awarded for "experimental discoveries regarding tunneling phenomena in superconductors" in 1960 while at the General Electric Research and Development Center, within easy walking distance of his home on Van Antwerp Road. Shortly after notification of the award, the center held a recognition reception for him, and Niskayuna proclaimed an "Ivar Giaever Day" in his honor. (Schenectady Museum.)

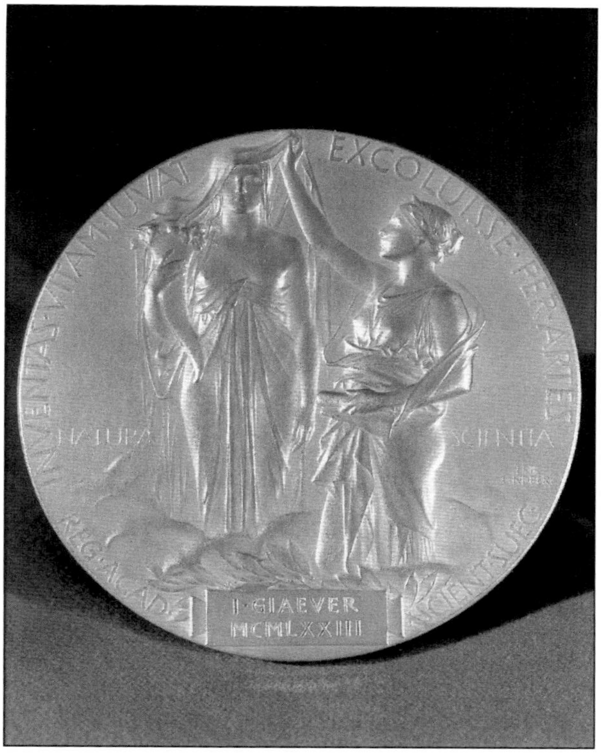

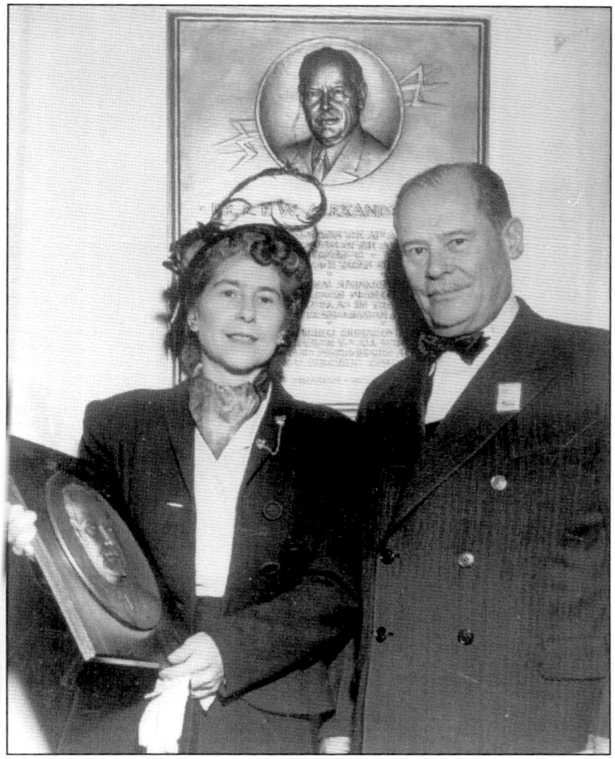

Ernst F. W. Alexanderson, shown here with his wife Thyra, was a radio and television pioneer. Born in Sweden in 1878, he came to the United States in 1901 to work with Charles Steinmetz. Pictures sent from his laboratory were projected onto a large screen at Proctor's Theater in Schenectady in 1930. This was a major step in the development of General Electric and television. Alexanderson died in 1975 and is buried in Vale Cemetery in Schenectady. (Efner City History Center.)

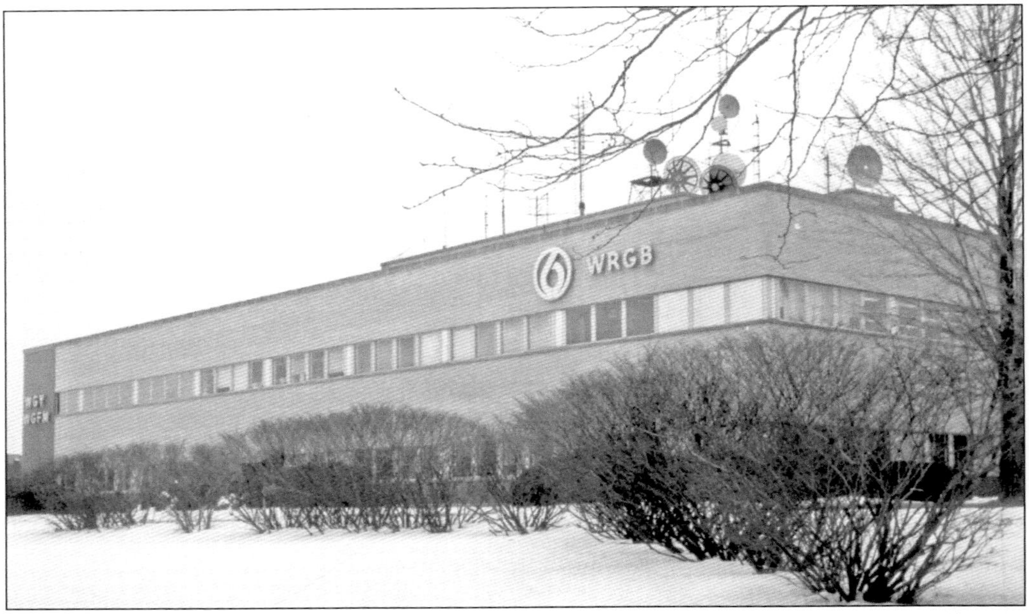

Television broadcasting came to Niskayuna in 1957 with the construction of this building at 1400 Balltown Road on land that was once part of Green's Farm. For many years, it housed both radio station WGY and television station WRGB. It was affiliated with NBC from the 1950s until 1981 when it joined CBS. General Electric owned WRGB until 1983 when it was sold to Unicom. The station is now called CBS6. (SCHS.)

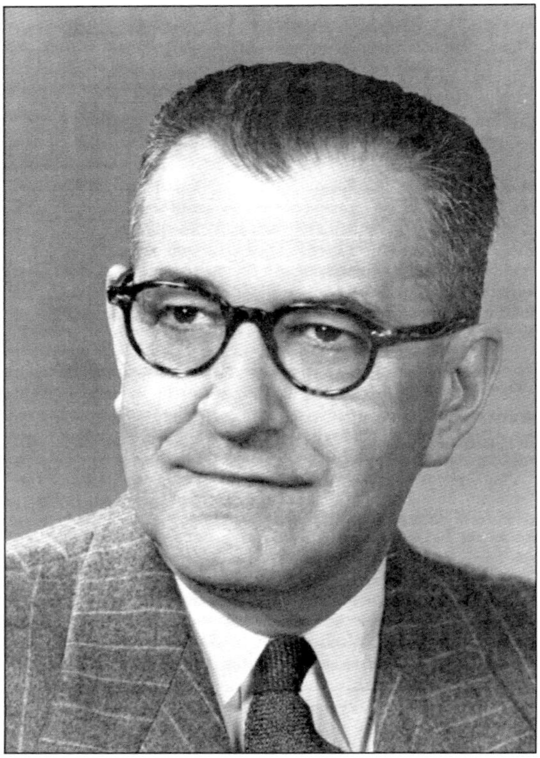

Television station WRGB owes its name to Dr. W. R. G. Baker, a telecommunications expert who became a vice president of General Electric in 1941. He worked closely with Ernst F. W. Alexanderson and was authorized by the Federal Communications Commission (FCC) in 1940 to establish a technical committee for standardization of television. The first public television demonstration and WRGB's birth date was January 13, 1928, when an experimental program was telecast and shown in Alexanderson's home at 1132 Adams Road in Schenectady. (SCHS.)

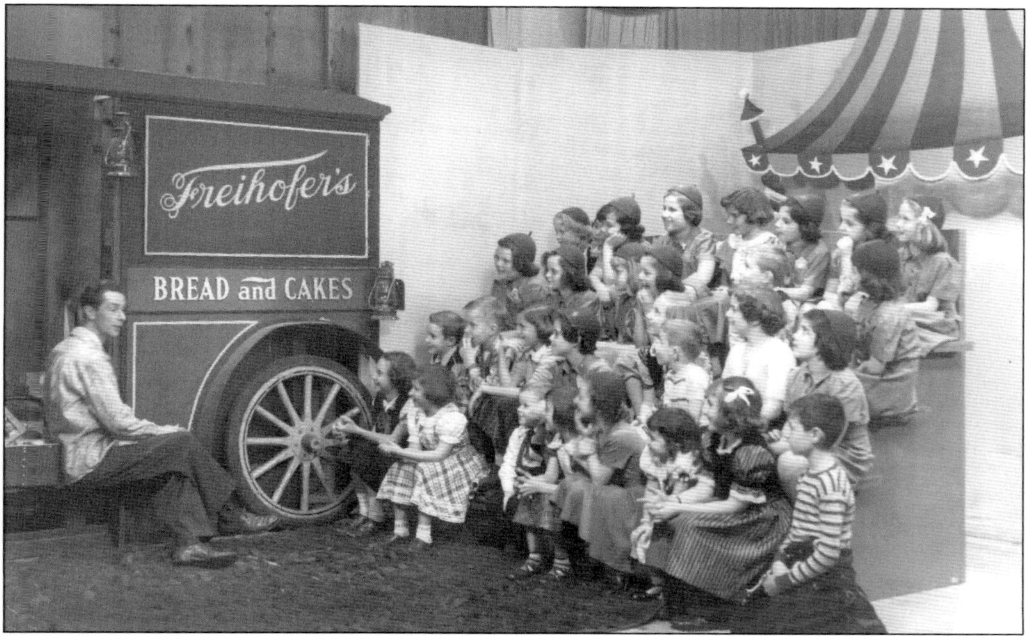

Breadtime Stories, better known as the *Freddie Freihofer Show*, was telecast from 1948 to 1965. Shown here is the first host, Ralph Kanna. The 15-minute children's show featured drawings called "squiggles," birthday "cakers," and the well-known Freihofer jingle—all fondly remembered by local residents. (Efner City History Center.)

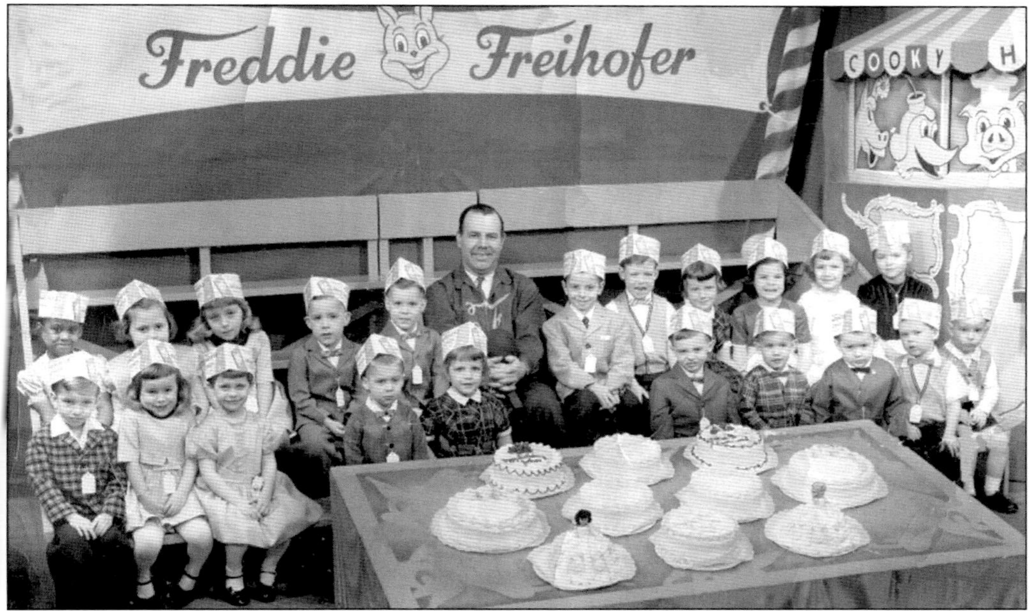

For its last 10 years from 1956 through 1965, the *Freddie Freihofer Show* was hosted by "Uncle Jim" Fisk, who is shown here in 1962 with 10 cakes and 21 children who had February birthdays. Fisk and his wife Mary Lou now live at the Glen Eddy retirement community in Niskayuna. Various Freihofer families lived throughout the New York State capital district, and the Curtis home at 2126 Union Street in Niskayuna is still often called the Freihofer House. (SCHS.)

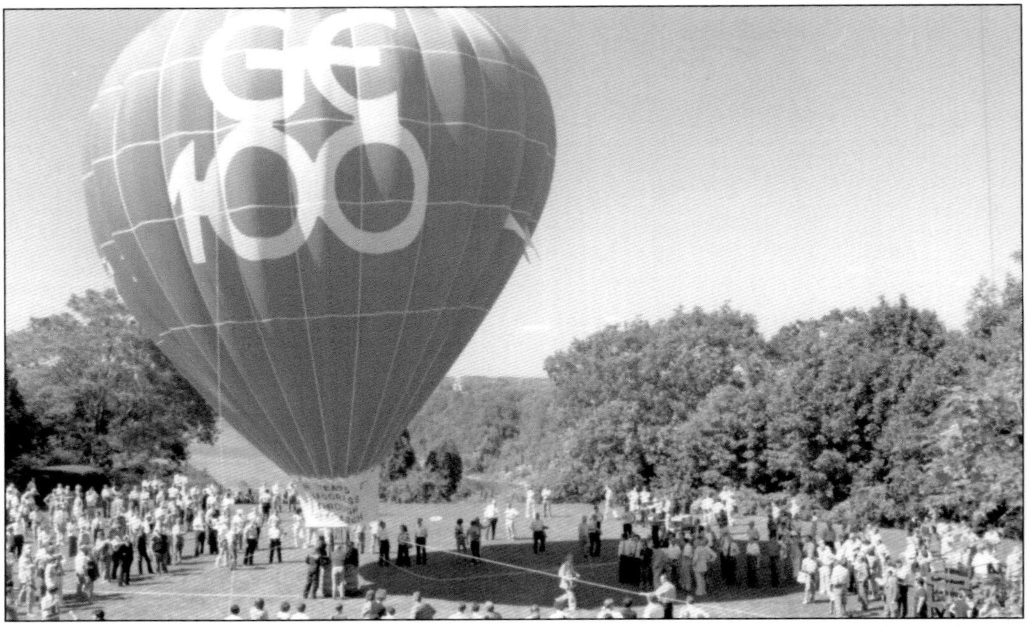

The 100th anniversary of General Electric, based on the 1878 formation of the Edison Electric Light Company by Thomas Edison with the financial help of J. P. Morgan, was celebrated worldwide in 1978. The balloon in this picture is lifting off from the General Electric Research and Development Center in Niskayuna. General Electric publications frequently cite research done at the center, now called GE Global Research, as the basis of the company's past success and future prospects. (Efner City History Center.)

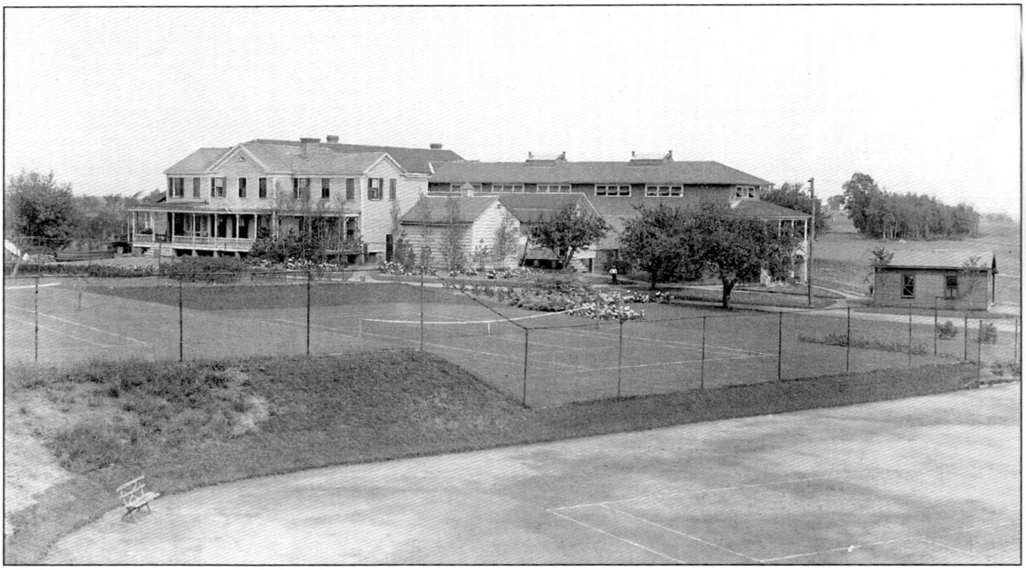

The Mohawk Golf Club of Niskayuna was incorporated in 1898 from a merger of the Schenectady Golf Course and the College Hill Golf Course. Its original site on Rosa Road was soon outgrown. In 1904, the new Mohawk course opened in Niskayuna. It was located on the site of the John Ellis summer home, later called the Smitley farm, on Troy Road at trolley stop No. 5. Depicted is the building destroyed in a 1907 fire. (Efner City History Center.)

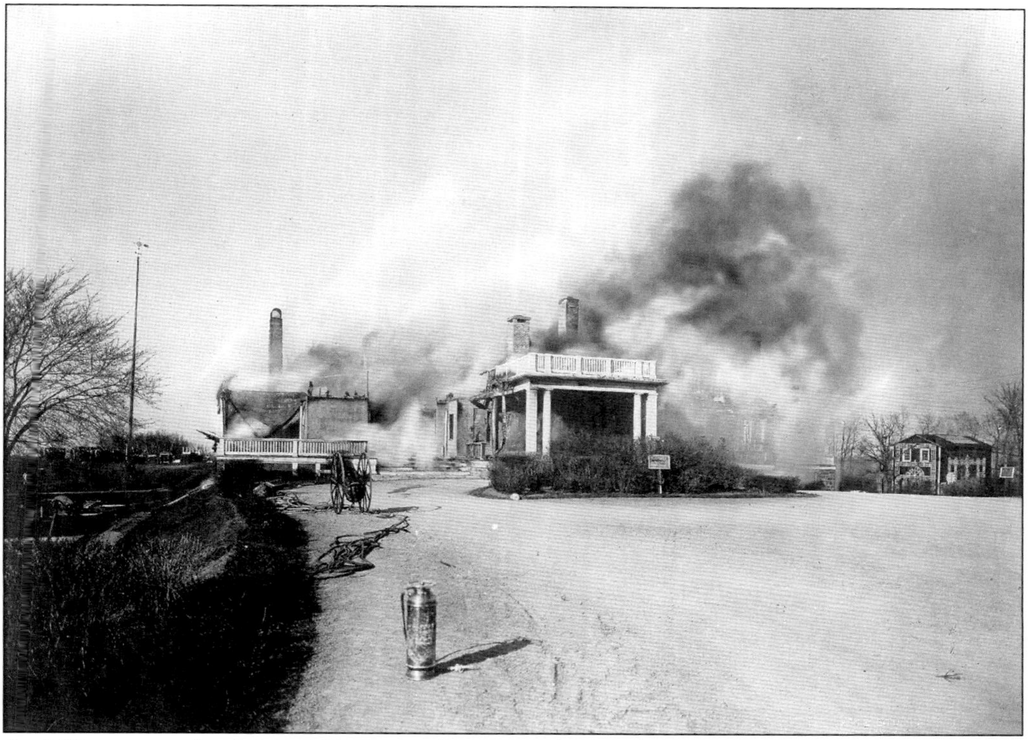

At 3:30 p.m. on April 26, 1923, flames from a workman's blowtorch started a fire that totally destroyed the second clubhouse within two hours. The first clubhouse was also destroyed by fire in 1907. That fire was caused by a defective flue. (Schenectady Museum.)

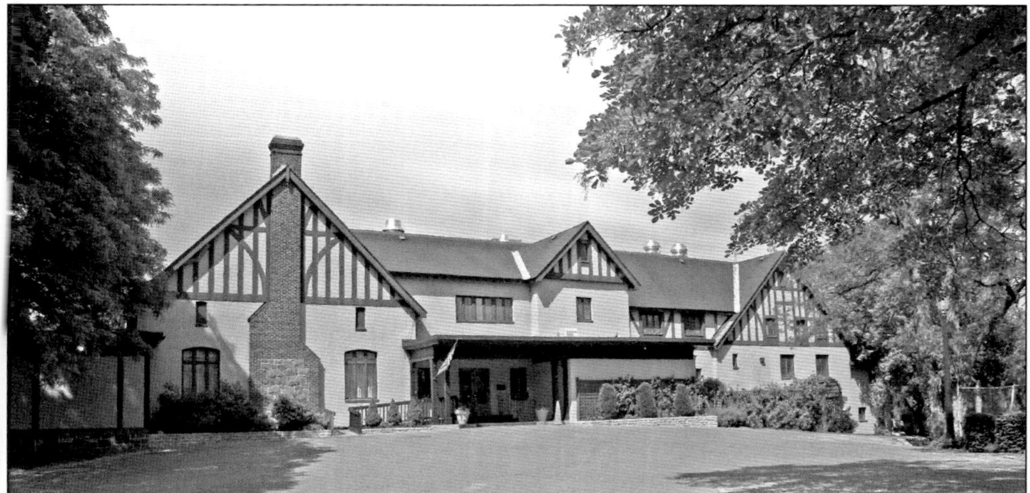

The current English Tudor Mohawk Golf Clubhouse at 1849 Union Street, the third building on the site, opened on New Year's Day in 1925. An aerial view of the club shows its magnificent star shaped 18-hole championship golf course almost completely surrounded by residential areas, except for the neighboring Bevis Hill Reservoir on Balltown Road to the northwest. North, South, and East Country Club Drives to the southeast are named for the club. (SCHS.)

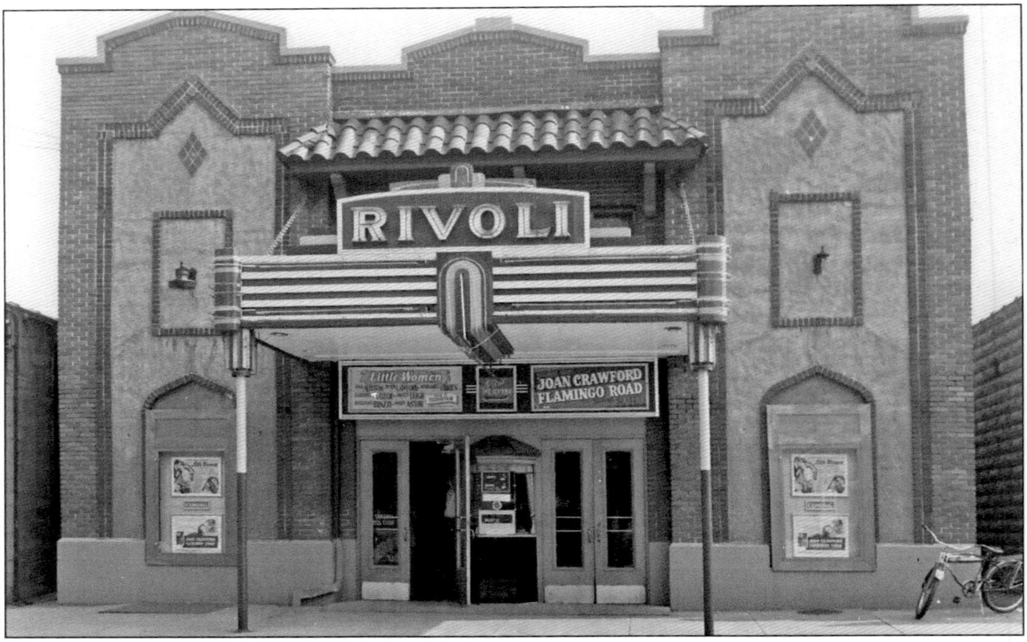

The Rivoli Theater with its Spanish facade at 1615–1617 Union Street opened in 1927. Although it is in the city of Schenectady just over the town line, this theater was the closest thing to Niskayuna having one of its own. It provided entertainment for both Niskayuna and Schenectady residents. The theater closed in 1950, and the building was subsequently used by various other businesses. (SCHS, Larry Hart Collection.)

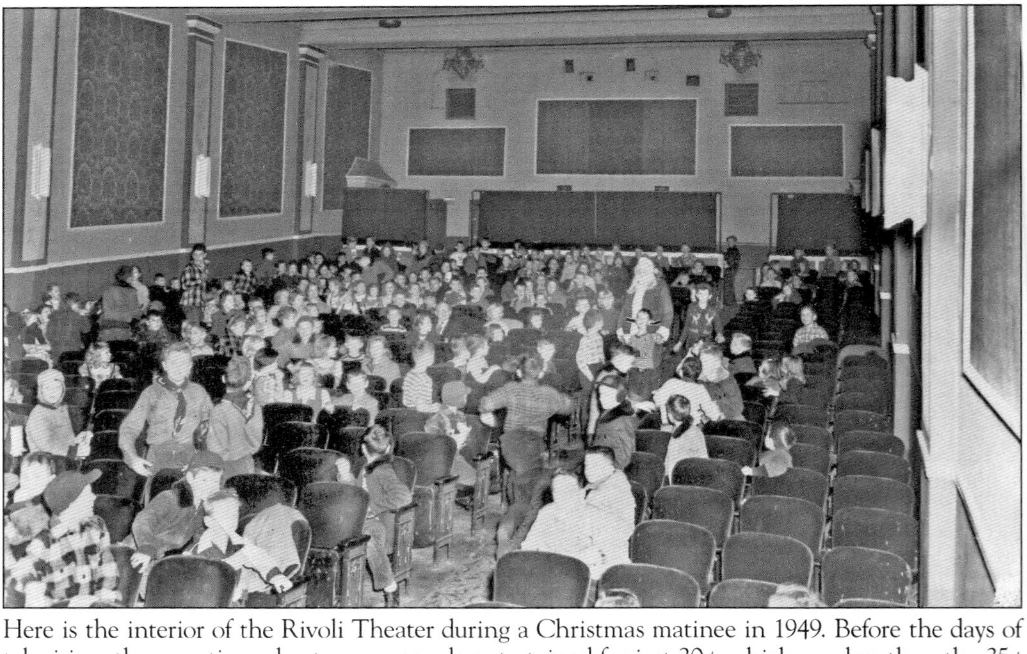

Here is the interior of the Rivoli Theater during a Christmas matinee in 1949. Before the days of television, these matinees kept young people entertained for just 20¢, which was less than the 35¢ or 50¢ being charged at downtown theaters. The Rivoli Theater seated about 500 moviegoers. Santa Claus can be seen here distributing packets of candy. (SCHS, Larry Hart Collection.)

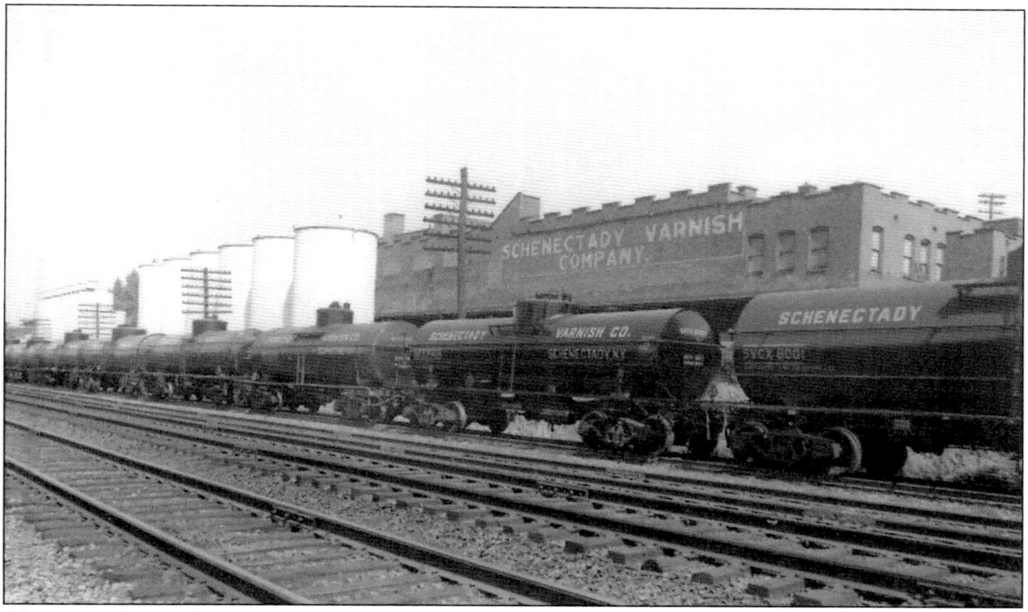

W. Howard Wright established the Schenectady Varnish Company in 1906 to manufacture versatile and economical electrical insulating materials. In 1907, a plant was built on Congress Street in Schenectady. In 1962, under the leadership of his son Henry D. Wright, the name of the company was changed to Schenectady Chemicals. (SCHS.)

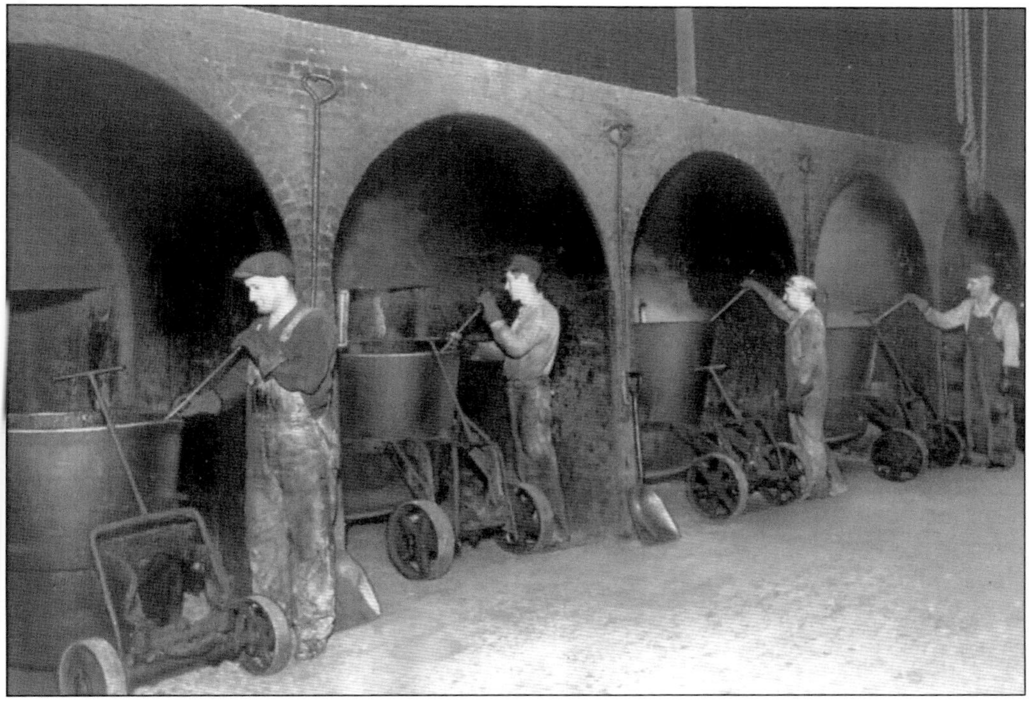

This is a production line at the Congress Street facility of Schenectady Chemicals. It is unknown whether this stirring group posed for the picture, but the four men appear to be working in synchrony. (SCHS.)

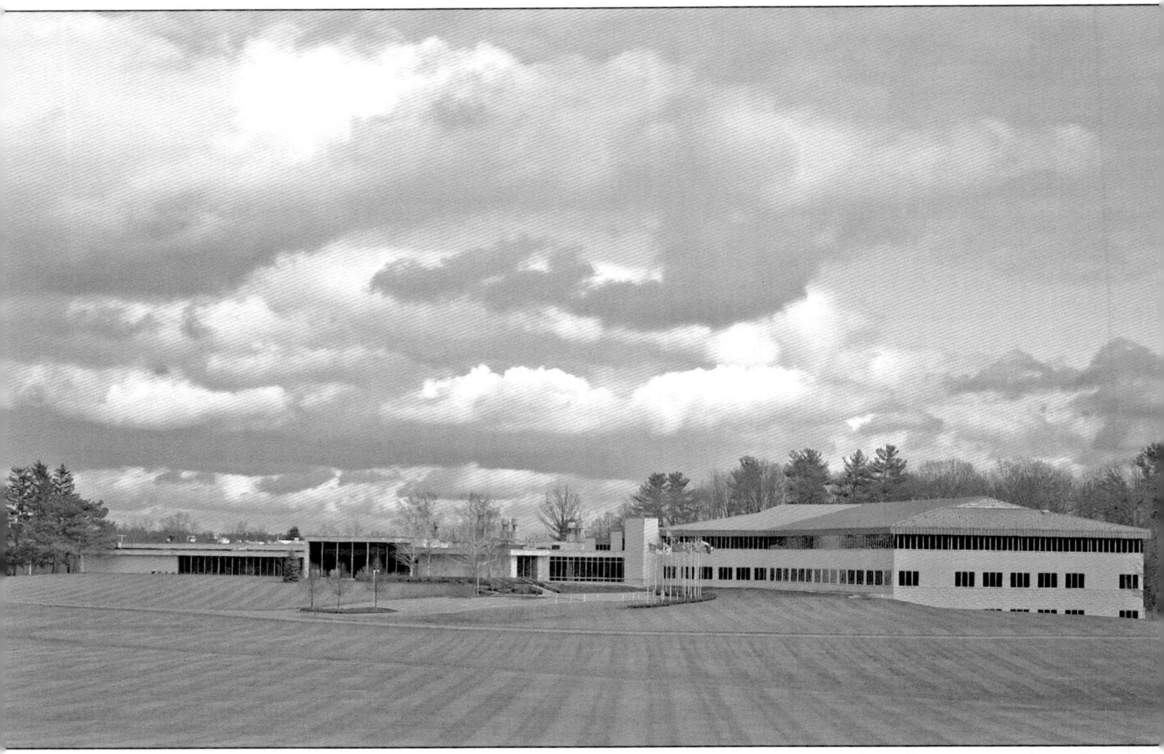

In 1993, Schenectady Chemicals became Schenectady International and is currently referred to as the SI Group. The Congress Street site seen in previous photographs is not in use today, and all local manufacturing is done at a site in Rotterdam Junction next to SCHS's Mabee Farm Historic Site. This is a current photograph of the SI Group's company headquarters and research laboratory on Balltown Road in Niskayuna. The facility was built in 1967 and substantially expanded in 2002. (SCHS.)

Four

Homes and Neighborhoods

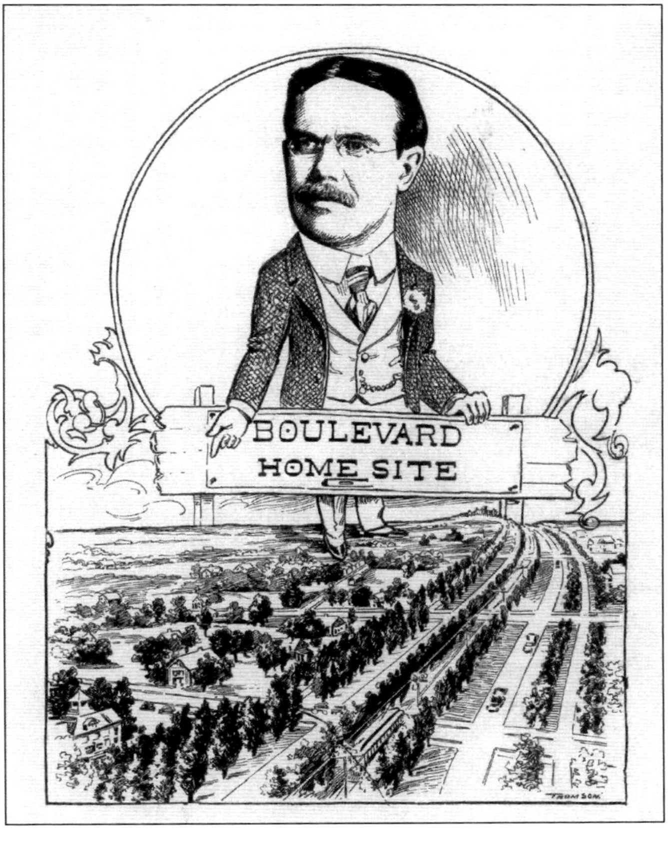

Beginning in 1900, W. Garner Bee (1868–1945) and his associates developed the Grand Boulevard area on the 140-acre farm purchased from Christian Schopmeier. This is a fanciful 1910 sketch of Bee and his development, one that was highly successful and produced an attractive neighborhood whose homes continue to be prized to this day. (SCHS.)

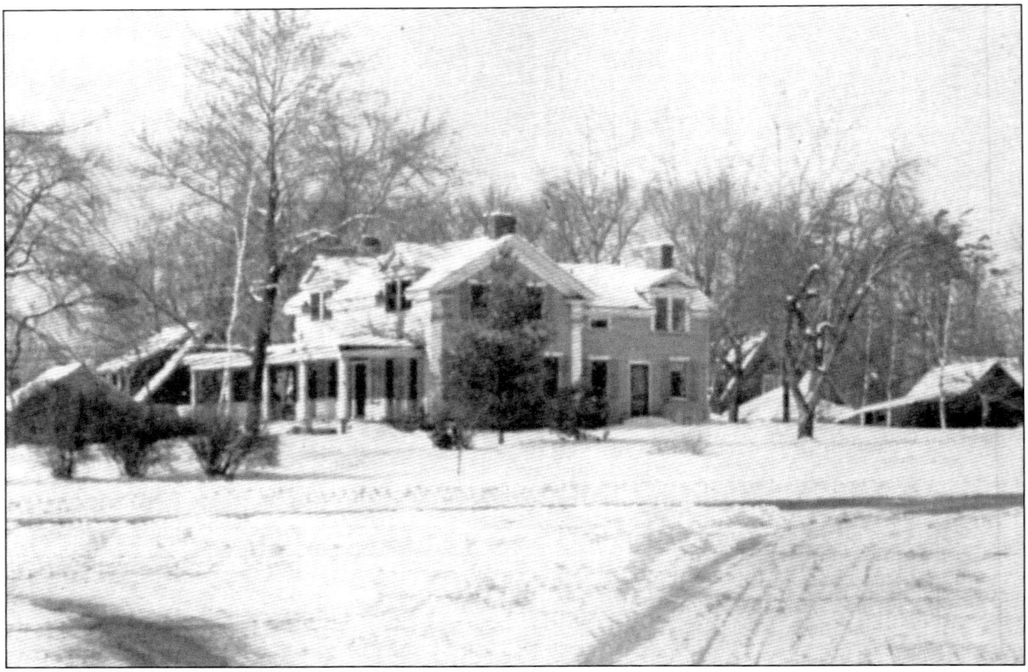

Here is the Schopmeier farmhouse in 1939. In the 1960s, this was the home of Dr. C. Guy Suits (1905–1991), vice president of General Electric and director of its research and development center from 1945 to 1965. Suits enlarged and modified the home extensively. The Suits-Bueche Planetarium at the Schenectady Museum is named in his honor and that of Arthur M. Bueche (1922–1982), who succeeded Suits as research and development director. (SCHS.)

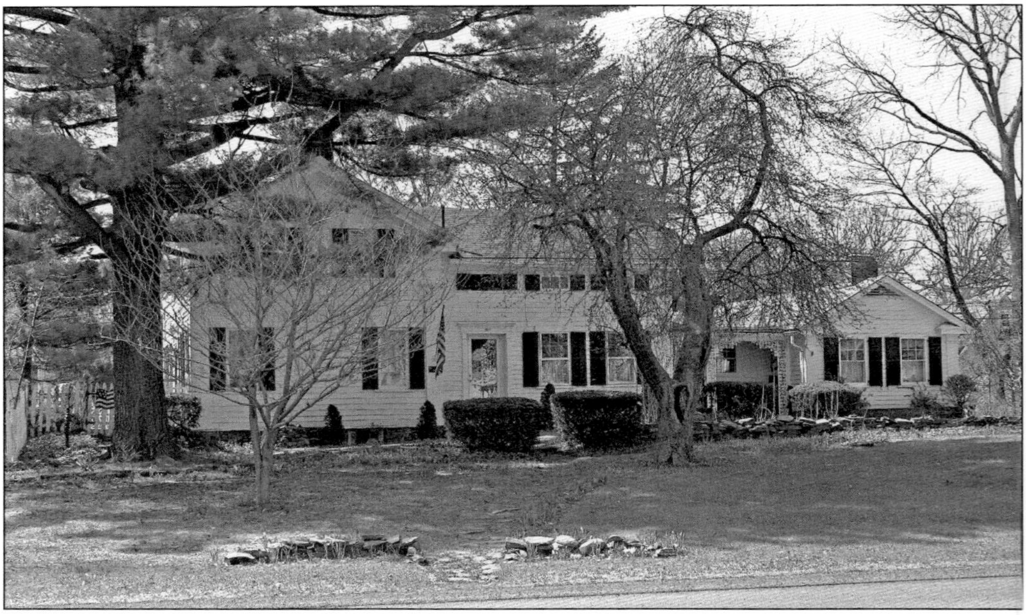

This is the Schopmeier farmhouse, today the home of David and Bridget Denofio. Taken 70 years after the previous photograph, the Y-shaped tree appears larger but is still protecting the home from cars coming down Story Avenue that fail to stop at Regent Street. (SCHS.)

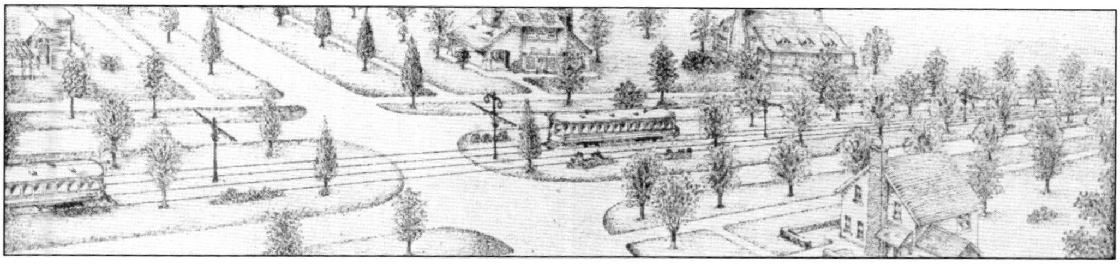

W. Garner Bee and his associates saw the advantages of developing a high-class suburban residential area from the 140-acre farm of Christian Schopmeier. By 1906, the property had been purchased and the area planned out. The center of the plot was Grand Boulevard, two roadways separated by a wide median with provision for a trolley line. There was a quarry for excellent building stone at the northwest corner of Grand Boulevard and Dean Street. (SCHS.)

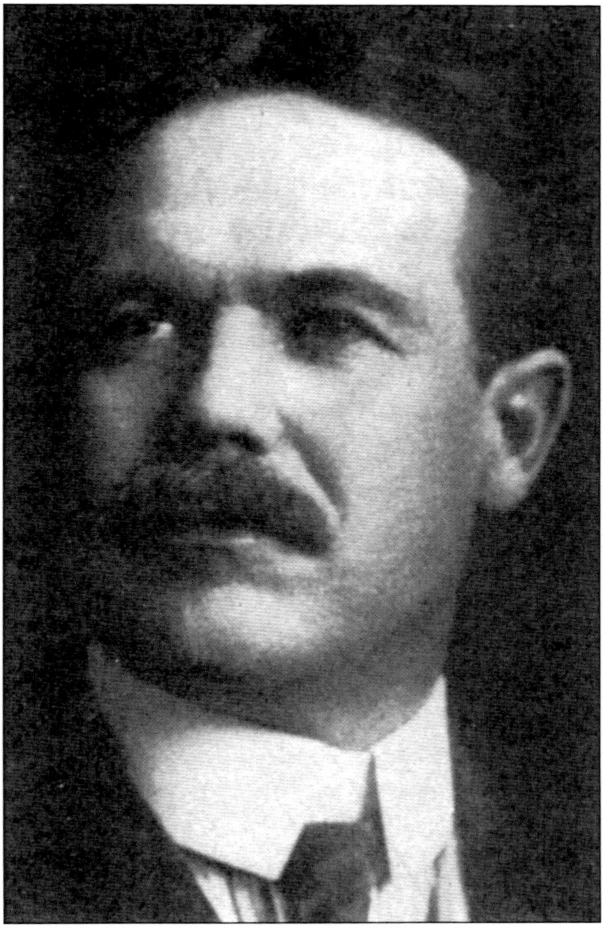

William Garner Bee, sometimes known as "the godfather of Niskayuna," was the builder and promoter of the development of Grand Boulevard. He was the force behind the growth of Niskayuna in the early 20th century, which started the town's change from rural to suburban. (SCHS.)

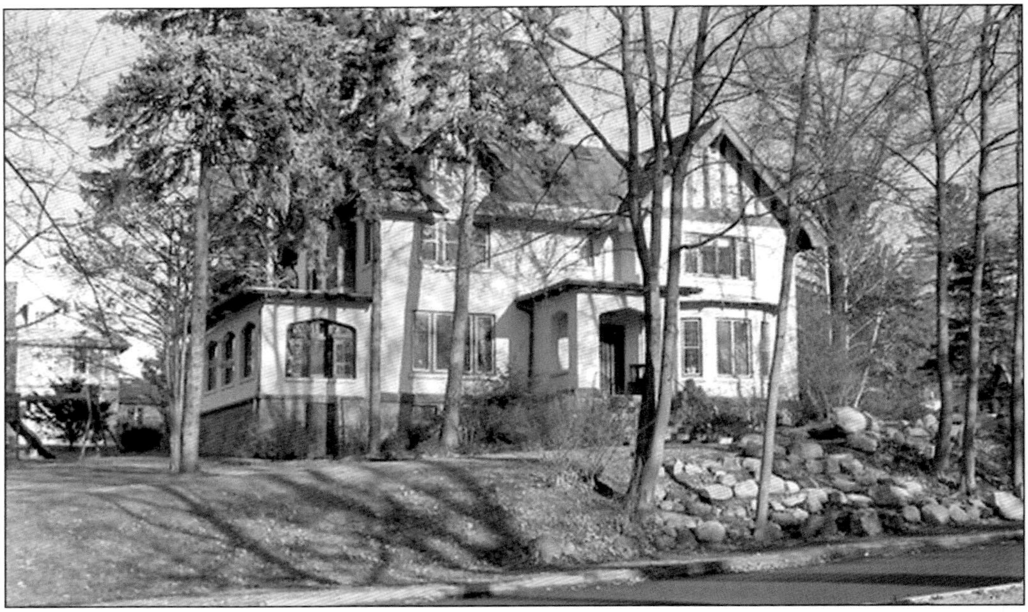

As W. Garner Bee worked his way up Grand Boulevard, he successively occupied several of the houses that he built. He eventually settled into the house at 2275 Grand Boulevard, one now known formally as the W. Garner Bee House and informally as "the Bees' Nest." The current owners are David and Kristy Guest. As suggested by David Guest, W. Garner Bee II, Garner Bee's grandson, was made grand marshal of Niska-Day in 2006. (SCHS.)

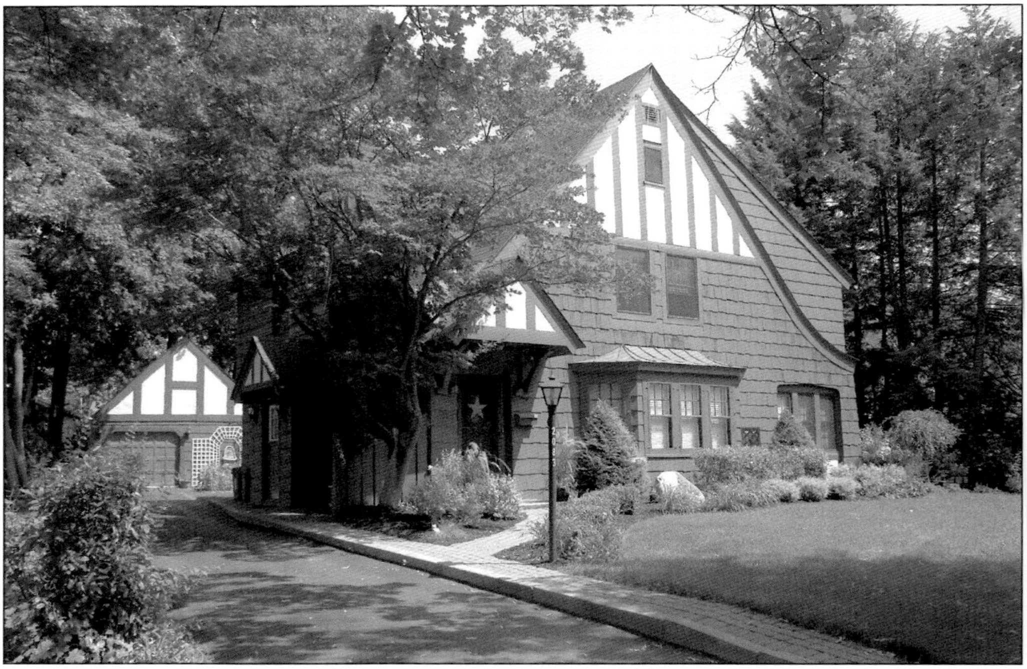

This home, located on the corner of Dean Street and Grand Boulevard, was built in 1927. It was occupied by Frank D. Barclay and his wife, Minnie Ida Barclay, daughter of W. Garner Bee. (Peg and Rick Mele.)

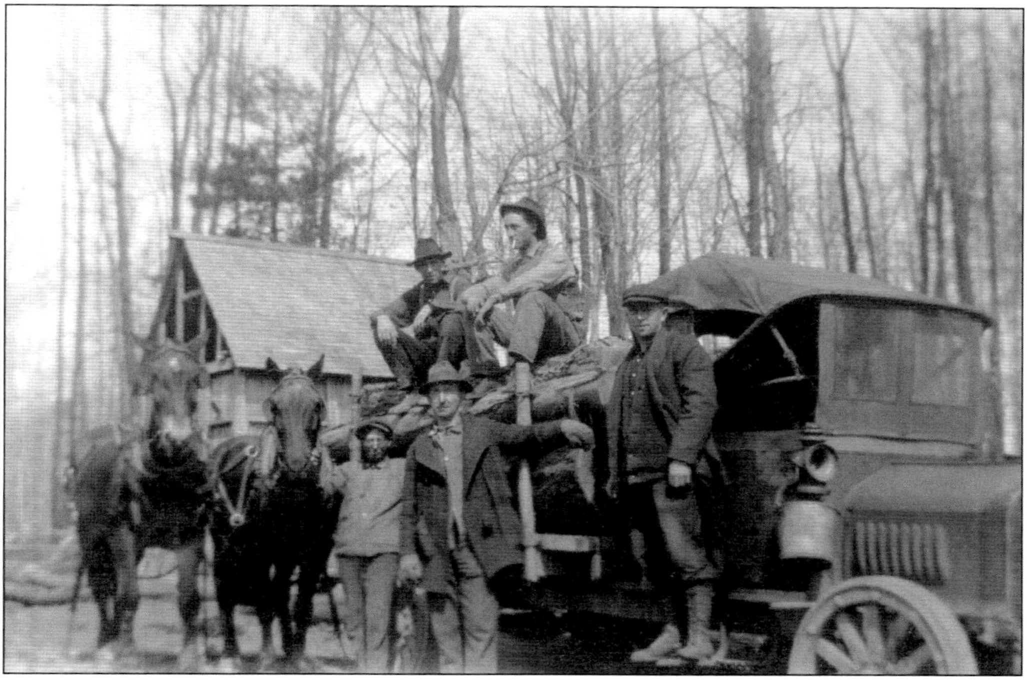

Construction of the Grand Boulevard neighborhood began about 1907 and continued into the 1920s. This photograph shows men, horses, and an early truck working on the area. (SCHS.)

Here is a wintertime construction scene on Grand Boulevard. The sleigh was a common type of wintertime vehicle consisting of a platform mounted on a pair of bobs. In this scene, the sleigh is being used to transport boxes of dynamite, commonly used in the early 20th century for constructive rather than destructive purposes. (SCHS.)

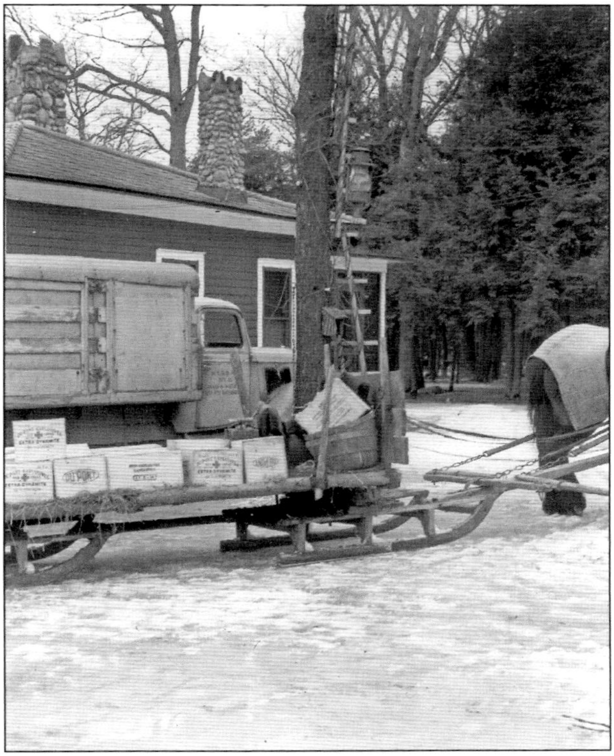

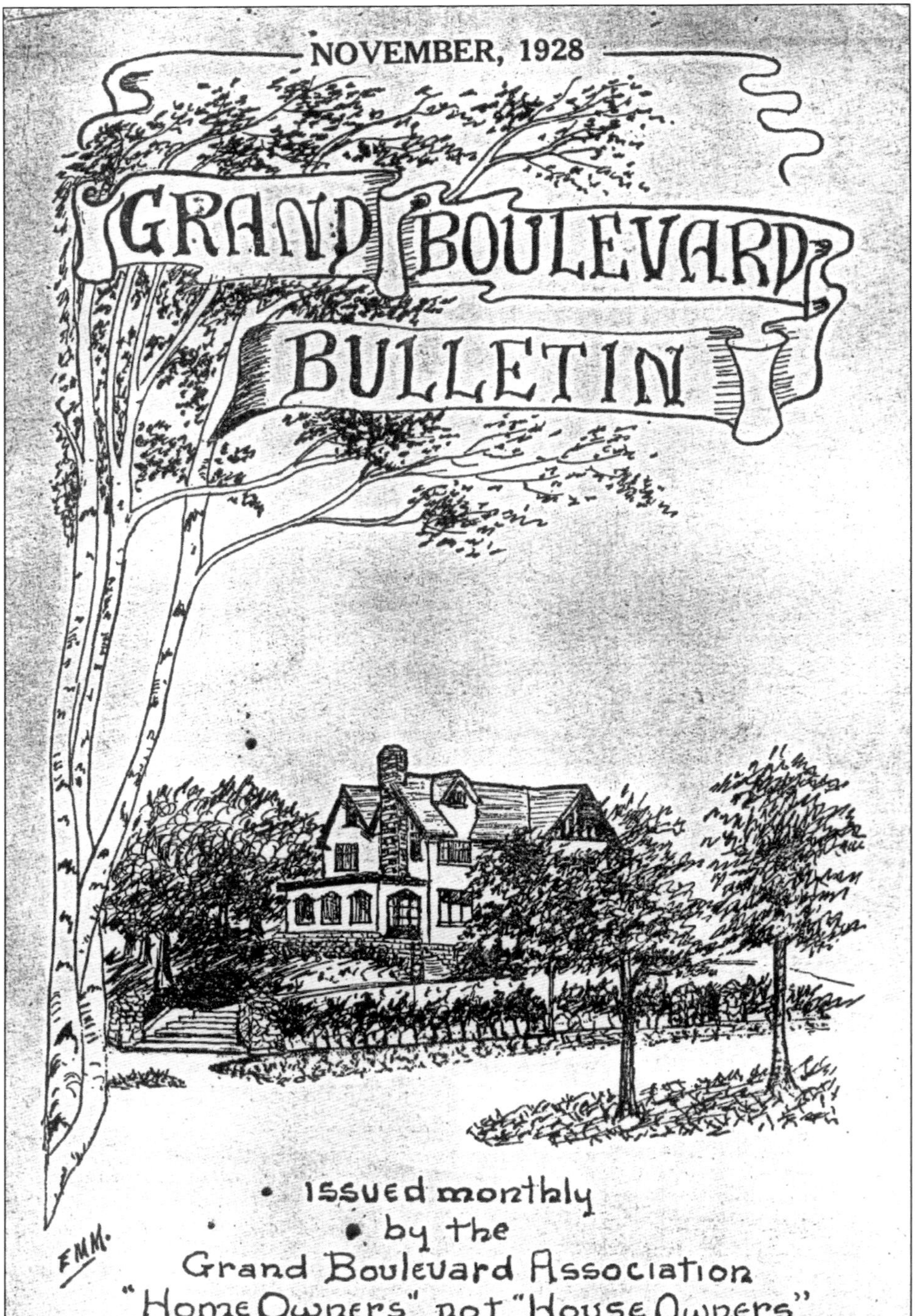

This issue of the *Grand Boulevard Bulletin* shows W. Garner Bee's home. Compare this to the corresponding photograph at the top of page 66. The *Grand Boulevard Bulletin*, an effort made to create a sense of community, was published monthly beginning in 1926 until its demise in 1970. (SCHS.)

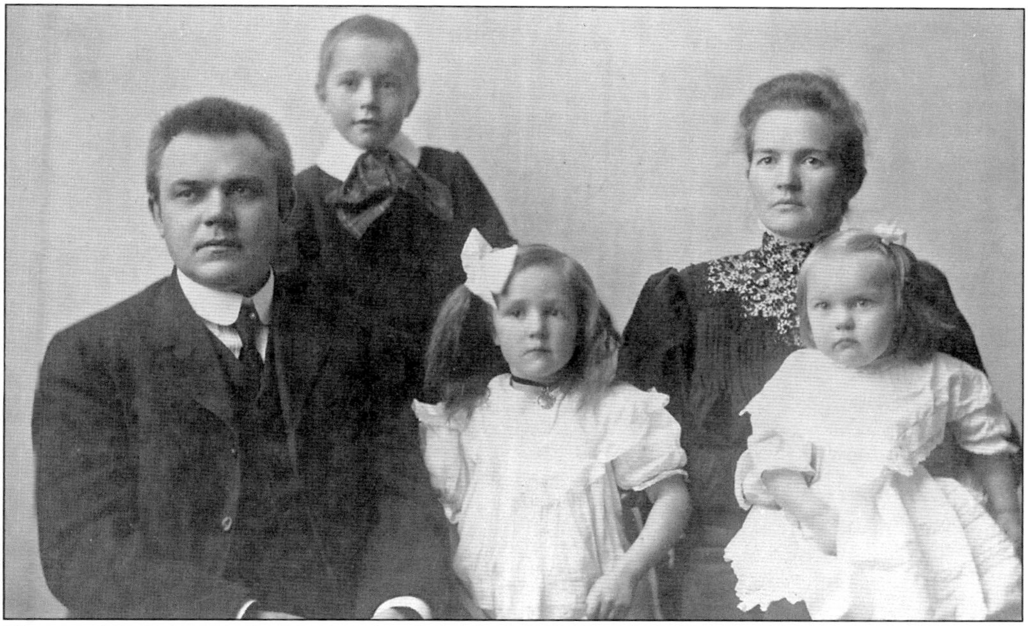

Here is the Christian Steenstrup family in late 1906. From left to right are Christian, his son Carl, his daughter Agnes, his wife Agnes Hjerrild, and his daughter Laura. Born in Denmark in 1874, Steenstrup immigrated to America in 1894 and joined General Electric in 1901. He is the inventor whose insight led to the General Electric Monitor top refrigerator that rapidly replaced the icebox in American homes. The patent for the innovative refrigerating machine was granted on April 15, 1930. (Schenectady Museum.)

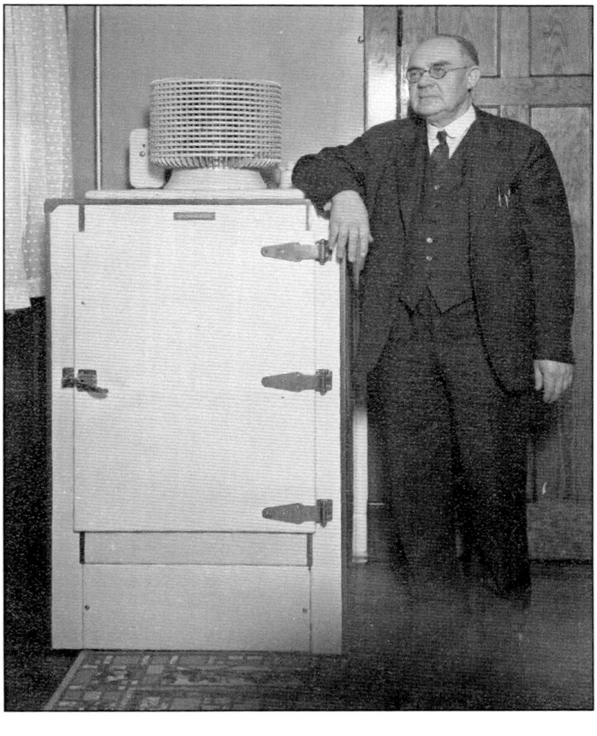

Christian Steenstrup (1874–1955) is seen here with a General Electric Monitor top refrigerator around 1935. Steenstrup chose the shape and design of the condenser at the top and called it a Monitor because it reminded people of the famous Civil War–era ironclad U.S.S. *Monitor*. Reconditioned Monitor top refrigerators are highly prized collector's items that now sell for upwards of $3,000 each. (Schenectady Museum.)

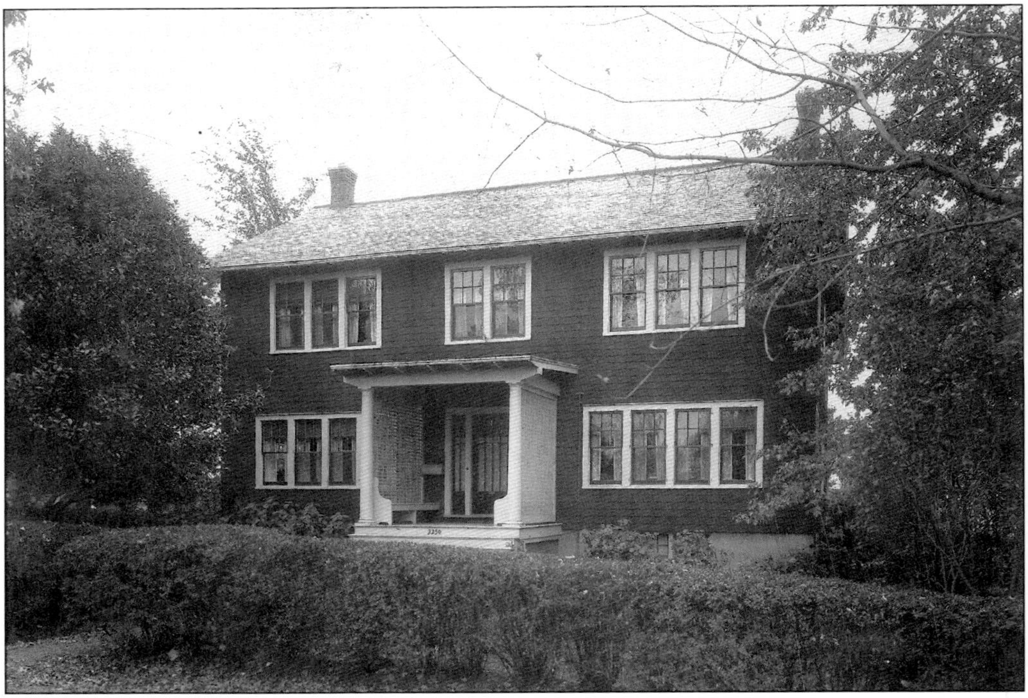

The Steenstrup residence is seen here at 2230 Grand Boulevard in Niskayuna. (Schenectady Museum.)

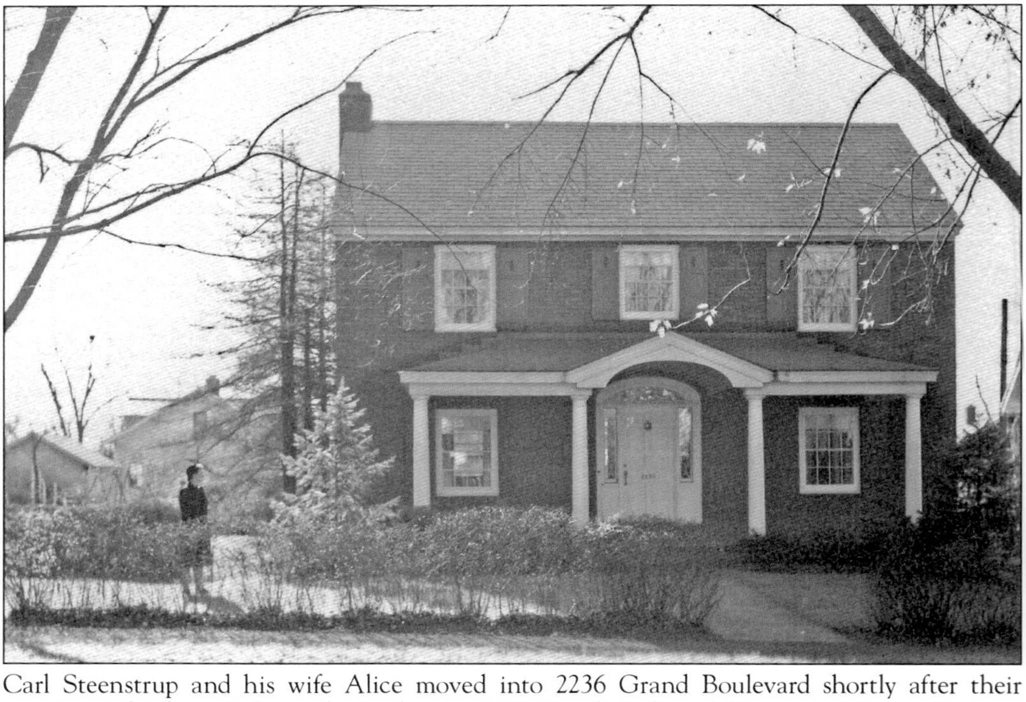

Carl Steenstrup and his wife Alice moved into 2236 Grand Boulevard shortly after their marriage. This home is located next door to 2230 Grand Boulevard, his parents' house. Carl was an electrical engineer who also worked for General Electric. (Jim Mancuso.)

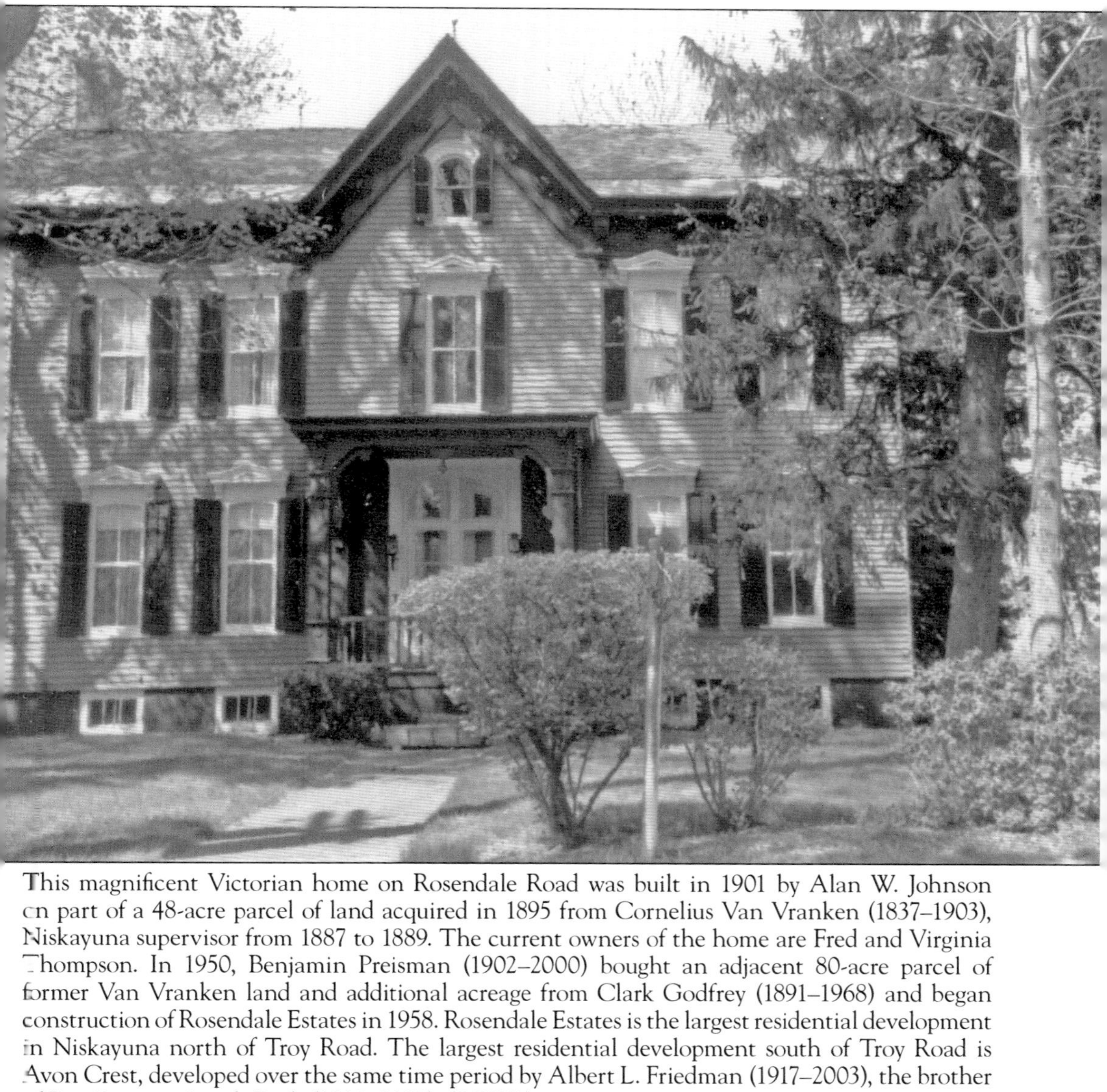

This magnificent Victorian home on Rosendale Road was built in 1901 by Alan W. Johnson on part of a 48-acre parcel of land acquired in 1895 from Cornelius Van Vranken (1837–1903), Niskayuna supervisor from 1887 to 1889. The current owners of the home are Fred and Virginia Thompson. In 1950, Benjamin Preisman (1902–2000) bought an adjacent 80-acre parcel of former Van Vranken land and additional acreage from Clark Godfrey (1891–1968) and began construction of Rosendale Estates in 1958. Rosendale Estates is the largest residential development in Niskayuna north of Troy Road. The largest residential development south of Troy Road is Avon Crest, developed over the same time period by Albert L. Friedman (1917–2003), the brother of Ben Preisman's wife Ruth (1909–2007). (SCHS.)

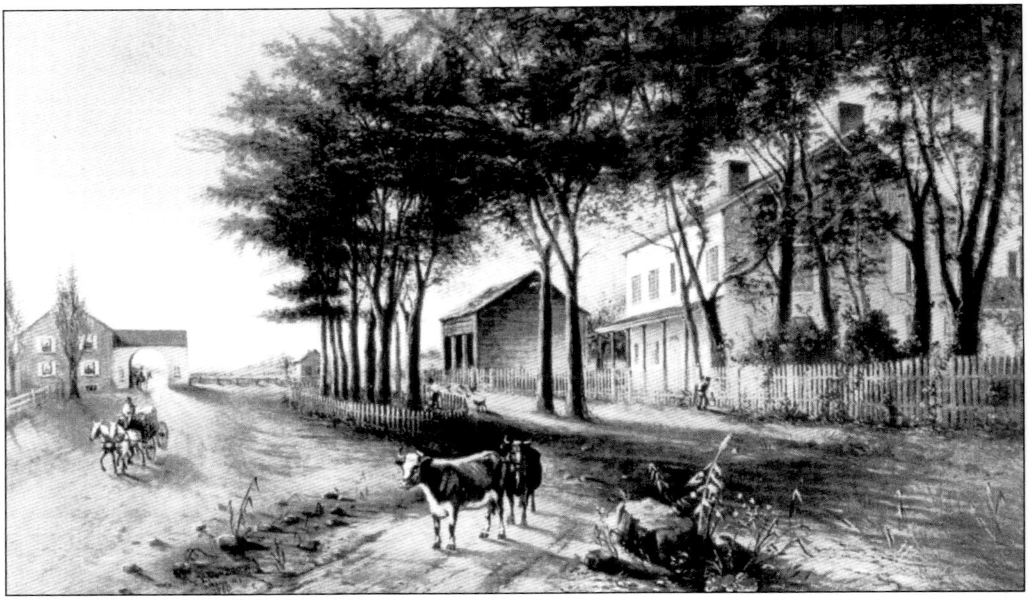

In 1840, Josiah and Elizabeth Stanford, parents of Leland and Charles Stanford, purchased the extensive Elm Grove Farm from Stephen and Harriet Van Rensselaer and converted its main house to the Elm Grove Hotel, depicted here. Elm Grove was on the Albany–Schenectady Turnpike in what is now the part of Colonie called Roessleville, about six miles southeast of the current Niskayuna border. A turnpike tollgate can be seen at the left of the drawing. (SCHS.)

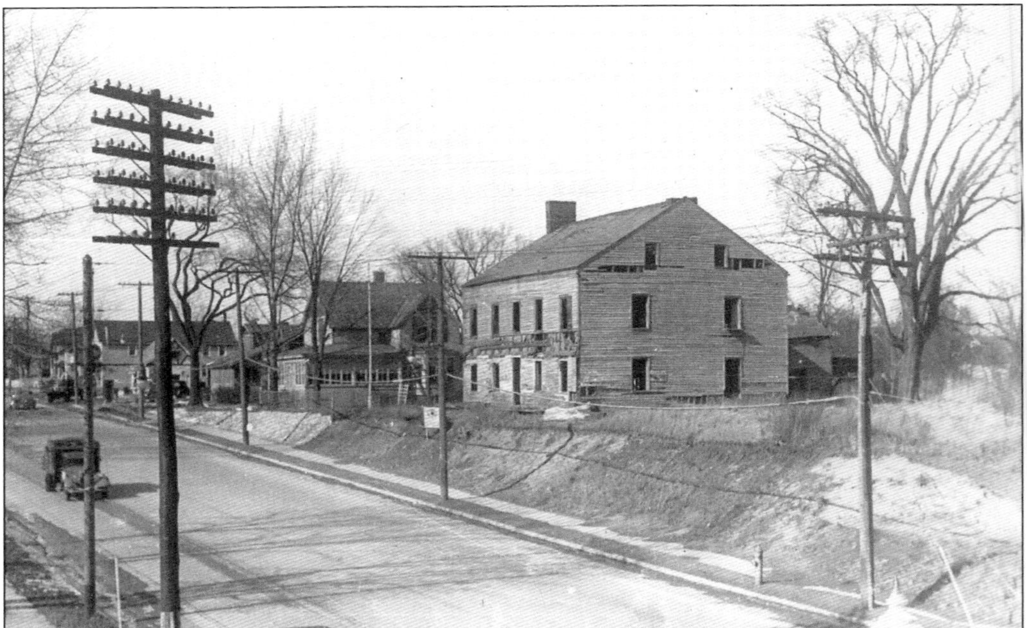

Here is the Elm Grove Hotel in the 1930s—vacant, devoid of its porch, and soon to be razed. Note that the tollgate is gone, the world has been electrified, the unpaved turnpike has become the smoothly paved Central Avenue, and all of the visible carriages are horseless. (SCHS.)

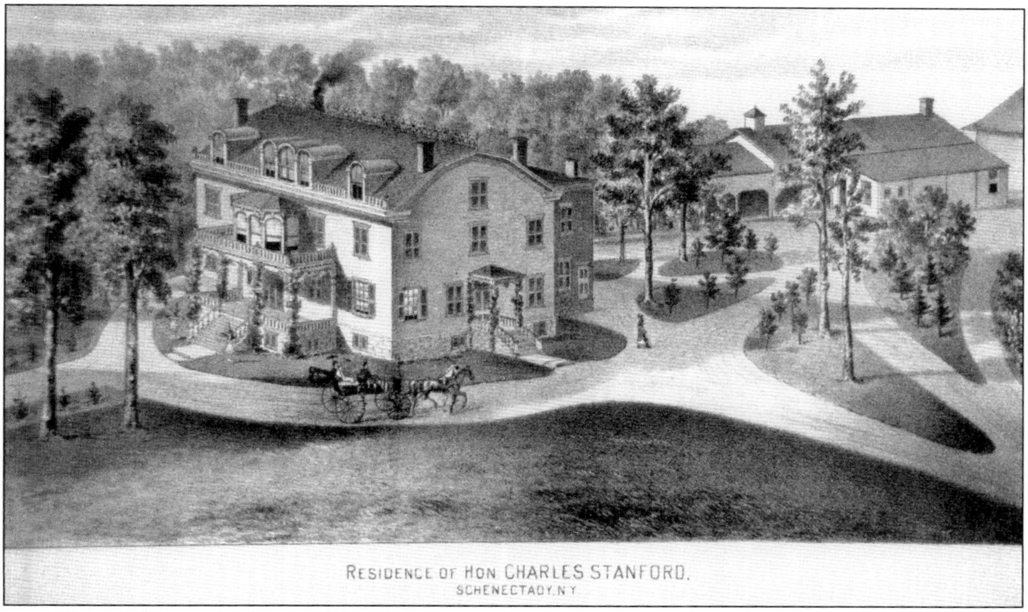

In 1859, Josiah Stanford moved his family to Locust Grove at the intersection of State Street and Balltown Road in Niskayuna, very close to the Schenectady border. Locust Grove was named for rows of locust trees on the property. The house was built around 1815 by Harmanus Schuyler, who served as Niskayuna town supervisor from 1817 to 1821. The appearance of the original building was altered to its present Victorian style by the Stanfords. (SCHS.)

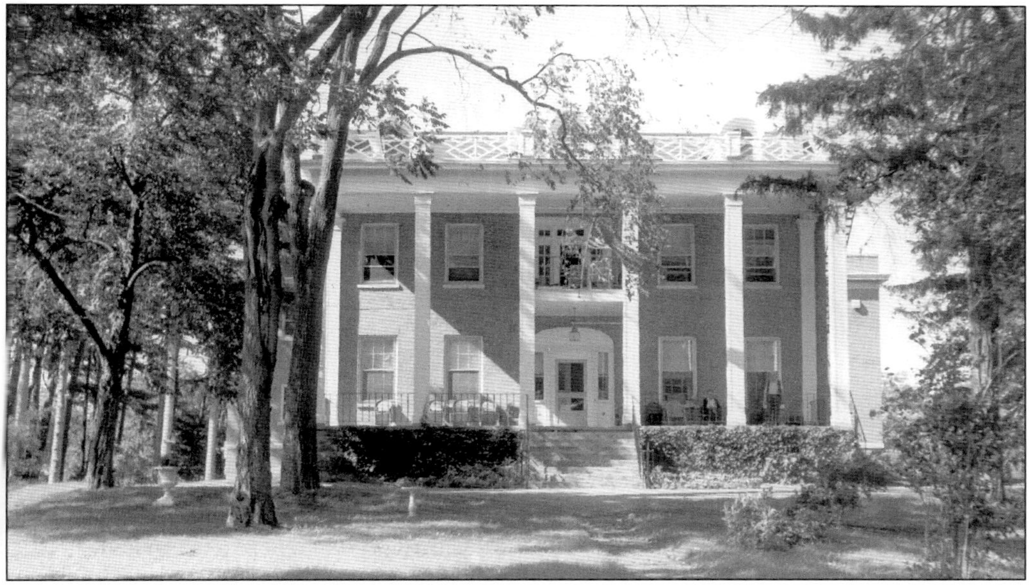

This is a current photograph of the Stanford mansion. In 1922, the 12-acre estate was purchased by the Ingersoll Memorial Trust, which was established by George T. Ingersoll (1847–1913), who had worked for Charles Stanford and was then hired by the City of Schenectady in 1885 as its first water superintendent. The Stanford mansion opened in 1823 as the Ingersoll Memorial Home for Aged Men. The Ingersoll home moved to a new facility on Consaul Road in 2008. (Efner City History Center.)

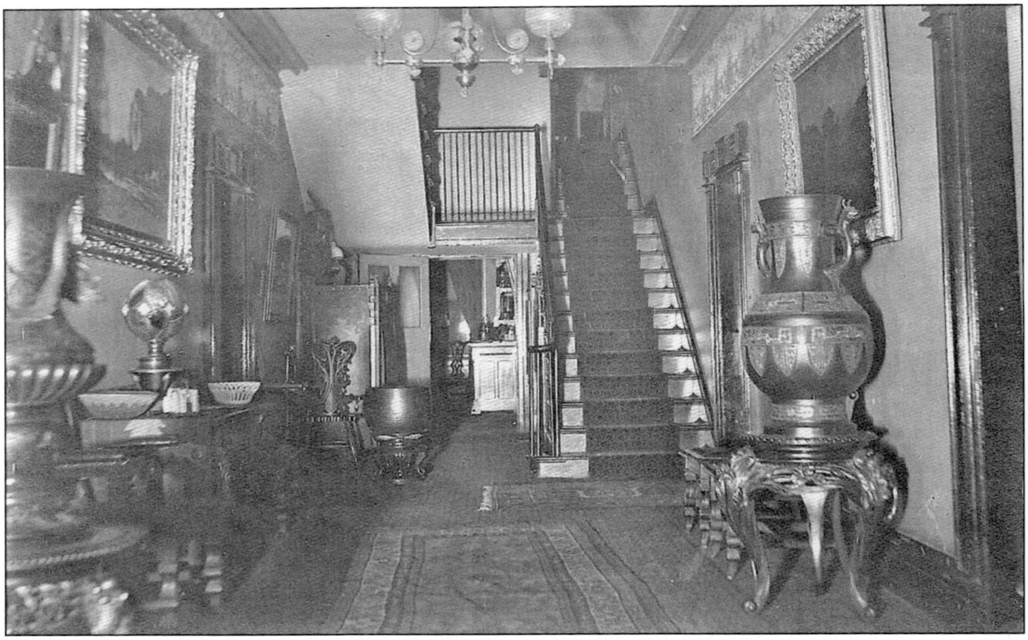

This photograph of the entrance of the Stanford home was taken around 1895 and shows the ornate decor typical of the times. This photograph, the one below, and several others of the Stanford property were shared with the historical society by Stanford descendant Glen Huntsberger III of California. (Glen Huntsberger III.)

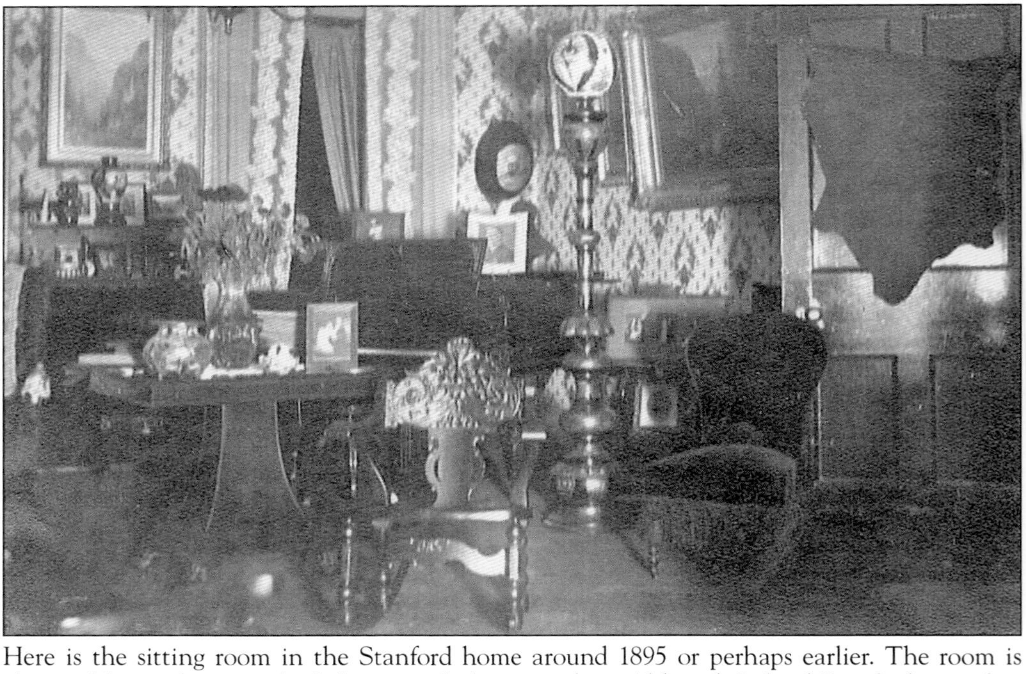

Here is the sitting room in the Stanford home around 1895 or perhaps earlier. The room is cluttered by modern standards but nonetheless nostalgic. Although Leland Stanford moved to California and never lived in the Stanford mansion, it is probable that he came back occasionally before 1885 to sit in this room and chat with his brother Charles. (Glen Huntsberger III.)

Charles Stanford inherited Locust Grove upon the death of his father in 1862. Charles was the brother of Leland Stanford, a United States senator and governor of California. In 1864, Charles was elected to the New York State Assembly and later to the state senate. He was president of the private water company that served Schenectady, one that he sold to the city on his deathbed in 1885. After his death, his son Welton inherited Locust Grove. (SCHS.)

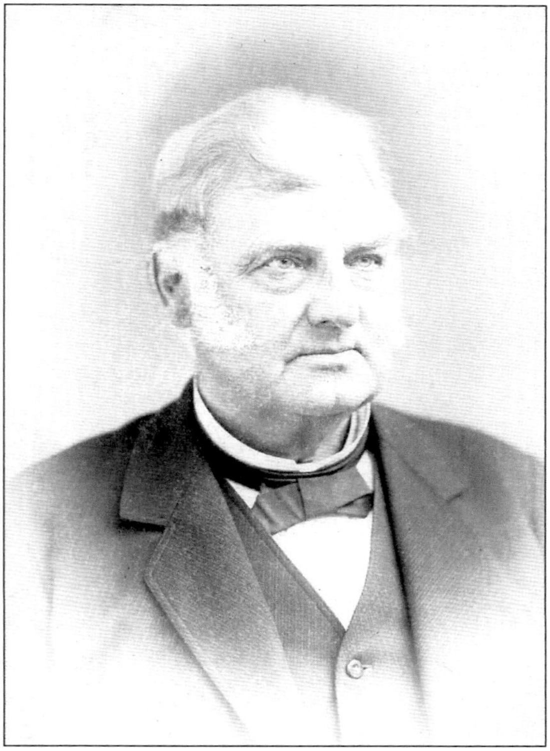

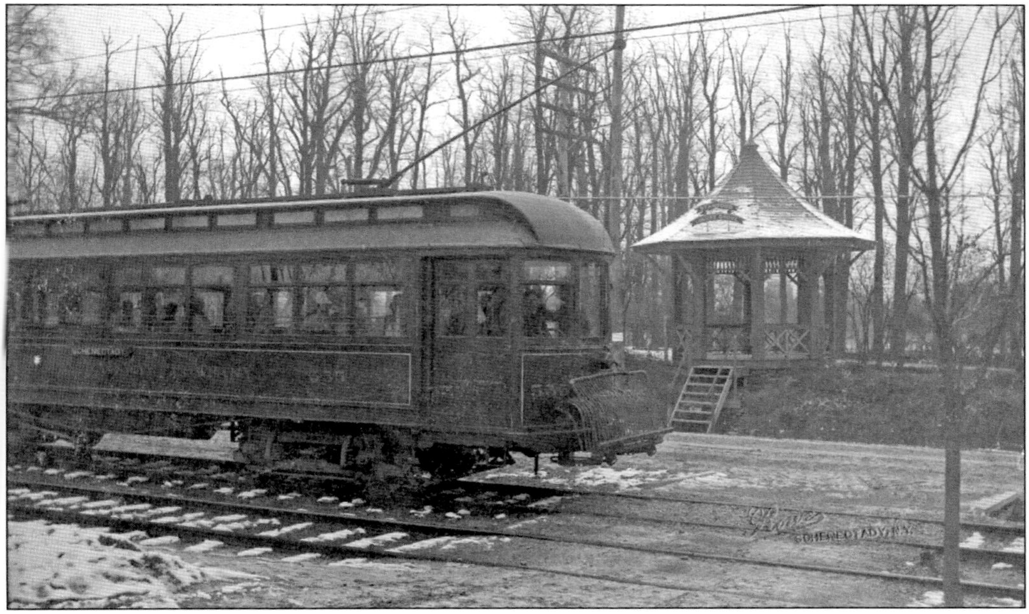

Trolley stop No. 6 in Niskayuna at the corner of State Street and Balltown Road is seen here. The topmost curved sign on the pagoda says "Stanford," and the one underneath it says "Locust Grove." Some stops, such as the one shown, had names as well as numbers, and in this case, passengers had a choice. The Schenectady Railway Company lines were extended to Troy, Albany, and Glenville in 1898. (Ralph Gasner.)

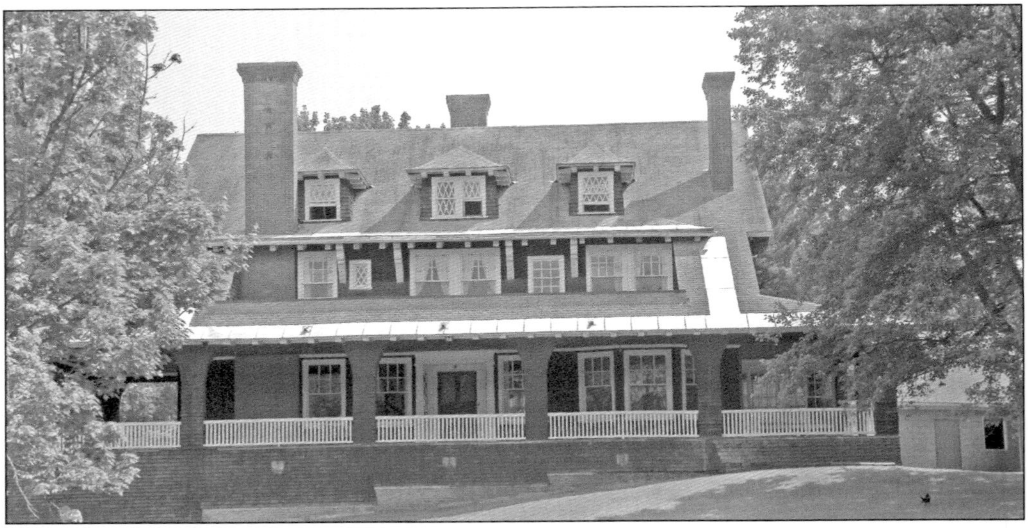

This large home was built in 1903 by George Westinghouse Jones, a cousin of the industrialist George Westinghouse Jr. and a cousin by marriage to General Electric inventor Charles W. Stone. The home, called *Caermarthen* to reflect Jones's Welsh ancestry, consisted of 26 rooms, servants' quarters, and eight fireplaces. The First Baptist Church purchased the house in 1955, and it was placed on the National Register of Historic Places in 1985. (SCHS.)

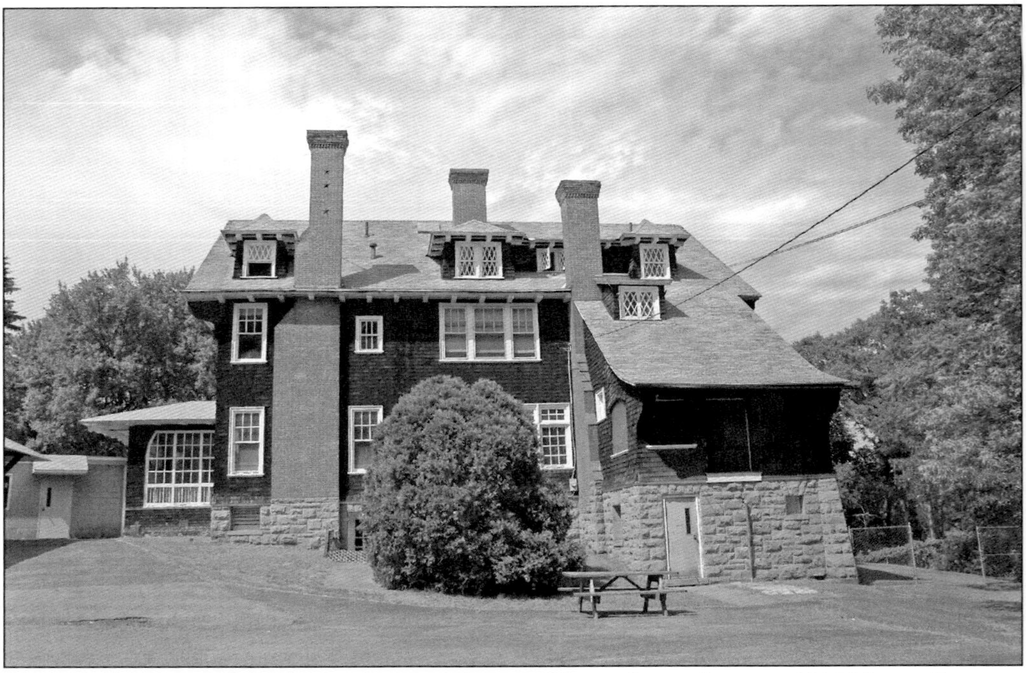

Here is a side view of the former home of George Westinghouse Jones at 1944 Union Street in Niskayuna adjacent to the First Baptist Church of Schenectady. The church uses the home for offices and its Sunday school. (SCHS.)

In 1702, Edward Hyde, Lord Cornbury (1661–1724), the governor of New York and New Jersey by appointment of Queen Anne, authorized construction of a Niskayuna fort on the land where this house stood. This home, built in 1756, was erected on the site of the 1670 homestead of Martin Cregier (1617–1713), one of the earliest settlers of Niskayuna. The house depicted was demolished in 1911 to make way for the New York State Barge Canal. (SCHS.)

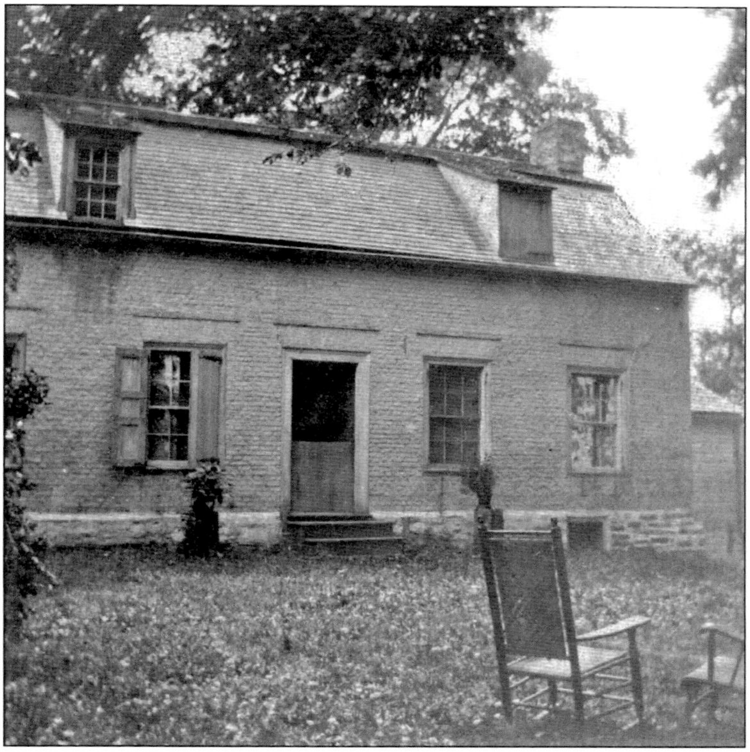

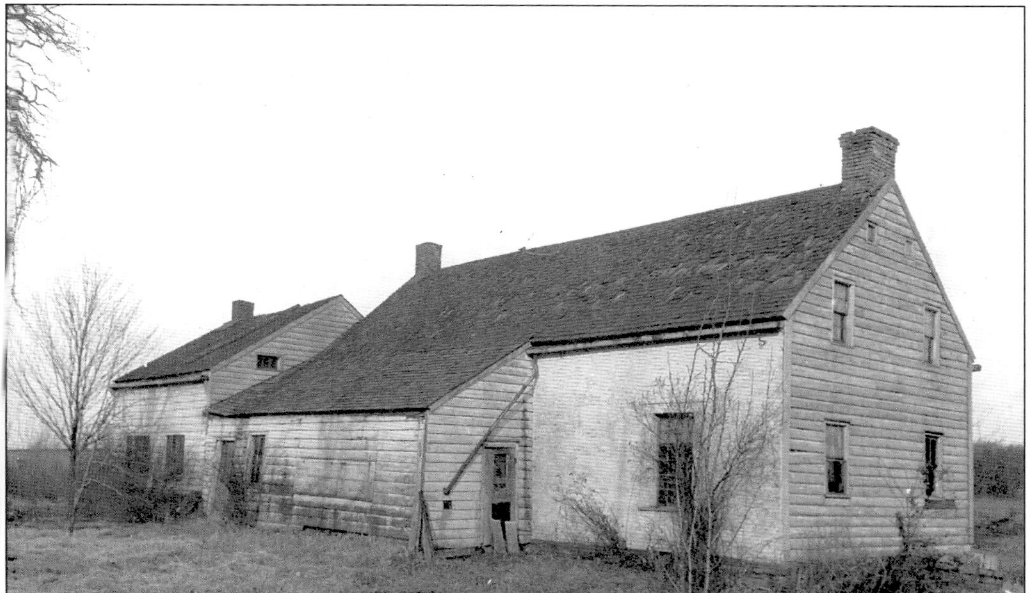

The Thymesen house was built very early by Cornelis Thymesen on land deeded from Jan Jacobsen Van Noorstrant and located "this side of Lysiens kill." Cornelis married Martie Ysbrantse in Albany. They settled in the Rosendale area around 1701. The photograph was taken in 1937. (SCHS.)

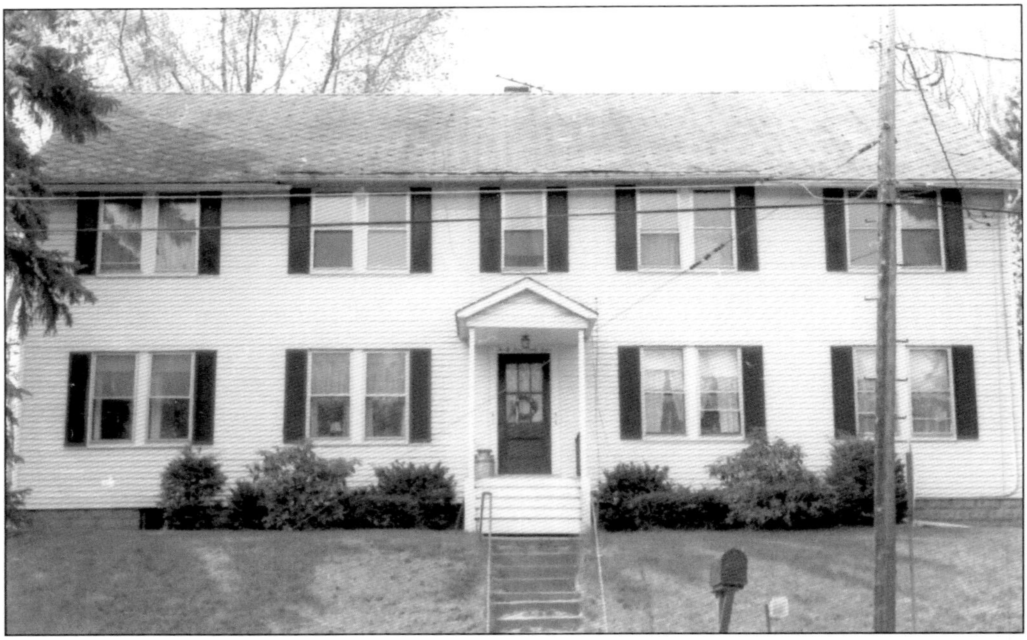

This house on Rosendale Road, affectionately called "the barn," was built around 1851. Currently an apartment house, the structure appears to be of Shaker design. The barn originally served as the stable for the MacIntosh Hotel. Around 1930, it was made into apartments by hotel owner Mary MacIntosh. (Efner City History Center.)

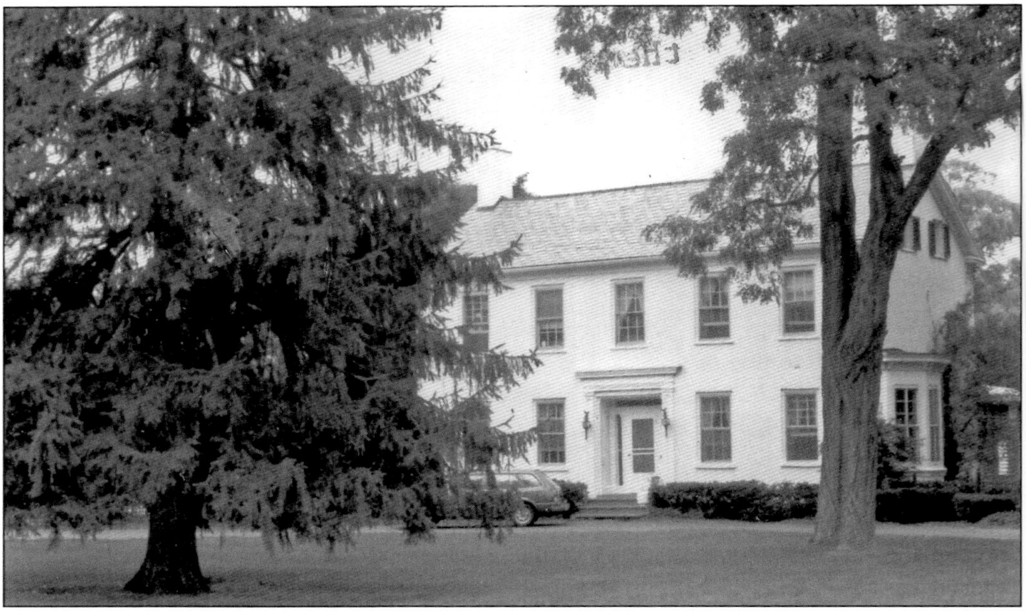

The Van Vranken Manor House of 1755 was one of five surviving houses built in the Rosendale/Lock 7 area by the Van Vranken family in the 18th century. It is located at what is now 1256 Lock 7 Road, the home of Howard and Patricia Goldstock. Five Van Vrankens fought in the American Revolution, and six of the first 28 men to serve as Niskayuna town supervisors were Van Vrankens. (Efner City History Center.)

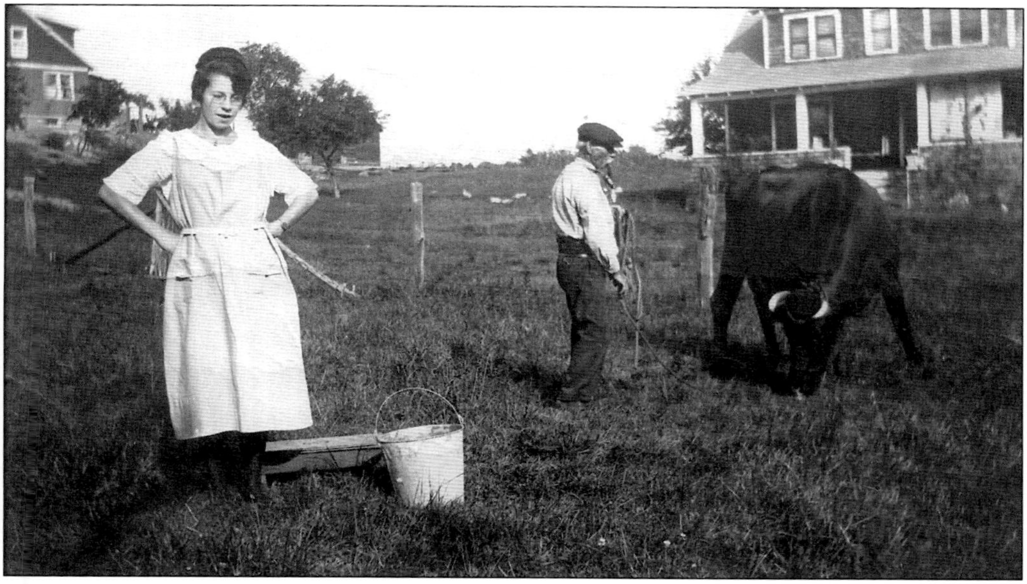

Here is an early-20th-century photograph of Frank Guthan at his farm on Consaul Road. The identity of the woman is unknown. When the Crosstown Arterial came through the area in the 1960s, the house in the background was moved to the corner of Consaul Road and Oregon Avenue. (Paul Pakan.)

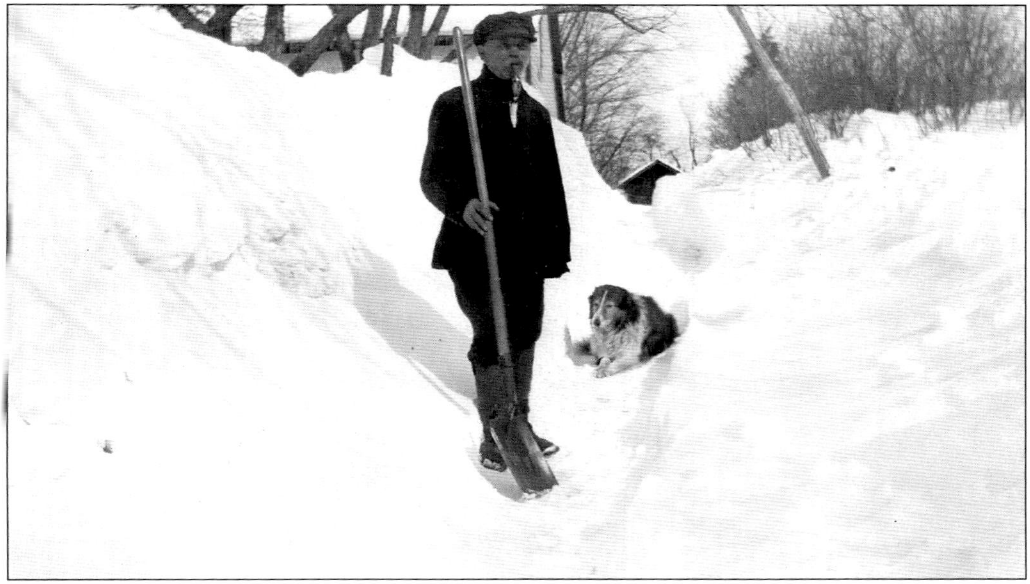

Frank Guthan is shoveling snow on January 21, 1914, the day of the largest snowfall of that winter. He is awaiting the arrival of the doctor and the birth of his granddaughter Bertha. (Paul Pakan.)

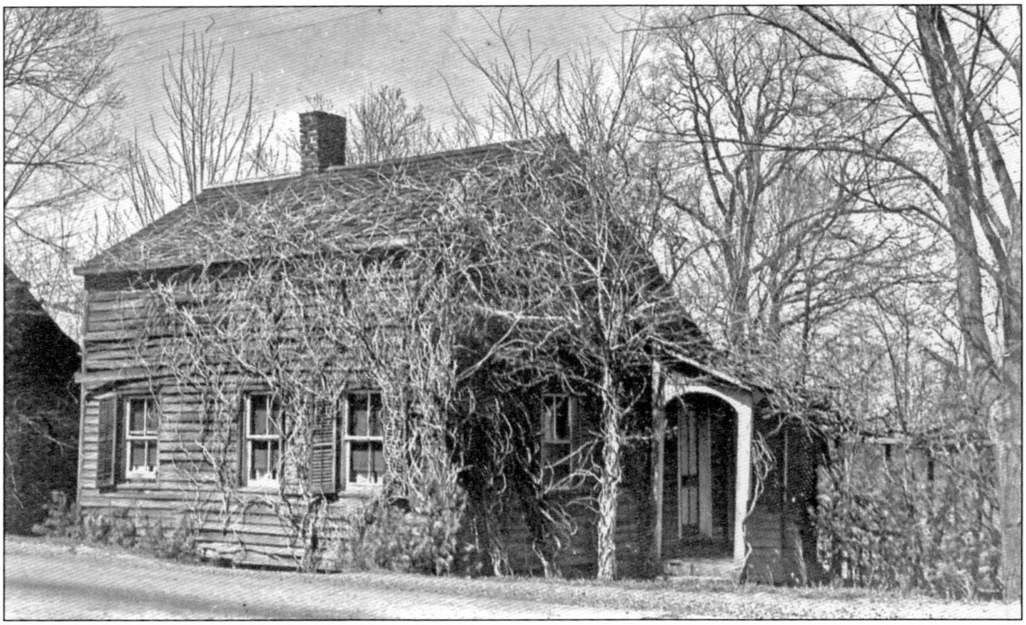

Pictured is the home of blacksmith Charles Marks and his wife, Helena Knabner Marks, in the late 19th century. The house was on Troy Road between the Niskayuna Reformed Church and the general store at the intersection of Rosendale and Troy Roads. The store is now best remembered as Denison's. (SCHS.)

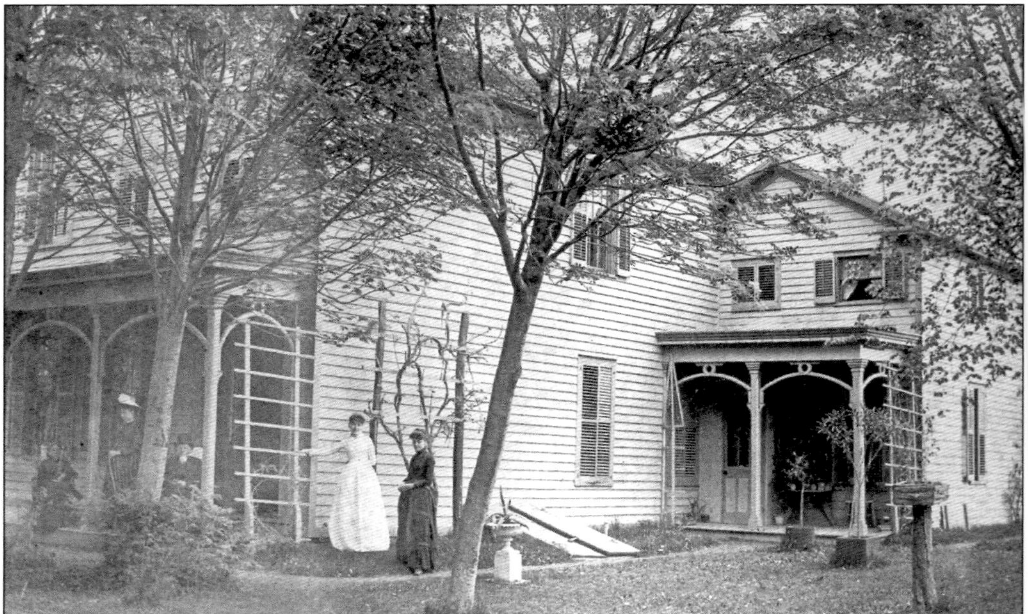

The Garnett Witbeck farmhouse was located at the intersection of Rosendale and Troy Roads. It had been in the Witbeck family since the American Revolution. In 1922, it was purchased by Howard Chadwick of W. A. Chadwick and Company Realtors. The house was razed, and residential subdivisions were laid out on the farmland. This photograph was taken in about 1885. (SCHS.)

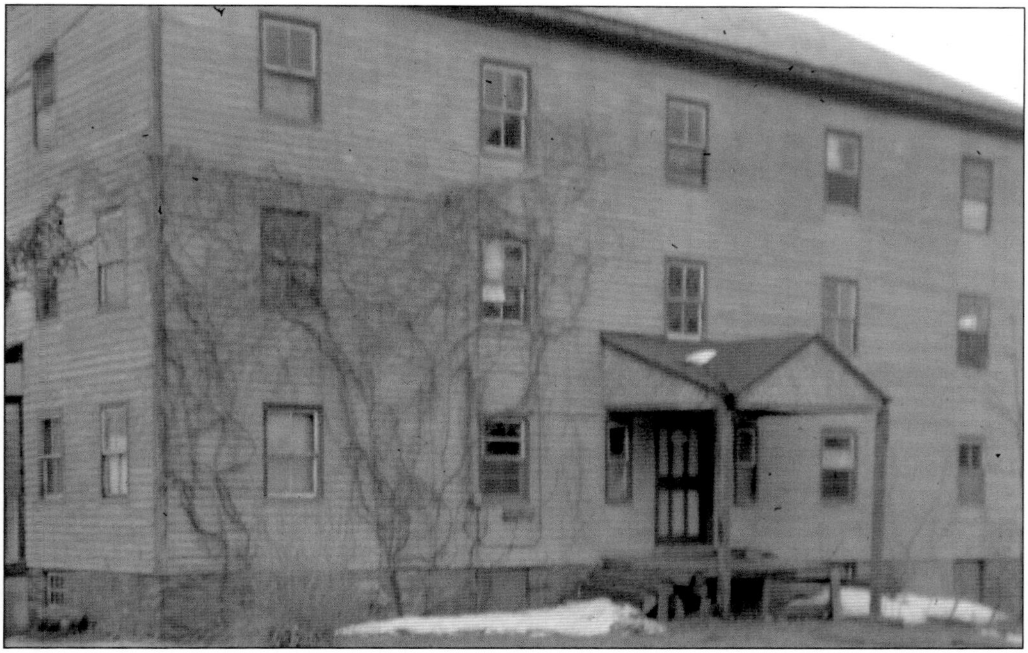

The Niskayuna hamlet was the Shakers' first stopping place when they and Mother Ann Lee (1736–1784) arrived from England in 1774. They developed the area now in the town of Colonie next to the current Albany International Airport. Only the buildings called South and West remain today and are private dwellings. The North building shown was taken for part of the airport. (SCHS, Laura Brown Collection.)

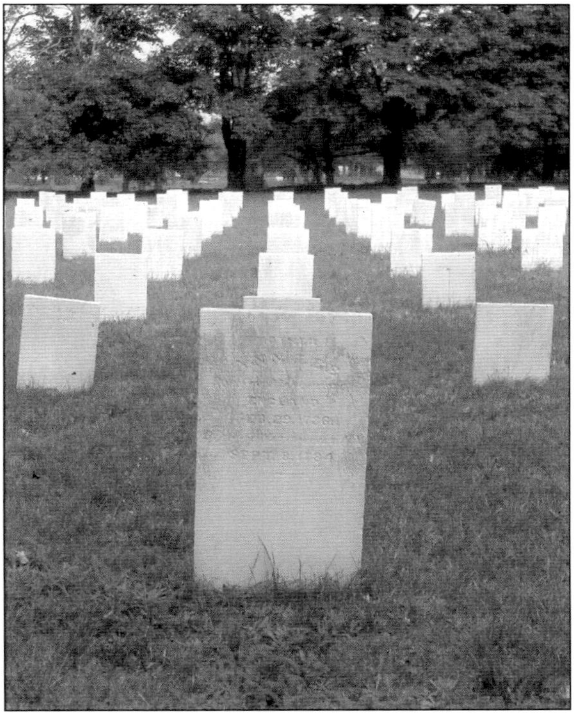

The Shaker Cemetery is located near the former Ann Lee home at the Albany International Airport. The stones are in straight rows and perfectly spaced. Lee's stone is larger than the others and is flanked by elders and eldresses. The last burial in the cemetery was in 1938. (SCHS, Laura Brown Collection.)

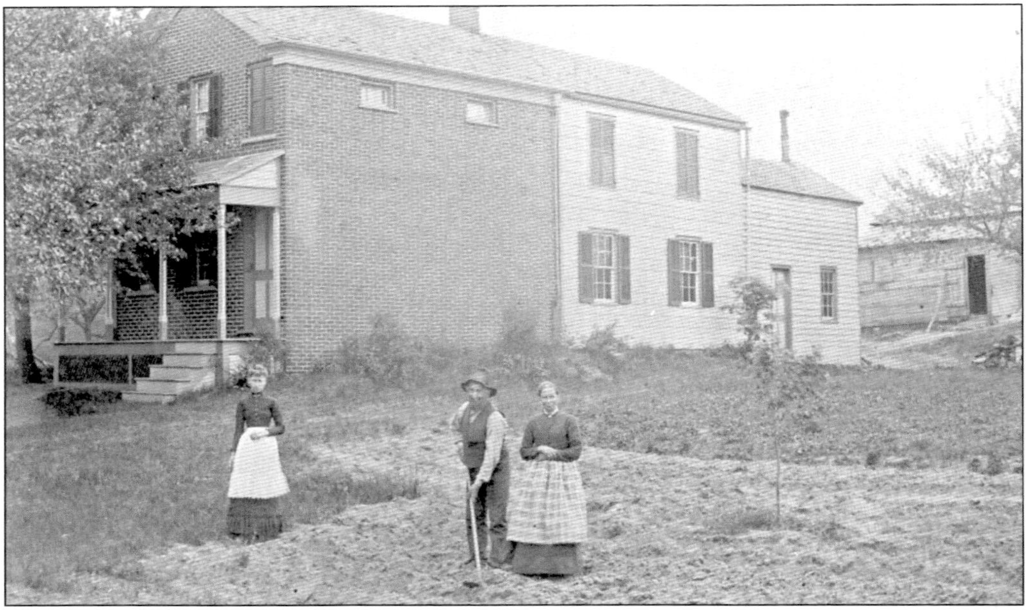

The Ruopp house at 3038 Troy Road, directly across from the Niskayuna Reformed Church, was built in 1870. Pictured from left to right in 1881 are Christina Ruopp at age 16 and her parents, Jacob and Anna Maria Ruopp. Christina married Charles William Male and became the mother of Charles T. Male Sr. and Maude A. (Male) Rice, Niskayuna's receiver of taxes for over 40 years. The shed in the background was a blacksmith shop. (SCHS.)

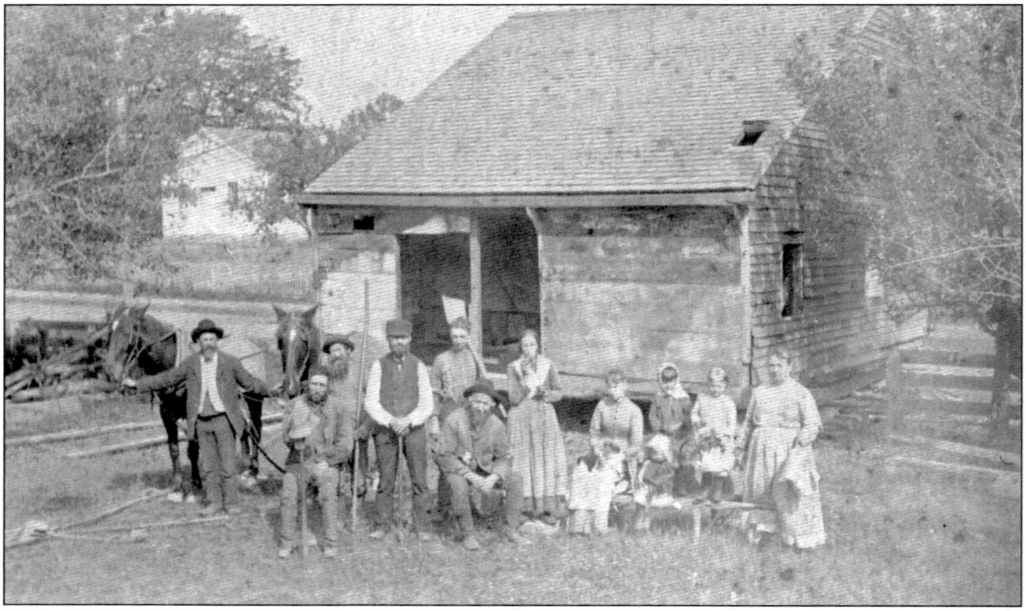

Here is the extended Ruopp clan posing behind the blacksmith shop in 1888. The man holding the horses is Civil War veteran Valentine Alheim. The others from left to right are James Moncton, Luke Marks, Charles Mouter, Charles William Male, Jacob Ruopp, Anna Maria Ruopp, Christina Ruopp Male, three unidentified children (one is probably Jennie Mouter), and Charles Mouter's wife Emma. (Janette Burger.)

Pictured are John Samuel Findlay Jr. and his wife, Alice May Burger Findlay, holding daughter Florence Marion Findlay in 1913. Florence grew up to marry John Nicholas Waterfield and gave birth to future Niskayuna deputy police chief J. Richard Waterfield (see page 120). (Janette Burger.)

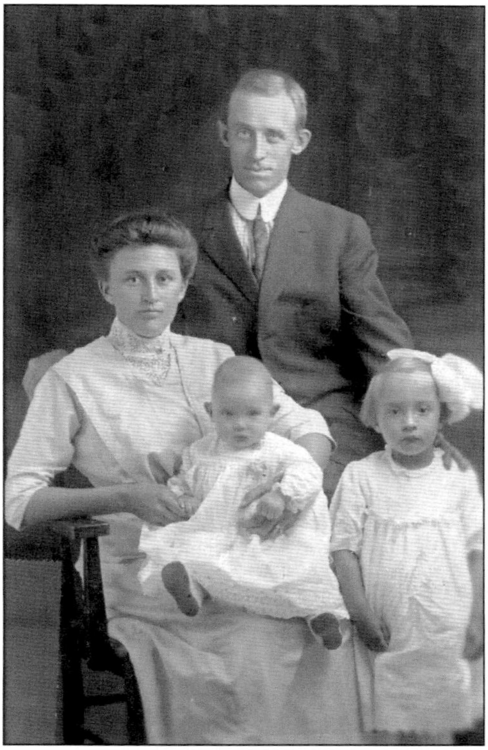

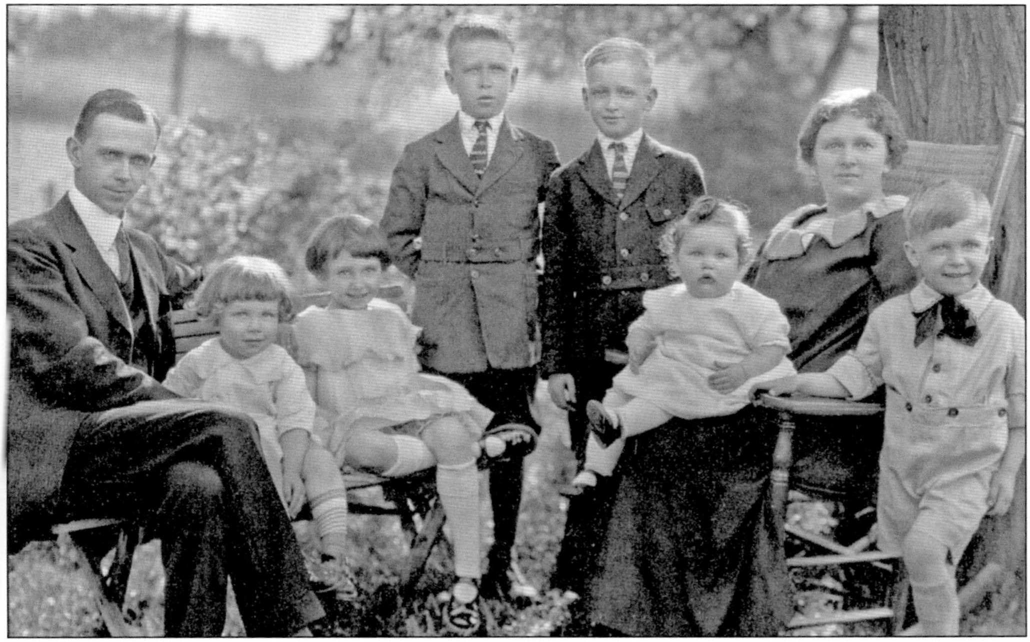

The Male family is shown here in 1925. From left to right are Charles T. Male Sr., son Donald, daughter Janette, sons Tom and Bill, son Ken on the lap of his mother, Mildred Schairer Male, and son Teddy at her side. Tom and Bill were born just 15 months apart and were always dressed alike. (Janette Burger.)

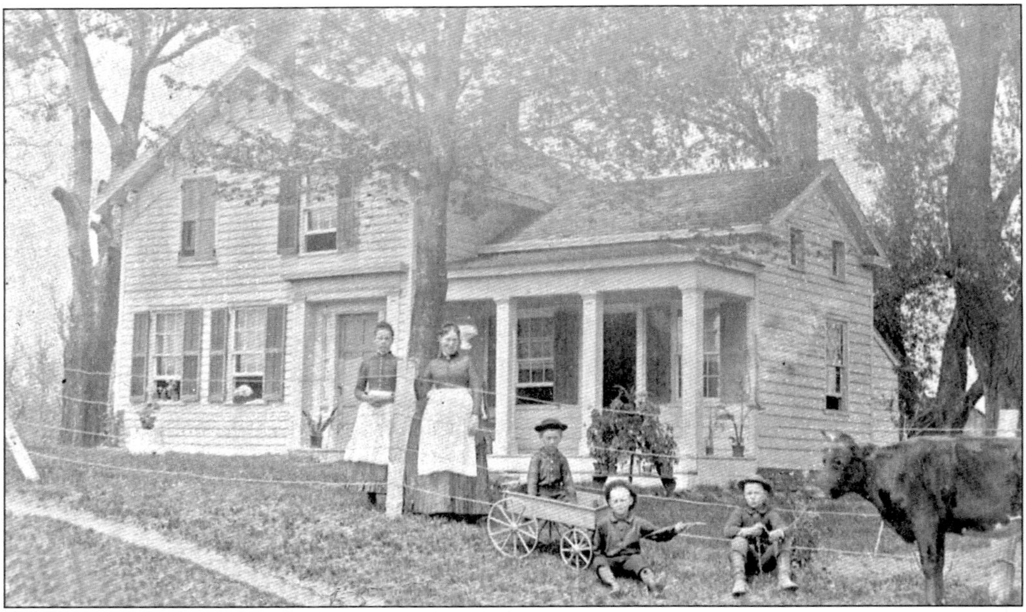

Here is the home of Luke and Ellen Marks in 1920, two years after Luke died. From left to right are "Aunt Grace" Marks and visitors Mildred Schairer Male and her children Janette Male (in the wagon), Bill Male, and Tom Male. Janette grew up to marry E. Melvin Burger Sr. The Burgers tilled farms on Troy Road and later Niska Isle where Janette still lives and graciously shares her extensive photograph collection with people who make books. (Janette Burger.)

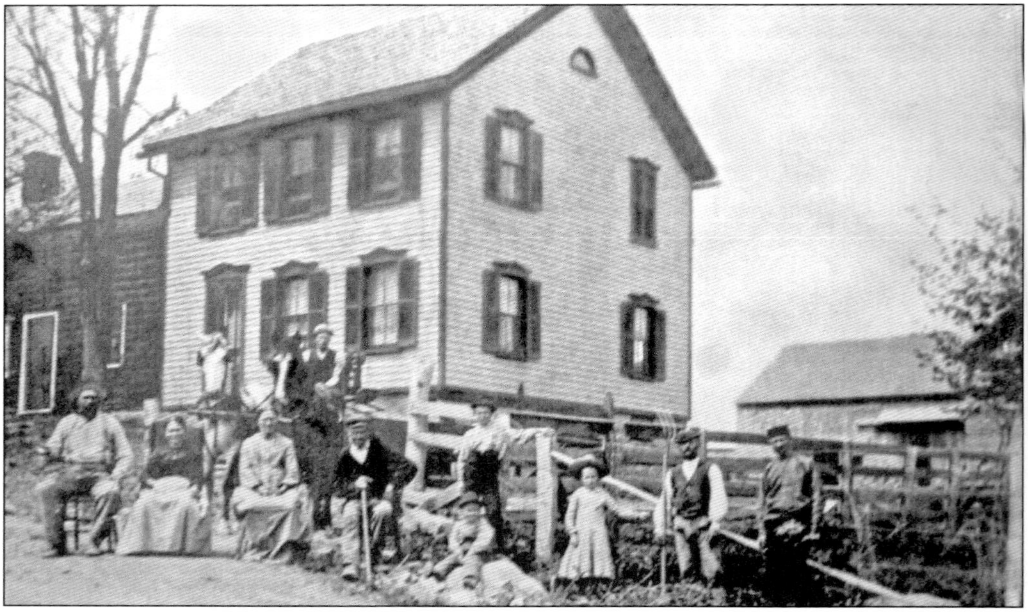

The Schairer farmhouse on Vly Road is pictured in 1887. The man on the horse is a hired hand. The others from left to right are John Schairer; sisters Dorothea Hauser Schairer and Anna Hauser Schuler; their father, Ludwig Hauser; Jacob Schuler Jr. with his hand on the post, and his brother Ludwig Schuler sitting down; Dora Schuler; a hired hand; and Jacob Schuler Sr. Somewhat later, a front porch was added to the house, which is still standing. (Carl Derwig.)

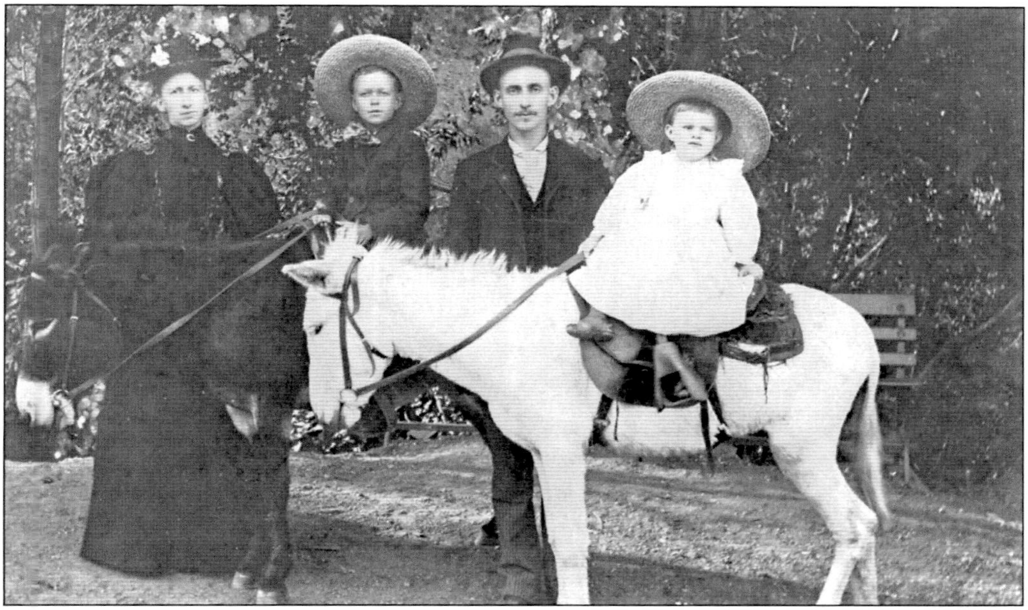

This photograph was taken in Colorado Springs in 1896. From left to right are Christina Ruopp Male; son Charles T. Male (age seven); Charles William Male; and Charles's sister Maude A. Male. The name of the pony is unknown. Charles T. Male was the founder of the engineering consulting firm C. T. Male Associates that did a significant portion of the surveying and engineering design for the infrastructure of the town of Niskayuna. (SCHS.)

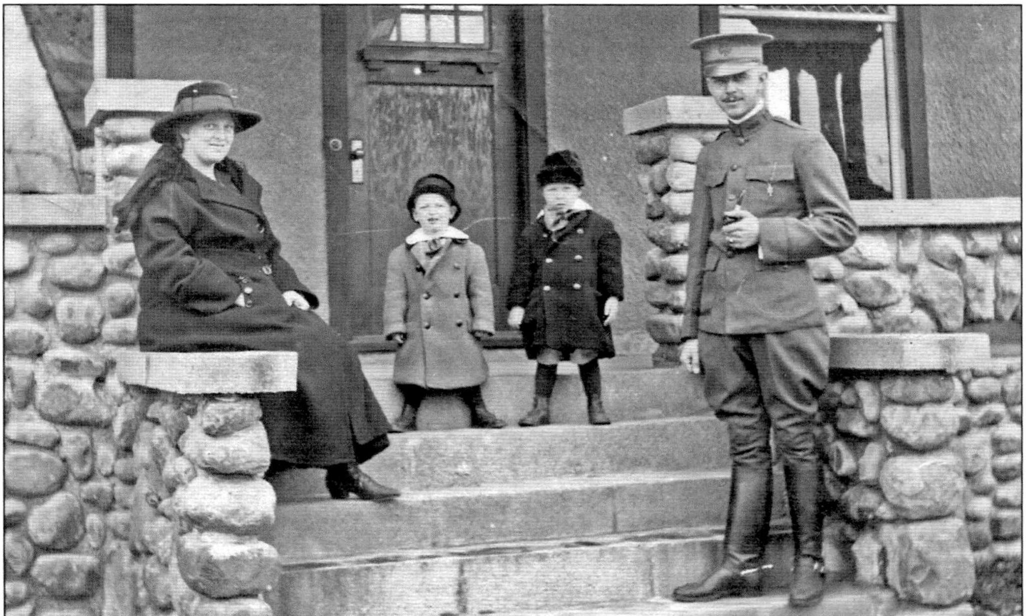

The Male family is pictured standing on the steps of their home on Troy Road across from Niskayuna Road. Shown from left to right are Mildred Schairer Male, William J. Male, Charles T. Male Jr., and Charles T. Male Sr. The photograph was taken in 1917 while Charles Sr. was serving in the army. (George Yager.)

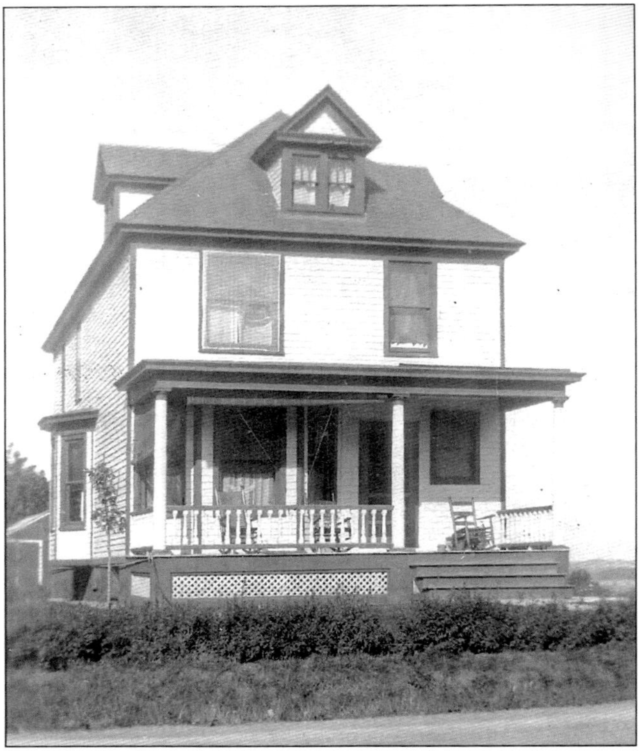

This 1911 photograph shows the house that was built by Pierce and Bridget Holohan at 2005 Troy Road (stop No. $19\frac{1}{3}$, also called Drydens). When they bought the property, they lived in an existing house until the new house was built. When Pierce died, Bridget moved to Schenectady. (Carolyn Veeder.)

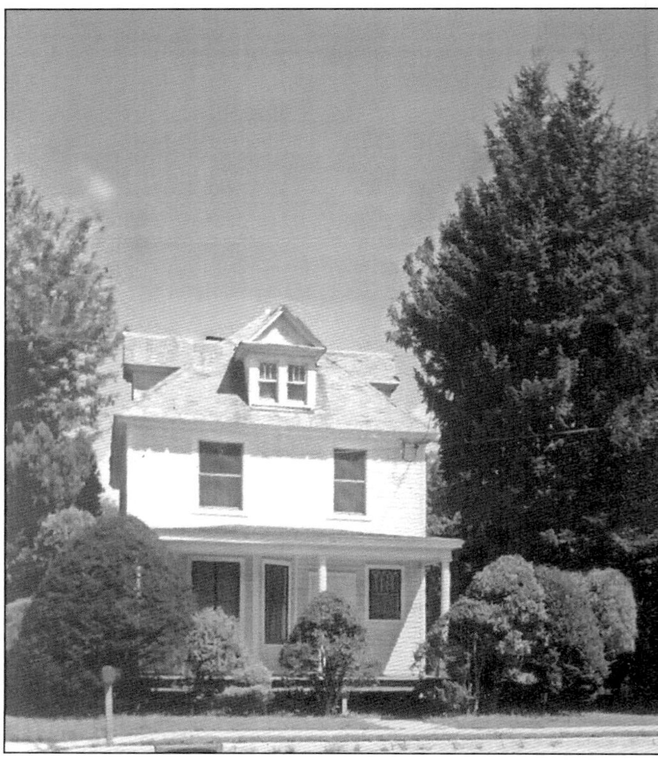

Here is the Holohan house as it looks today. (Carolyn Veeder.)

Pierce Holohan is looking very dapper in this 1870s photograph. He and his wife Bridget owned the Niskayuna Hotel at the corner of River and Rosendale Roads until 1910. Pierce was born in 1855 and died in 1919. (Carolyn Veeder.)

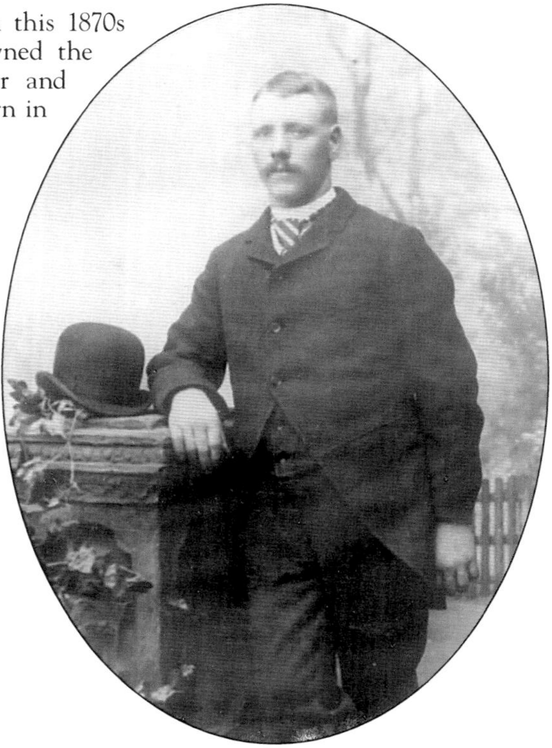

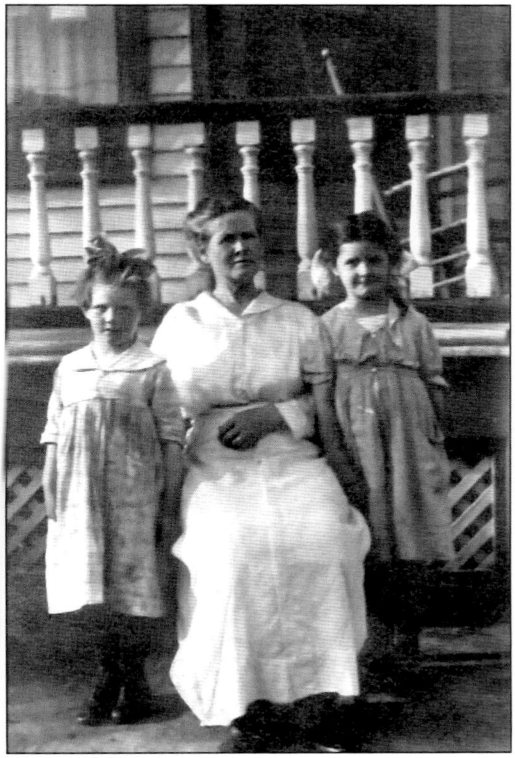

Bridget Holohan is pictured with two of her grandchildren, Margaret Keith (left) and Elsie Clement. The photograph was taken around 1917 at the house on Troy Road. Bridget was born in 1865 and died in 1955. (Carolyn Veeder.)

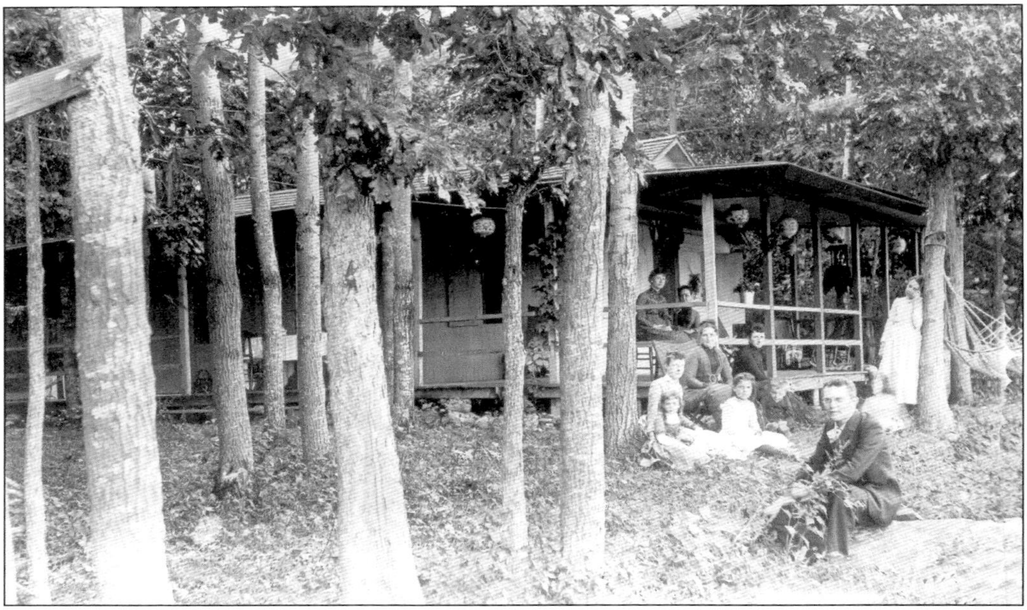

Here is Fred Kingsbury's summer camp, which was typical of several located along the Mohawk River in Niskayuna in the late 19th century. The photograph was taken on July 21, 1890. (SCHS.)

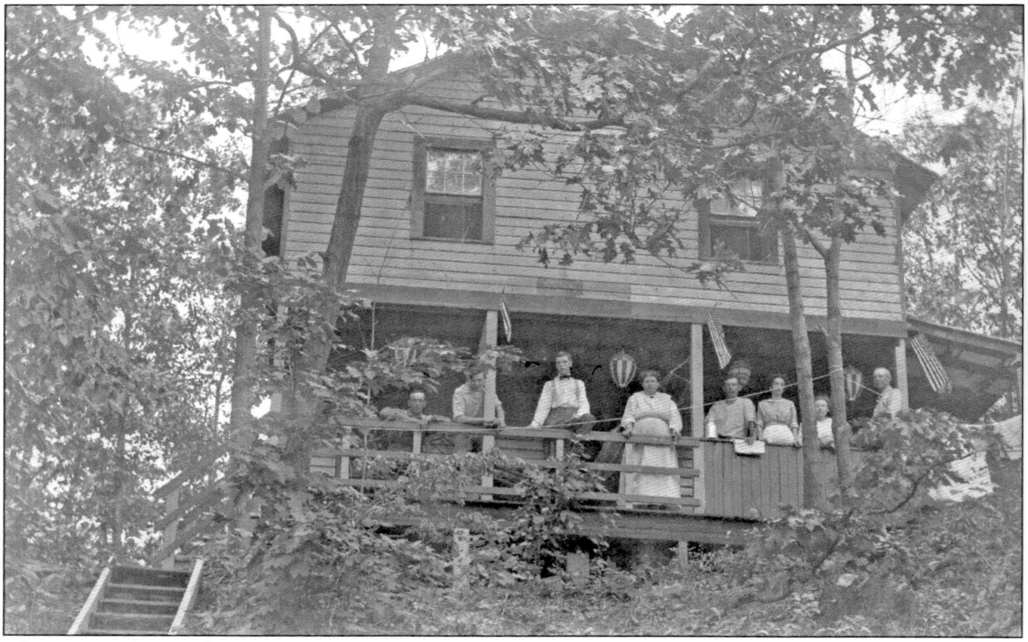

This is another early summer camp, one overlooking the Mohawk River on old River Road near the Colonie border. (SCHS.)

Five

Public Places

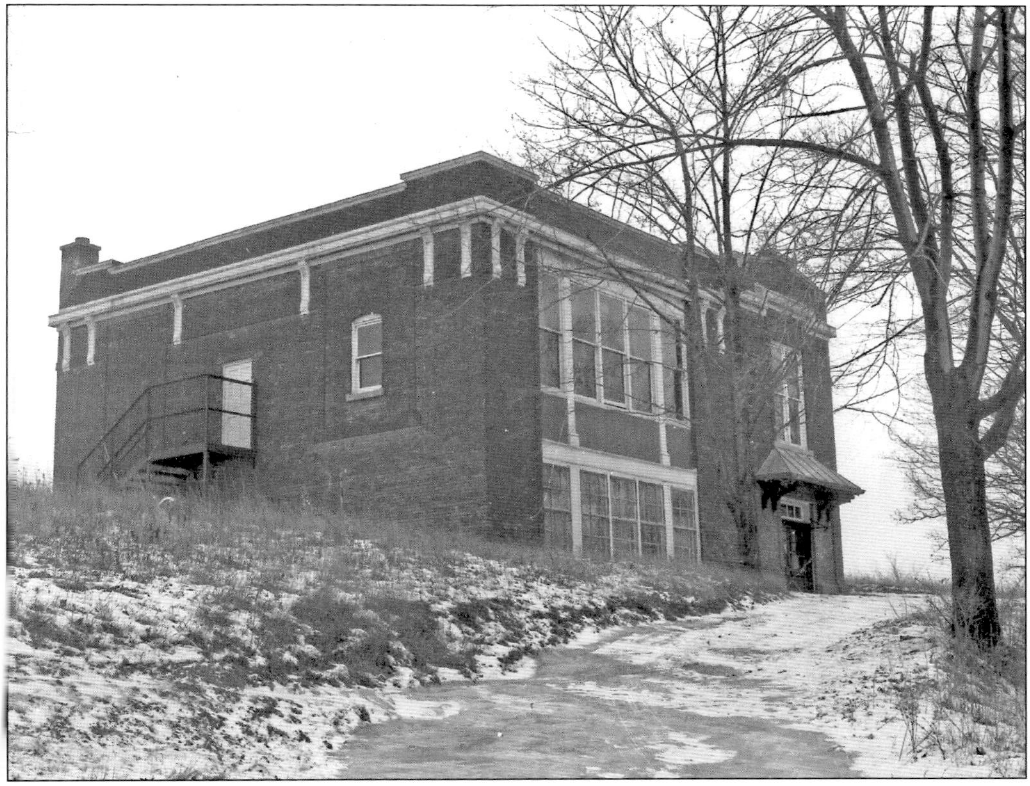

The Craig School of 1914 was a two-story, two-room redbrick building housing 40 to 60 students. It was constructed on Balltown Road on the site of an earlier and smaller school built in 1877. When the current Craig School was constructed farther to the south in 1948, this building was sold to Schenectady Chemicals, painted white, and used for storage. More recently, it was sold again and converted for use as a residential home. (SCHS.)

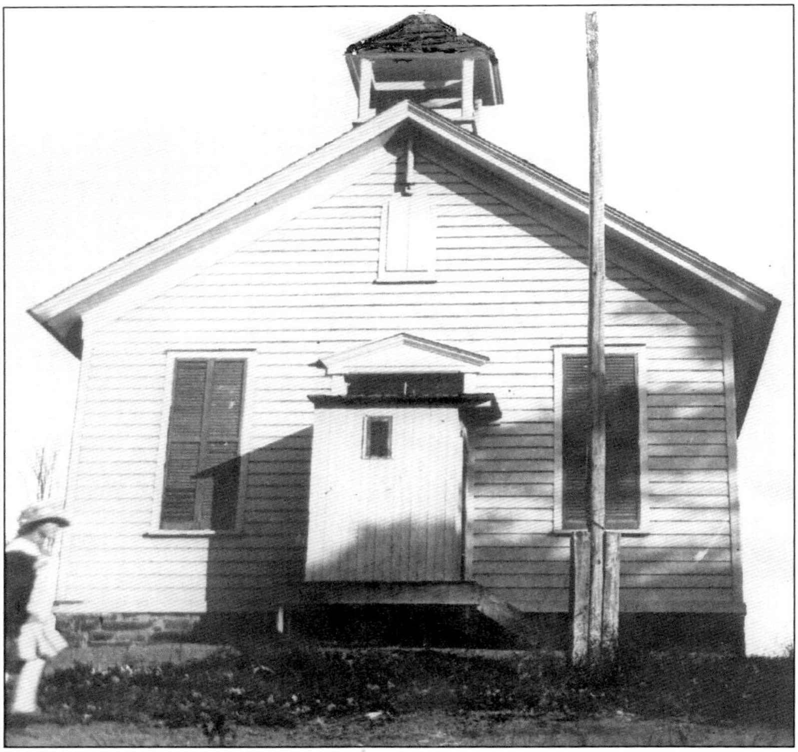

The Craig School District (school district No. 2) was named for the Craig family, who donated the land it is on. This building dates to 1877. One teacher taught 20 to 30 pupils in grades one through six. The building was later moved and used as a private home. (Efner City History Center.)

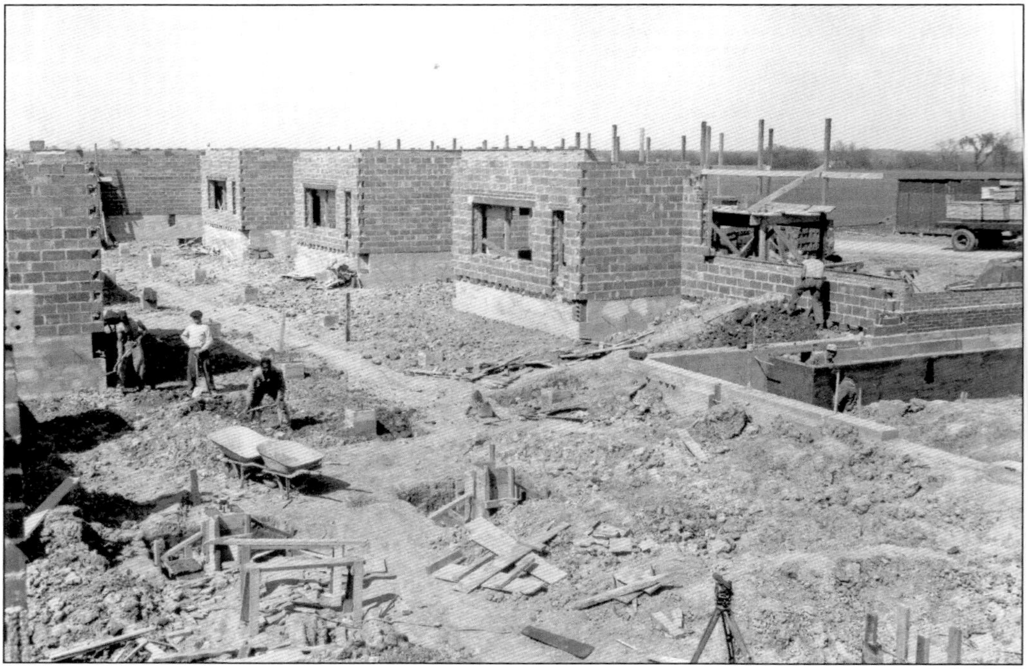

The current Craig School building on Balltown Road is seen here under construction in 1946 on the site of the prior one. The building was opened in 1948 and expanded in 1951 and again in 1953. Its innovative design allowed each classroom to have three walls of windows. (SCHS.)

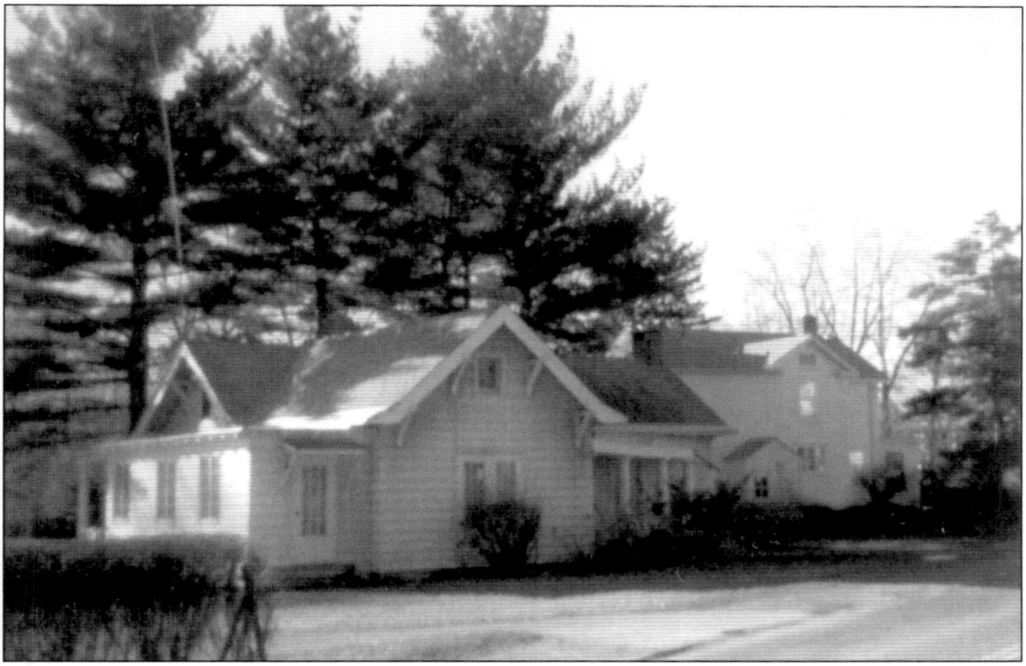

First built as a one-room school in 1877, the Van Antwerp School (Niskayuna Five) had a second classroom added in 1898. After a new school building was erected in 1910, it was later converted into a house, which still exists at 1204 Van Antwerp Road. (SCHS.)

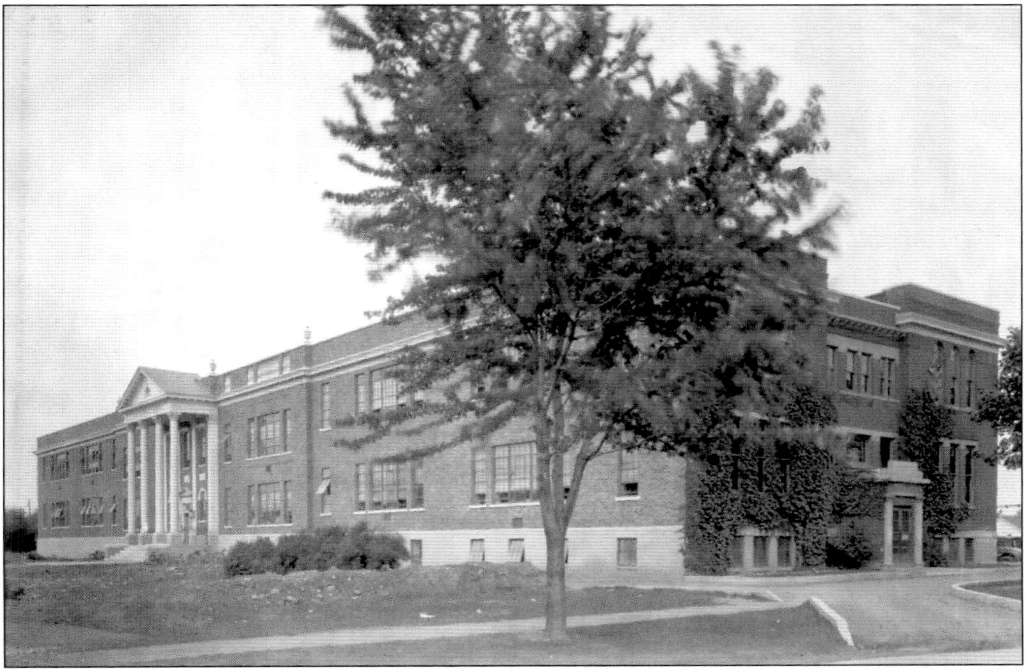

The Van Antwerp School, constructed in 1910, was doubled in size with an addition in 1925. A second addition was made in 1930. A third addition in 1949 included a library, a second gymnasium, and 10 more classrooms, creating the building shown here. (Efner City History Center.)

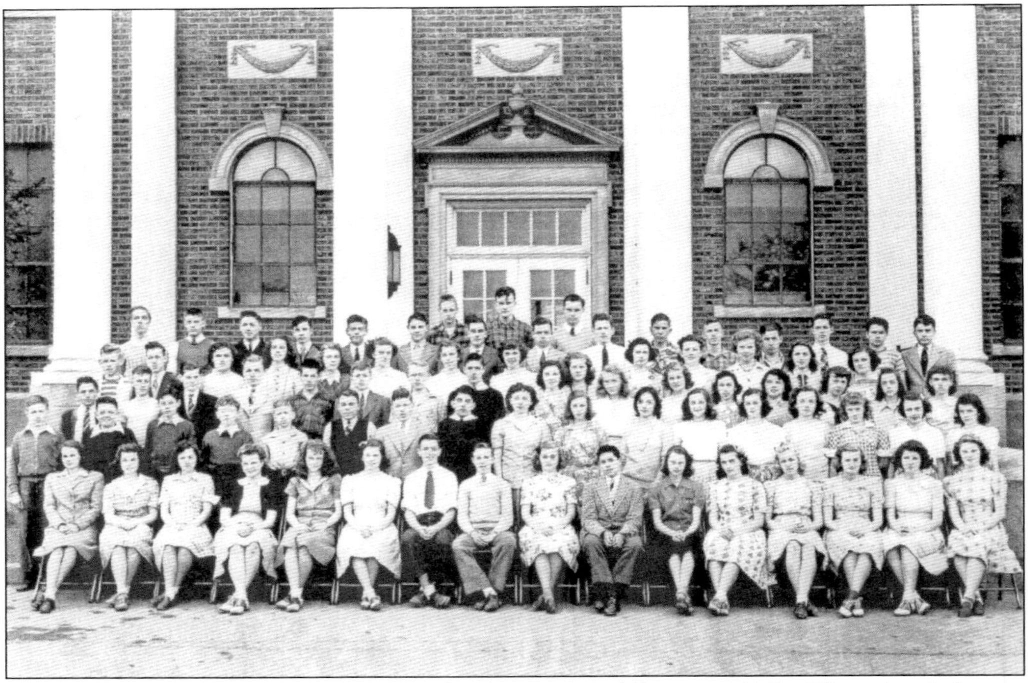

The ninth grade of Van Antwerp School is pictured here in 1943. The school district converted Van Antwerp to a middle school for grades six through eight in 1958 and built a second middle school, Iroquois, in 1969. Van Antwerp was closed from 1982 to 1993. Part of the building was leased to the town for use as a community center, and the other part was used by Schenectady County as the Niskayuna branch of the public library. The school reopened in 1993. (Al Finke Jr.)

Van Antwerp School Class of 1943

6th row: Jerry Meader, X, Bob Smith

5th row: X, X, Art Samson, John Ostrom, Murray Gobeli, Bob Broady, X, X, John Robb, Al Finke, Harvey Howell, X, Peter Darling, X, Dan Mead

4th row: Cornelius Wood, Donald Glindmyer, X, X, Barbara Ryan, X, X, Marjorie Pingon, X, Beth ?, X, X, X, X

3rd row: X, X, Leroy Wyman, John Ostrom, X, William McFarland, Charles Green, X, Phyllis Killam, Bernetta Felthousen, Nancy Prout, X, X, X, X, X

2nd row: X, X, X, Evan Richards, John Boink, X, X, Richard Yowell, Ellen ?, X, X, Phyllis Hughes, Virginia McCullock, Peggy ?, Jacky Roberts, X, Marian Smith

Seated: X, Joan Denny, X, X, X, Joan Morton, John Carroll, Edward Sheridan, Pauline Gaudet, X, X, Janet Hatch, Carol Chestnut, Arlene Shoemaker, X, X

This is the key to the class picture. Each *X* represents an unidentified person. (Al Finke Jr.)

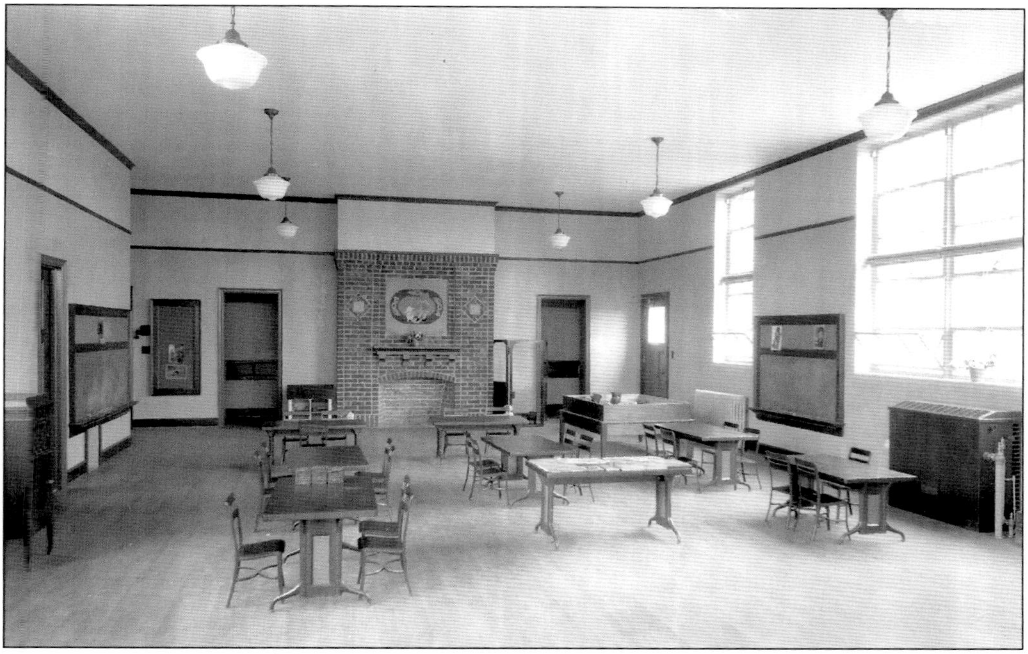

A Van Antwerp School kindergarten classroom with a fireplace in 1930 is showing that Niskayuna was in the forefront of the movement to include kindergartens in its public school system. (Efner City History Center.)

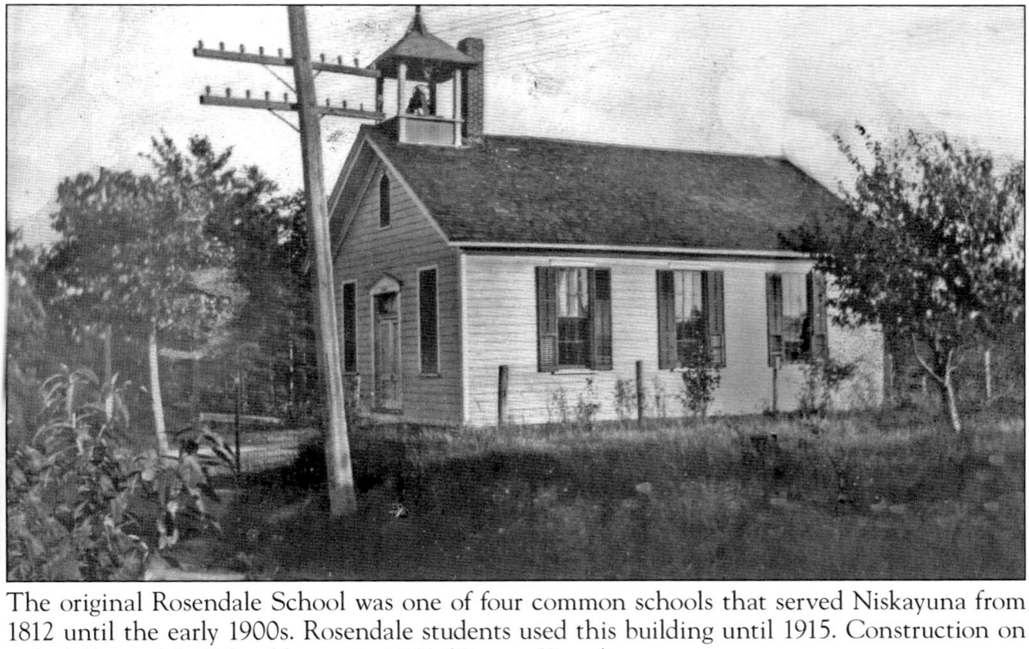

The original Rosendale School was one of four common schools that served Niskayuna from 1812 until the early 1900s. Rosendale students used this building until 1915. Construction on today's Rosendale School began in 1955. (George Yager.)

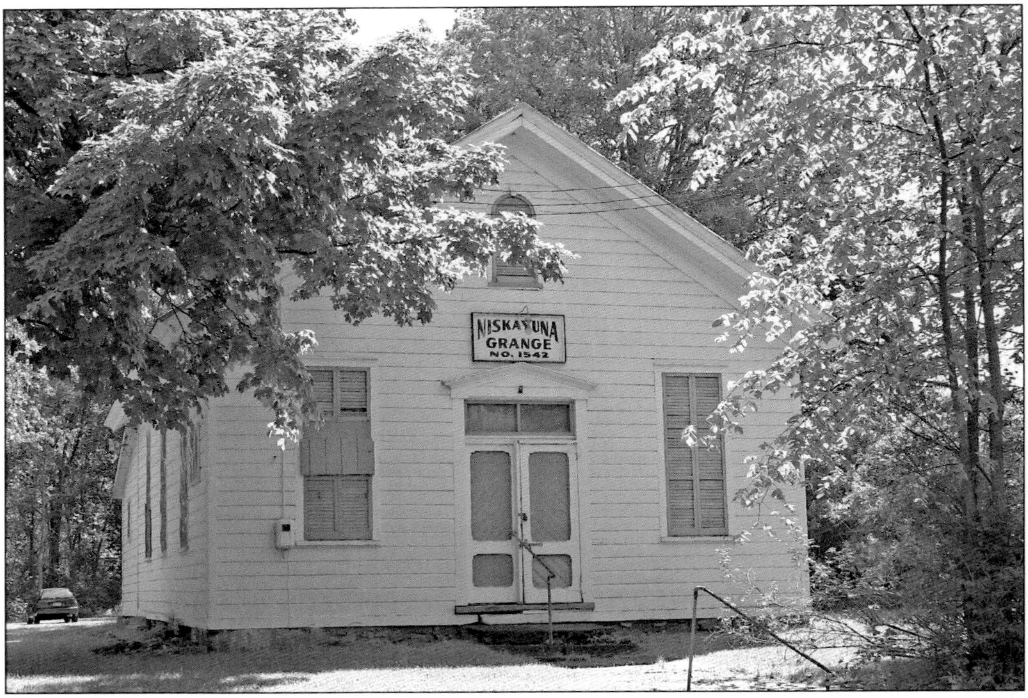

The original Rosendale School became the Niskayuna Grange hall, depicted here. The Grange disbanded in 1988 and gave the building to the town of Niskayuna. (SCHS.)

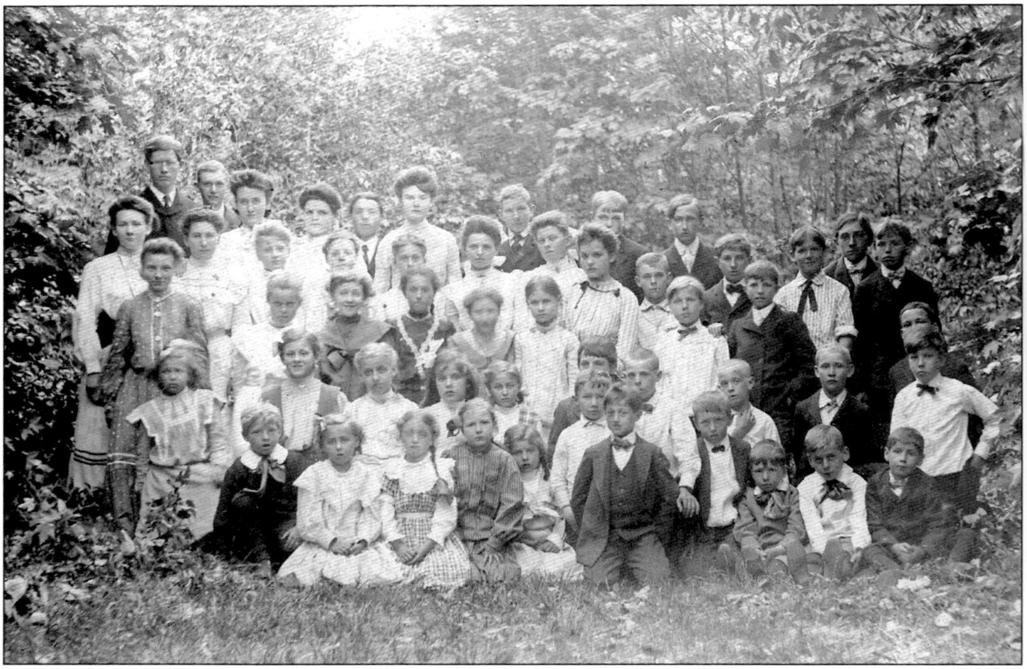

Almost 50 children comprised the student body of Rosendale School in this early-1900s picture. Lillian Yager (Dewar Kilkenny) is shown in the front row, fourth from the left. Blanche Beals (Clute) is on her left. In front of the teacher is Lizzie Yager (Myers). (George Yager.)

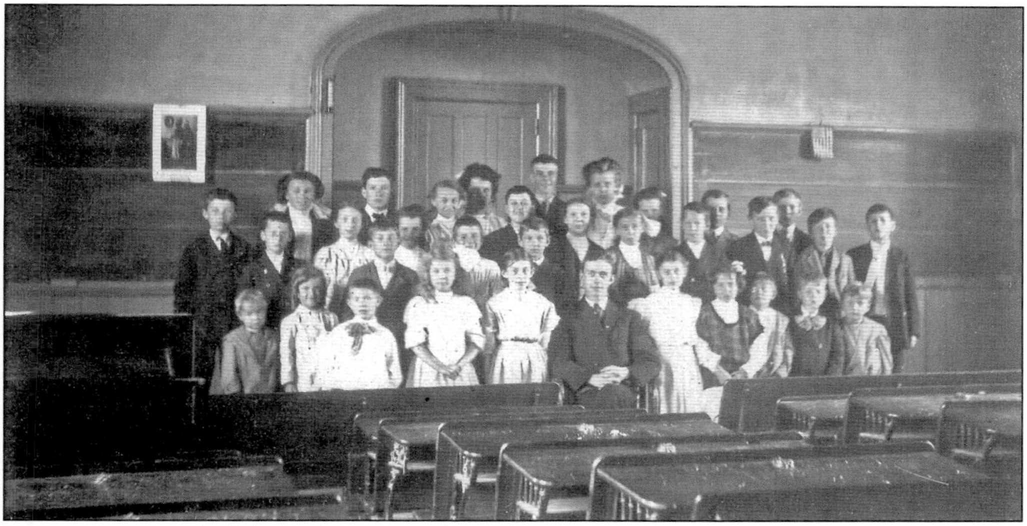

Here is the ungraded class of 1908 at Rosendale School. The teacher is Charles T. Male, who stated in his diary on September 14 that he was paid $11 per week for 36 weeks. He then listed his pupils in the following order: George L. Yager, John W. Lansing, Bertha Bradt, Irene Wallard, Christopher Yager, VanDorn Bradt, Elmer Riley, Joseph Johnson, Hubert Male, Isabella Beals, Lansing Vedder, Harold J. Pearse, Isabella Wallard, Bertha Inman, Lillian Yager, Edward J. Lansing, Florence J. Male, Lawrence Strobel, Lulu May Willey, Blanche Beals, Katie May Wallard, Chester Vedder, Palmer Vedder, Minnie Riley, Tony Padula, Ritie Lansing, Frank Willey, Arthur Loucks, Clarence Wallard, Daisy Dooley, Grazilda Beals, Edith V. Strobel, Harmon G. Altrock, and Edward Willey. (George Yager.)

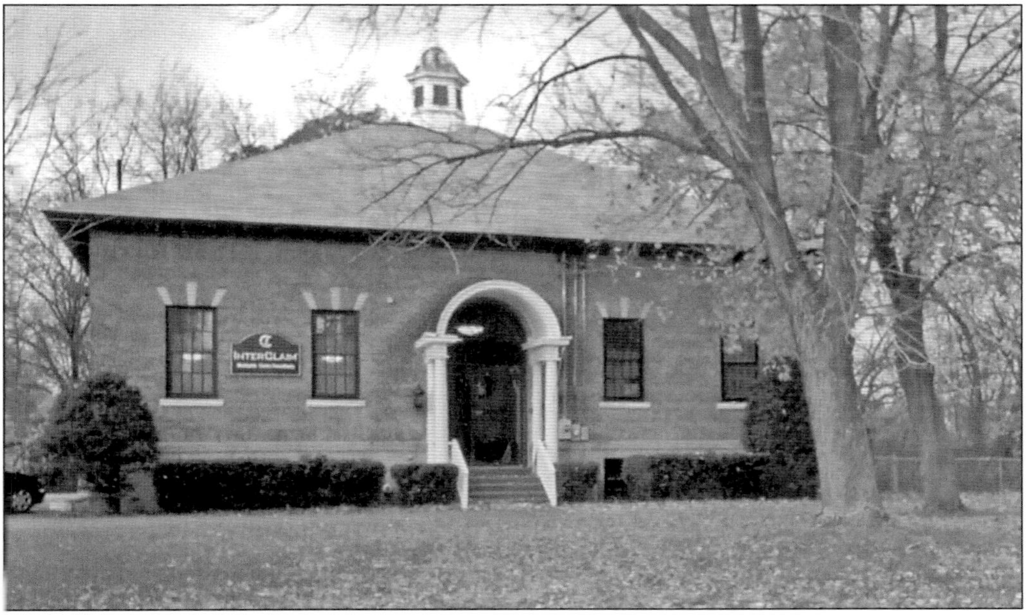

This brick building on Rosendale Road near its intersection with Troy Road is the precursor of today's Birchwood Elementary School. Built in 1850, it was known as Niskayuna Four. Since then, it has housed Ona Curran Antiques, a day care center, and a center for the deaf. (Carolyn Veeder.)

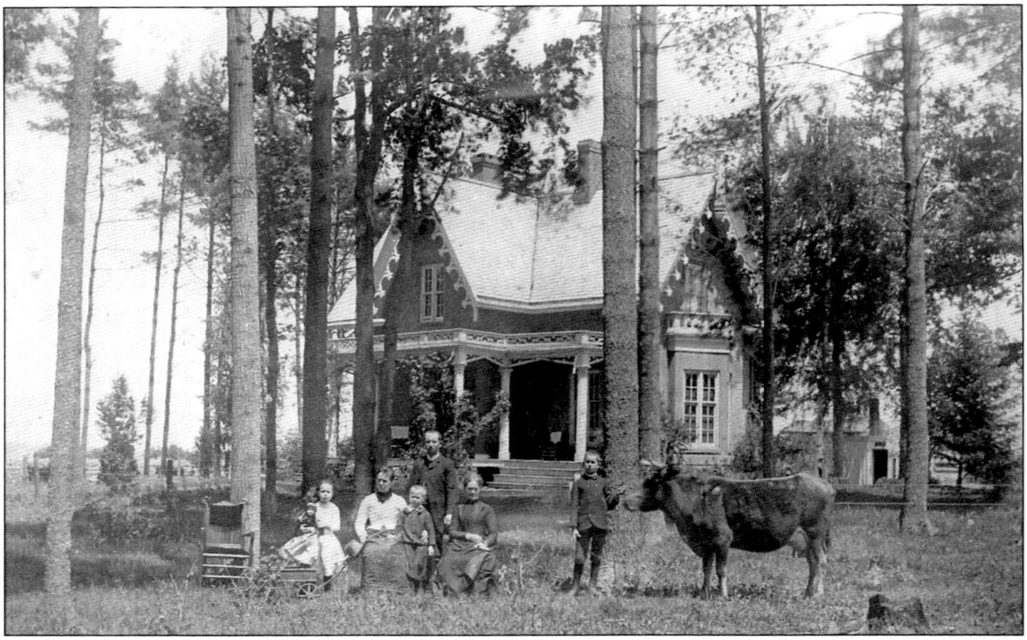

The "Gingerbread House," dating to 1856, was built as a summer home by Dr. William N. Duane. In later years, it also became home to the families of D. Carpenter and then Edward J. Quackenbush. The site became the new home for the relocated Calvary United Methodist Church in 1955. An education wing of the church replaced the house after it was razed in 1964. (SCHS.)

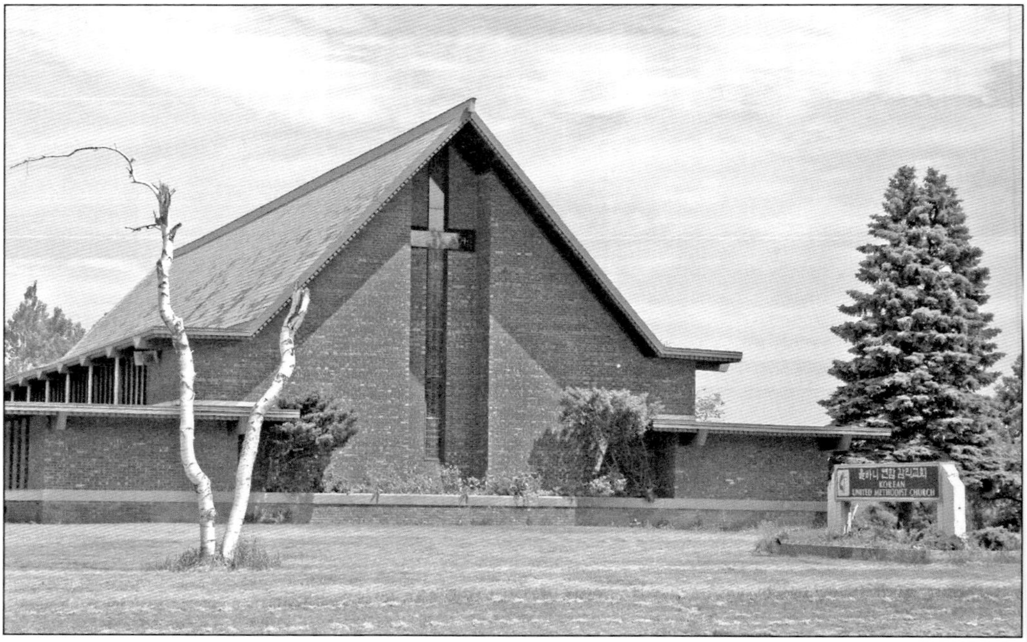

Calvary United Methodist Church was founded in 1872 to serve Schenectady's German-speaking Methodist population. Originally located at Union and Lafayette Streets in Schenectady, its congregation relocated to Balltown Road in 1955. In the 1990s, it became the Korean United Methodist Church, a center for the capital district's Korean community. (SCHS.)

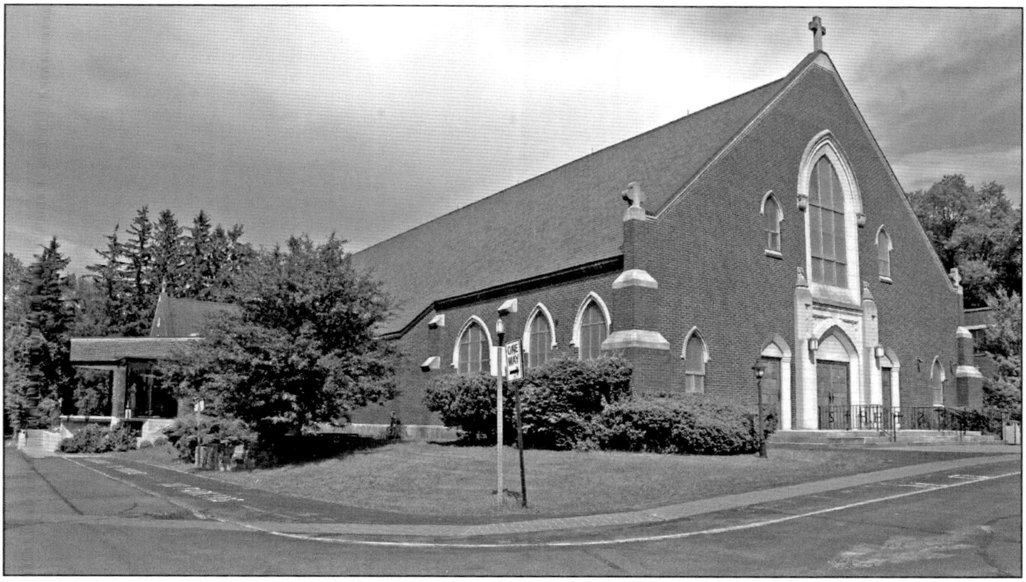

St. Helen's Roman Catholic Church, formed in 1926, was originally housed in a prefabricated Sears building at Union Street and Woodland Avenue in Schenectady, currently the site of a branch of Trustco Bank. The current church at 1803 Union Street in Niskayuna was dedicated in 1954. A rectory and convent were soon added to serve a rapidly growing suburban population. (SCHS.)

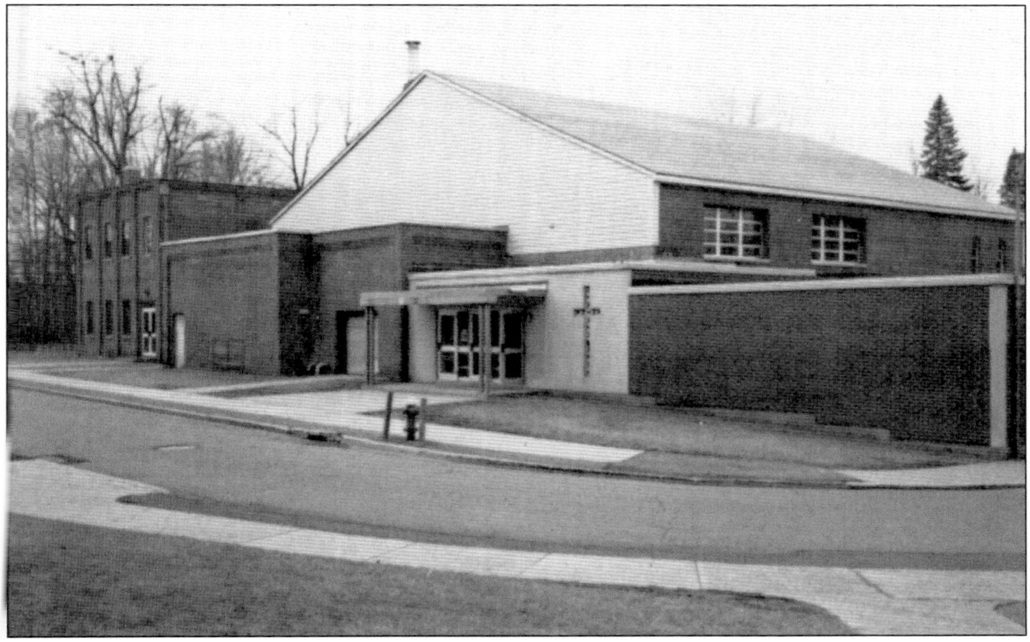

St. Helen's School was opened in 1955 in the renovated Rindfleisch Cleaners building, a portion of which can be seen at the far left. A gymnasium and additional classroom space were added over the period of 1956 to 1962, bringing the appearance of the complex to that of this 1970s photograph. In 2003, the front of the building was brought closer to the curb to enclose space needed for a new library and computer center. (Leona Jeffes.)

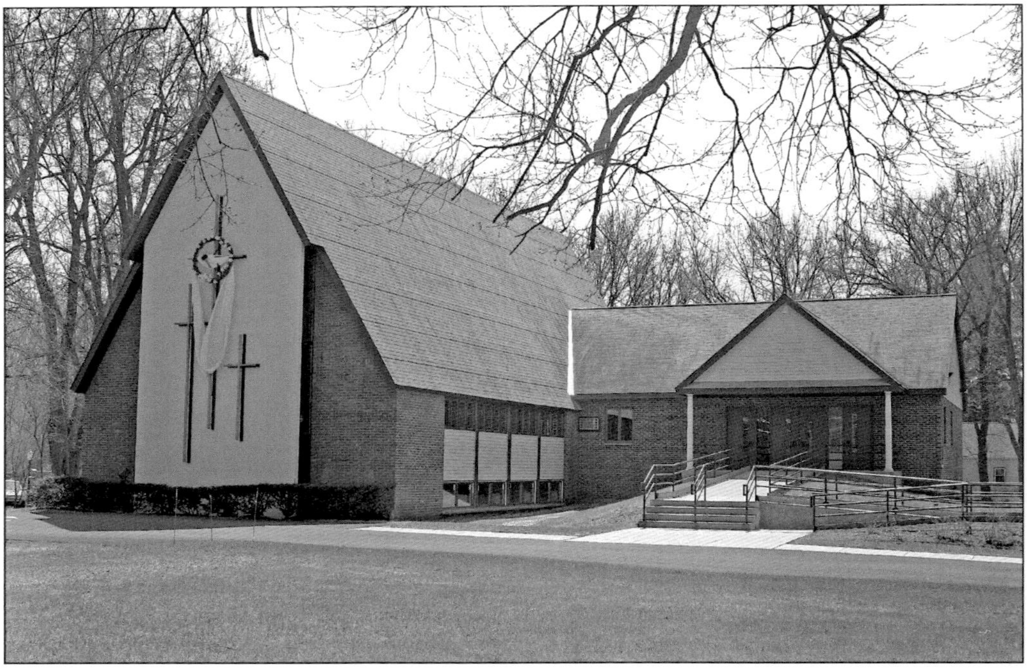

Immanuel Lutheran Church, founded in 1902 in Schenectady, moved to Niskayuna following World War II. As the suburban population expanded, the need for more space led to the construction of this building in 1958. (SCHS.)

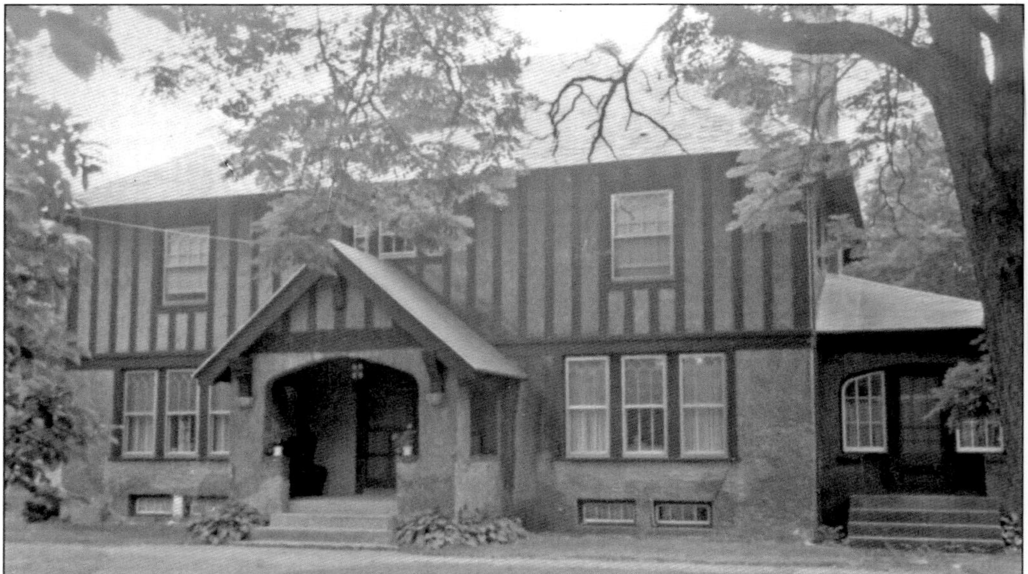

The Lutheran parsonage at 1850 Union Street is located next door to the Immanuel Lutheran Church of Niskayuna. (Efner City History Center.)

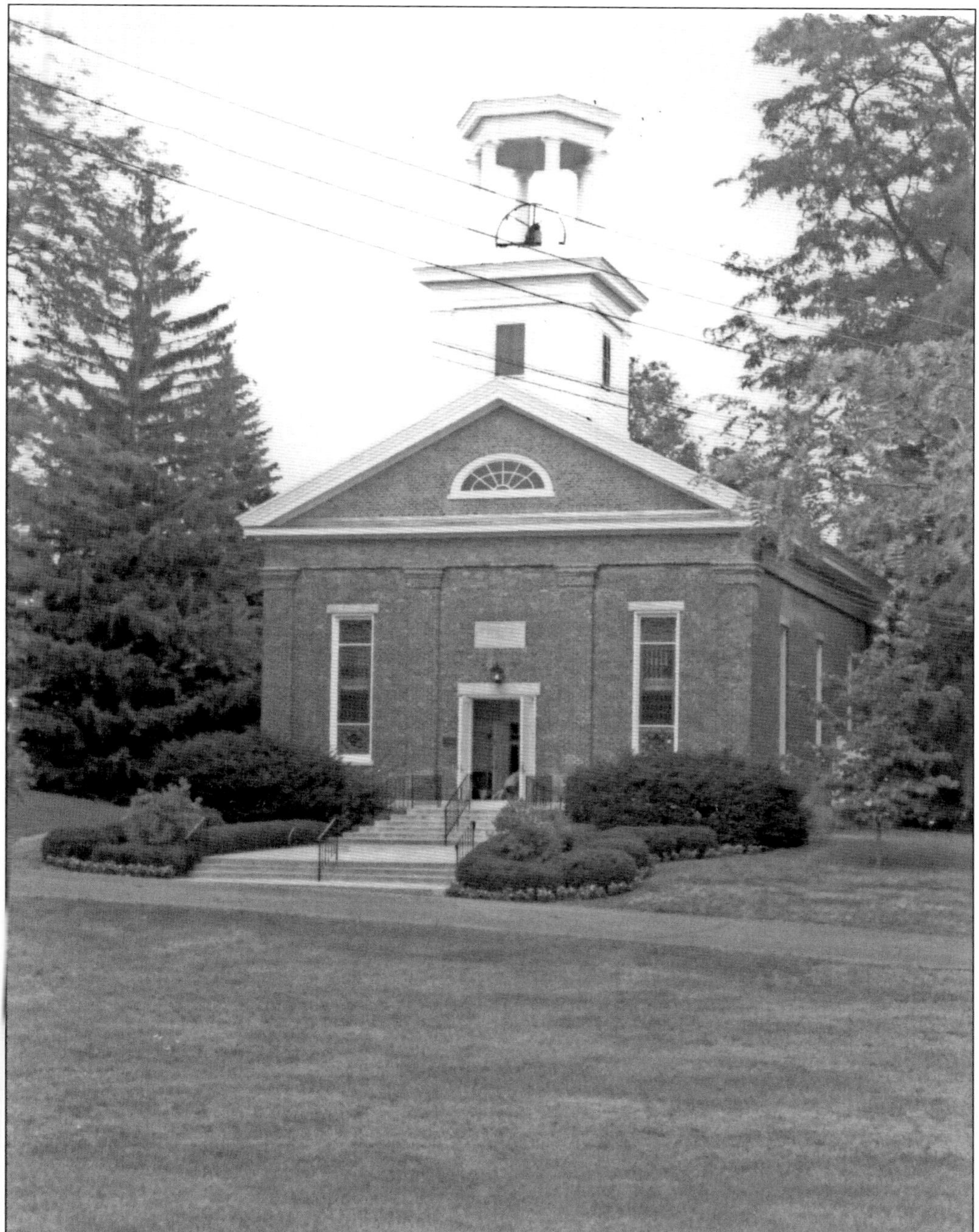

Here is the Niskayuna Reformed Church at 3041 Troy Road. The original church was a log building known as the Gabat House, or Prayer House, which was erected at the intersection of River and Niskayuna Roads about 1680. Formal organization of the congregation of the reformed church in Niskayuna occurred about 1750. In 1760, a new church building was completed at the corner of Rosendale Road and Troy Road. In 1828, the congregation moved to a frame structure erected upon the site now occupied by the present church. It was replaced by the current brick structure in 1852. (SCHS.)

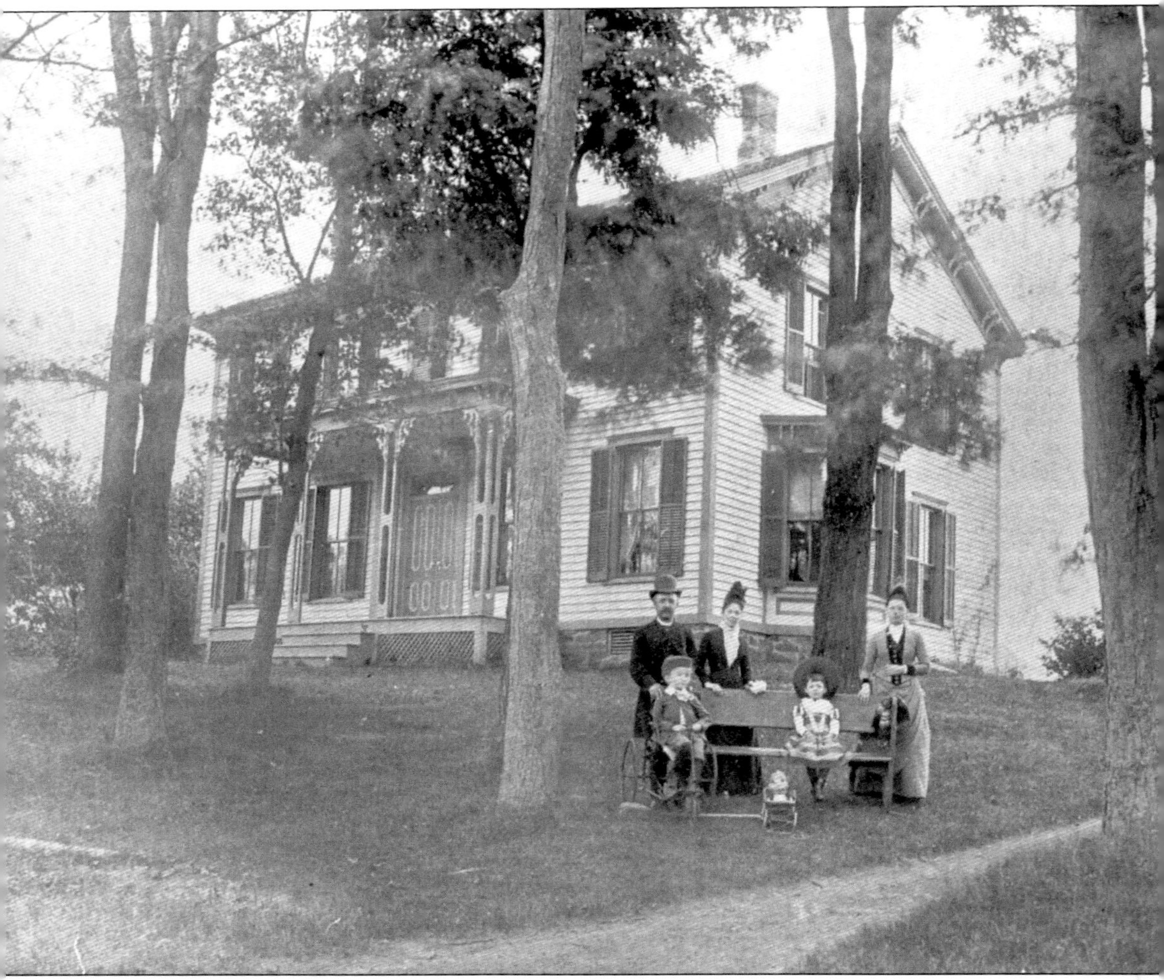

The original Niskayuna Reformed Church parsonage was built just west of the church in 1832. It was used until 1873 when it was replaced by this Colonial-style home. The new parsonage incorporated materials from the original building. Pictured by the bench in 1885 are Rev. Cornelius Ditmars; his wife, Leah Schairer Ditmars; their children Charles and Ida; and Emma Schairer, mother of Mildred (Schairer) Male. (SCHS.)

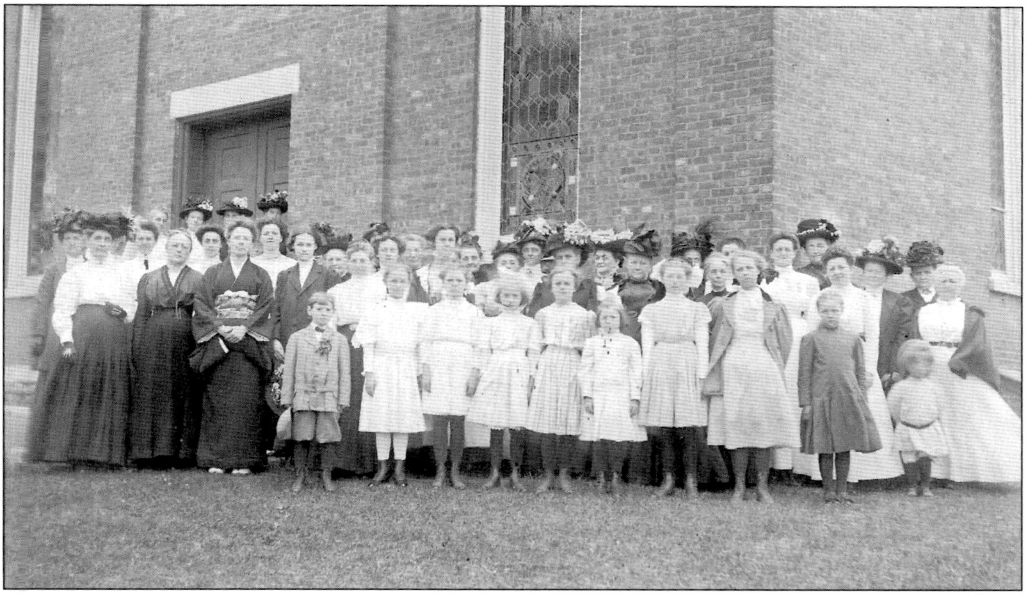

This 1906 photograph of the Women's Missionary Society includes many prominent local women who are identified in the diagram below. The group is posed outside the Niskayuna Reformed Church on Troy Road. (Niskayuna Reformed Church.)

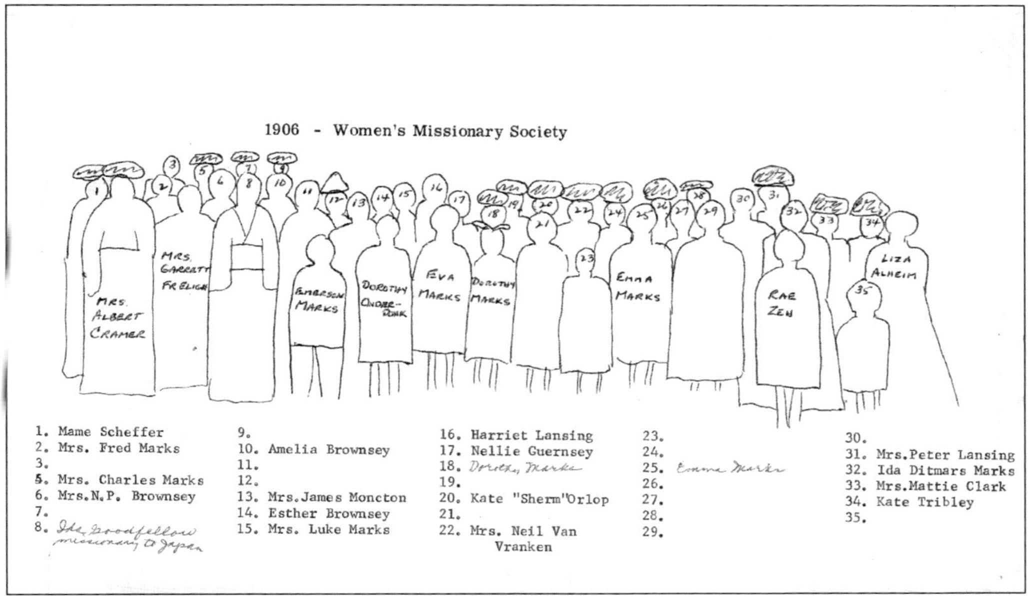

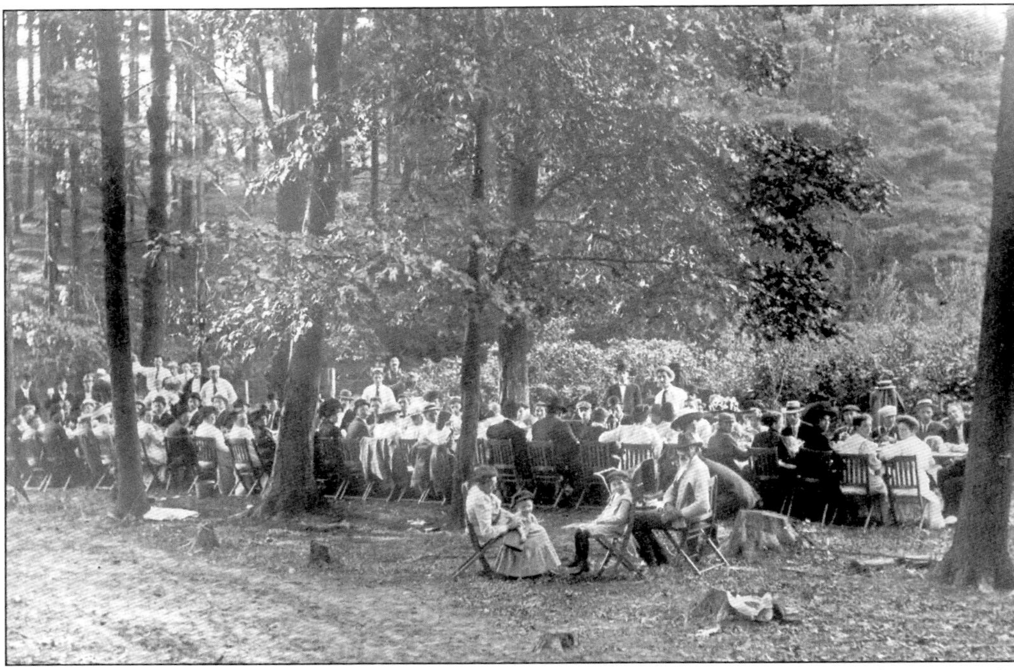

Pictured here is a church picnic for the Niskayuna Reformed Church in the early 1900s. The event was held in the woods that stood at the corner of Mill Road and Troy Road in Colonie. (Niskayuna Reformed Church.)

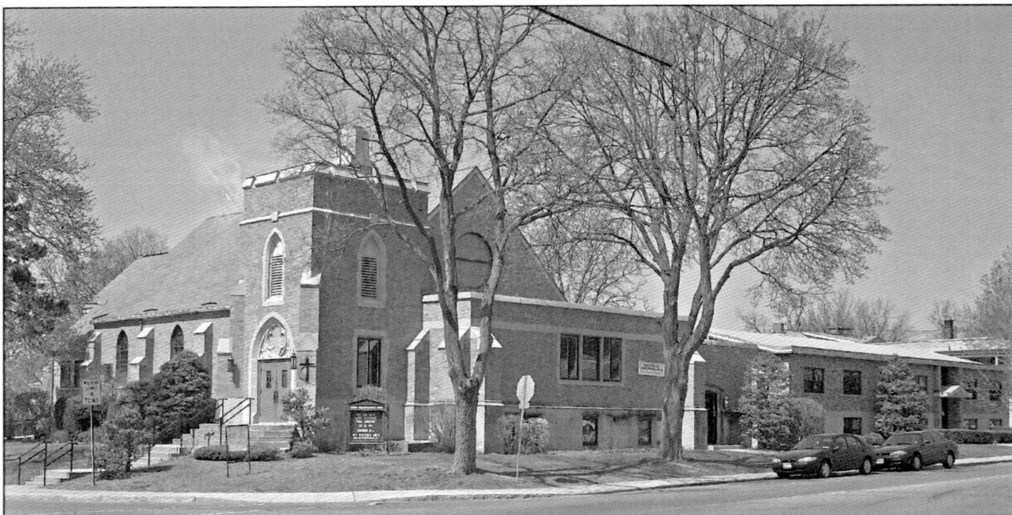

The Eastern Parkway United Methodist Church on Ashmore Avenue in Schenectady is just over the Niskayuna border, but its parsonage and a substantial part of its congregation is in Niskayuna. Construction began in 1926 to replace a chapel that dated to 1903. From time to time in the past, the church basement has housed the Schenectady Inner City Ministry (SICM), the Mohawk Pathways Girl Scout Council, and other social service organizations. (SCHS.)

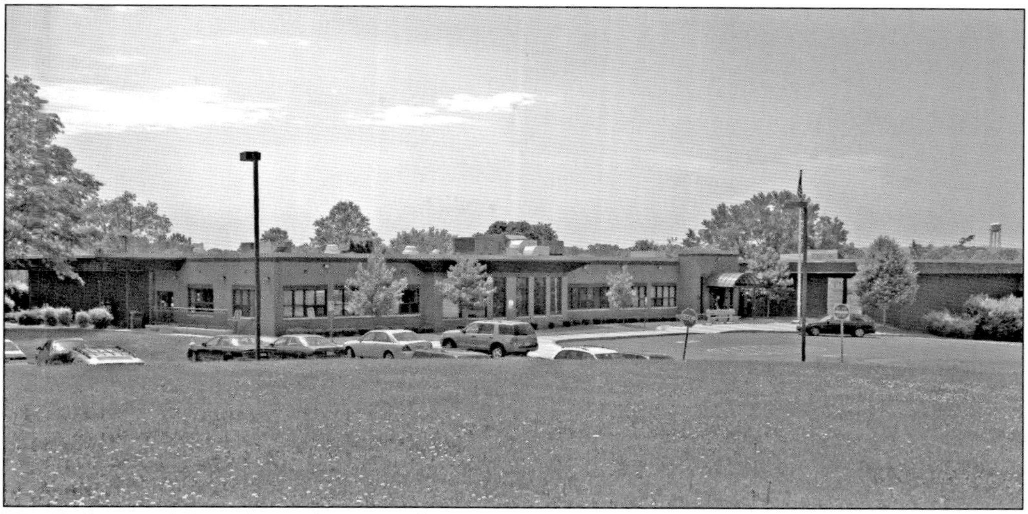

The Robert and Dorothy Ludwig Jewish Community Center (JCC) at 2565 Balltown Road was built on land purchased in 1960 by Schenectady County's Jewish community. Dedicated on April 23, 1967, the JCC houses meeting rooms, a nursery, an indoor swimming pool, and a health club. Additions since then have included the William and Estelle Golub Family Park in 1988 and a new fitness center. Membership is open to all. (SCHS.)

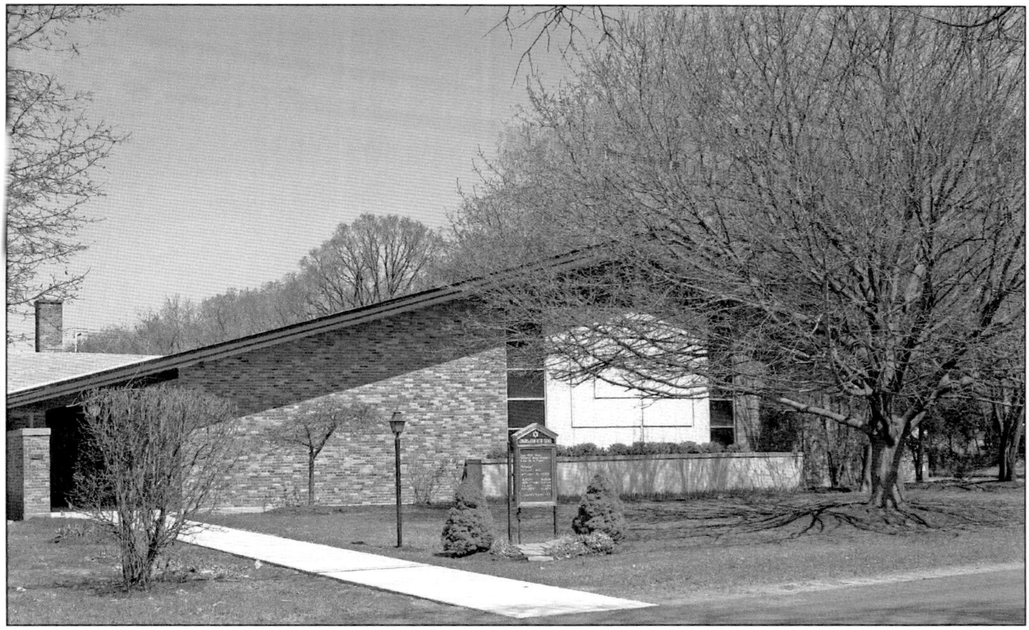

In 1971, the Orthodox Congregation Beth Israel moved from Schenectady to 2195 Eastern Parkway in Niskayuna. The site is across from the Van Buren Apartments and just a short distance to the city boundary. (SCHS.)

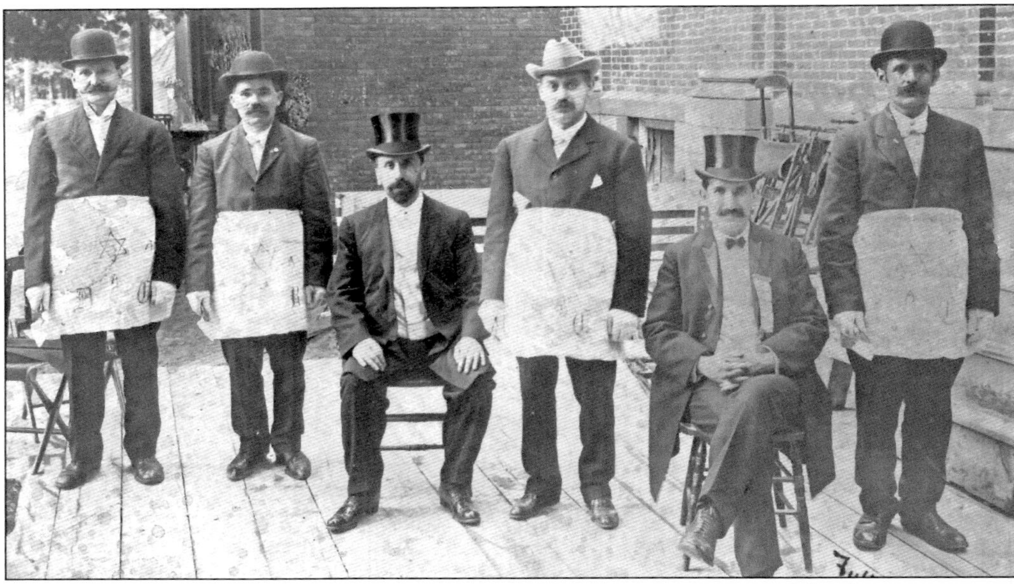

Pictured is a June 5, 1908, ceremony for the laying of the cornerstone of the first sanctuary of Congregation Agudat Achim on Nott Terrace in Schenectady. From left to right are David Cohen; Morris Baker; Rev. Samuel Hinden, the congregation's first rabbi; Jacob Cohen; Abraham Seaman, first president of the congregation; and Israel Cohen. The four men wearing Masonic aprons were members of the board of directors of the congregation. (Congregation Agudat Achim.)

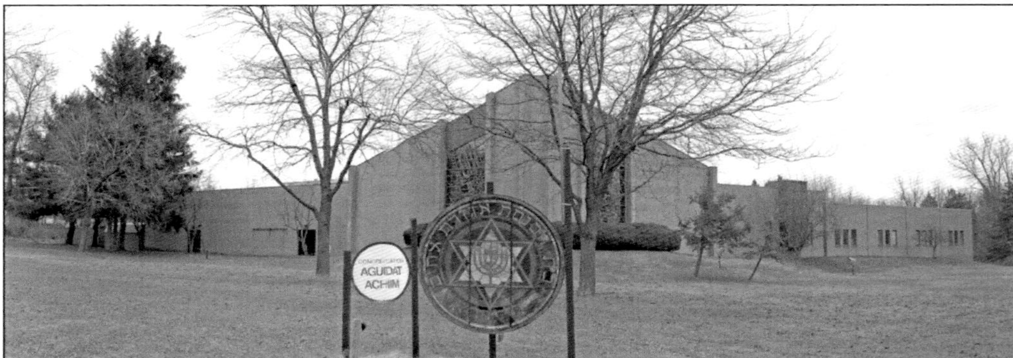

Congregation Agudat Achim, literally "an assembly of brothers and sisters," is located at 2117 Union Street. The congregation was founded in 1891 by five families who met in homes until their first sanctuary became available in 1909. Just a few months after Beth Israel's move into Niskayuna, the congregation moved its Torah into this new facility on November 21, 1971. As of that date, Niskayuna became home to all or part of all three Schenectady County synagogues. (SCHS.)

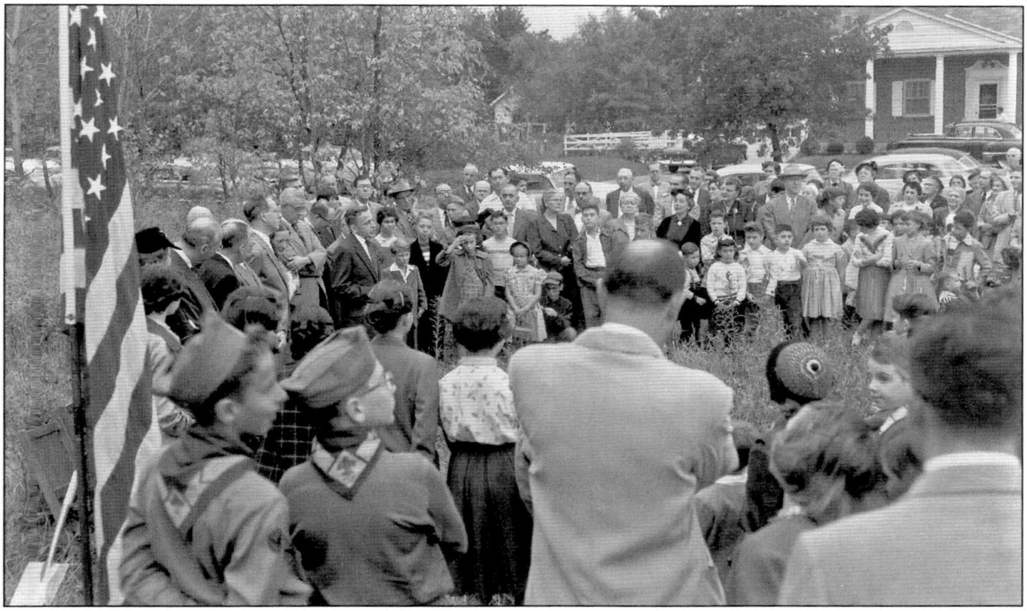

The groundbreaking ceremony for the new Temple Gates of Heaven, originally known as Congregation Shaarai Shamayim, was a festive occasion in September 1954, with officials from both Schenectady and Niskayuna on hand. The boundary between the municipalities passes through the building site. Speaking here is attorney Alexander Diamond, as Schenectady mayor Archibald Wemple stands with his back to the camera. (SCHS.)

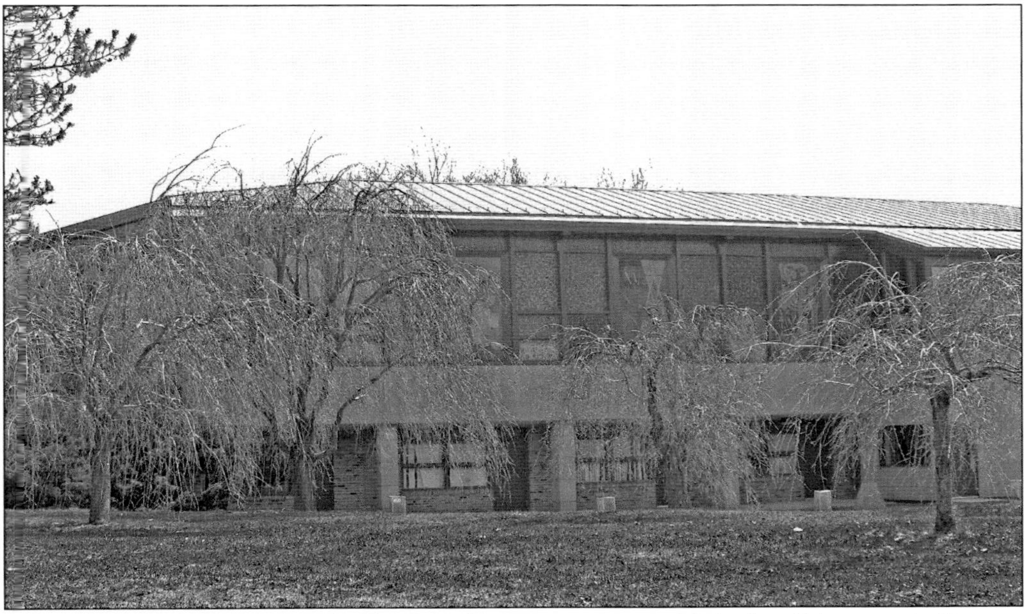

Temple Gates of Heaven was the first Jewish congregation established in Schenectady County. Founded by German immigrants, the congregation purchased its first property on Ferry Street in 1865. After several relocations, the current temple was built in 1954 at the corner of Ashmore Avenue and Eastern Parkway. The cherry trees in the photograph are in bloom, but black-and-white photography does not do them justice. (SCHS.)

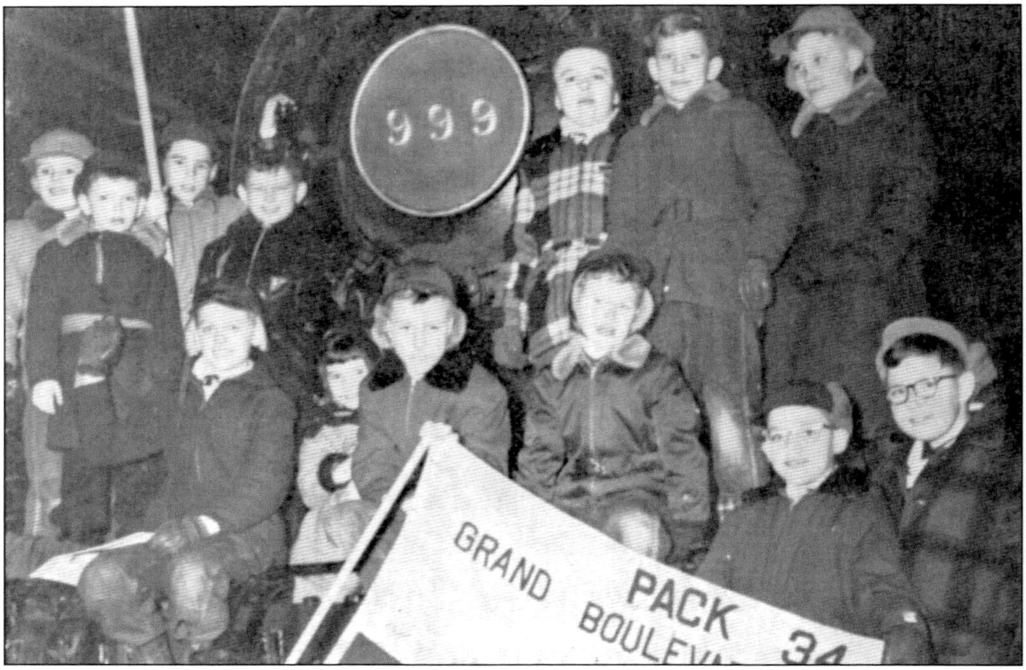

Cub Scout Pack 34 of Niskayuna gathers around engine No. 999, the first locomotive ever to go 100 miles per hour, at the Selkirk engine house. The scouts took a train trip on the New York Central Railroad from Schenectady to Selkirk, the station just south of Albany, on January 22, 1955. (SCHS.)

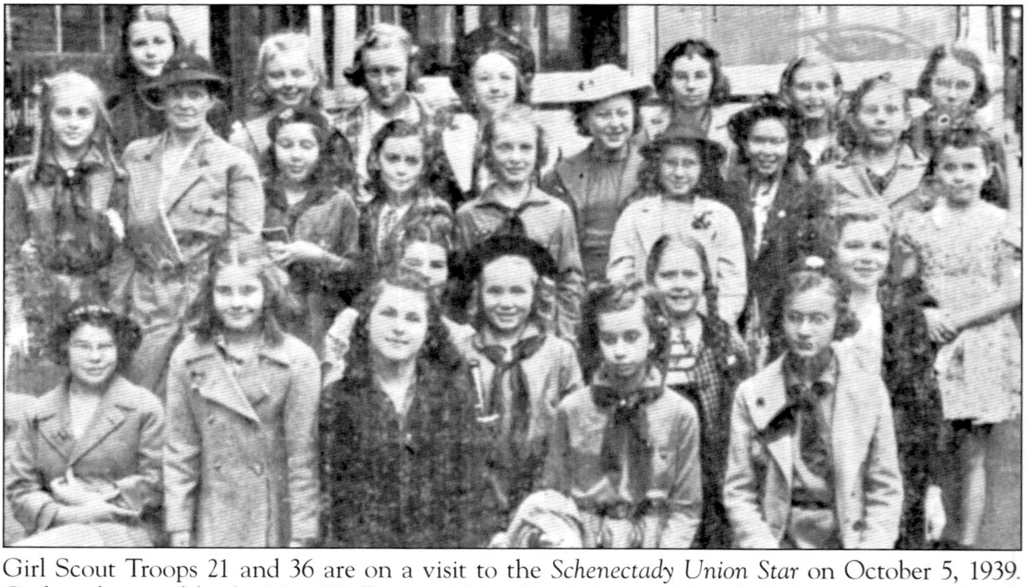

Girl Scout Troops 21 and 36 are on a visit to the *Schenectady Union Star* on October 5, 1939. Gathered around leader Vera Weller are Altha Cox, Marjorie Mansfield, Jane Verwoert, Perrie Jane Jones, Muriel Randles, Barbara Ryan, Marion Smith, Bernetta Felthousen, Doris Kelley, Peggy Cooper, Eunice Bancker, Evelyn Fiestelmann, Joya Kennan, Doris Kennan, Joan Nessler, Virginia McCulloch, Marilyn Havens, Barbara Havens, Christina Schweiker, Pauline Gaudet, Patricia Snell, Ann Kastensmith, Helen Sarchet, Joanne Bailey, and Marion Frederick. (SCHS.)

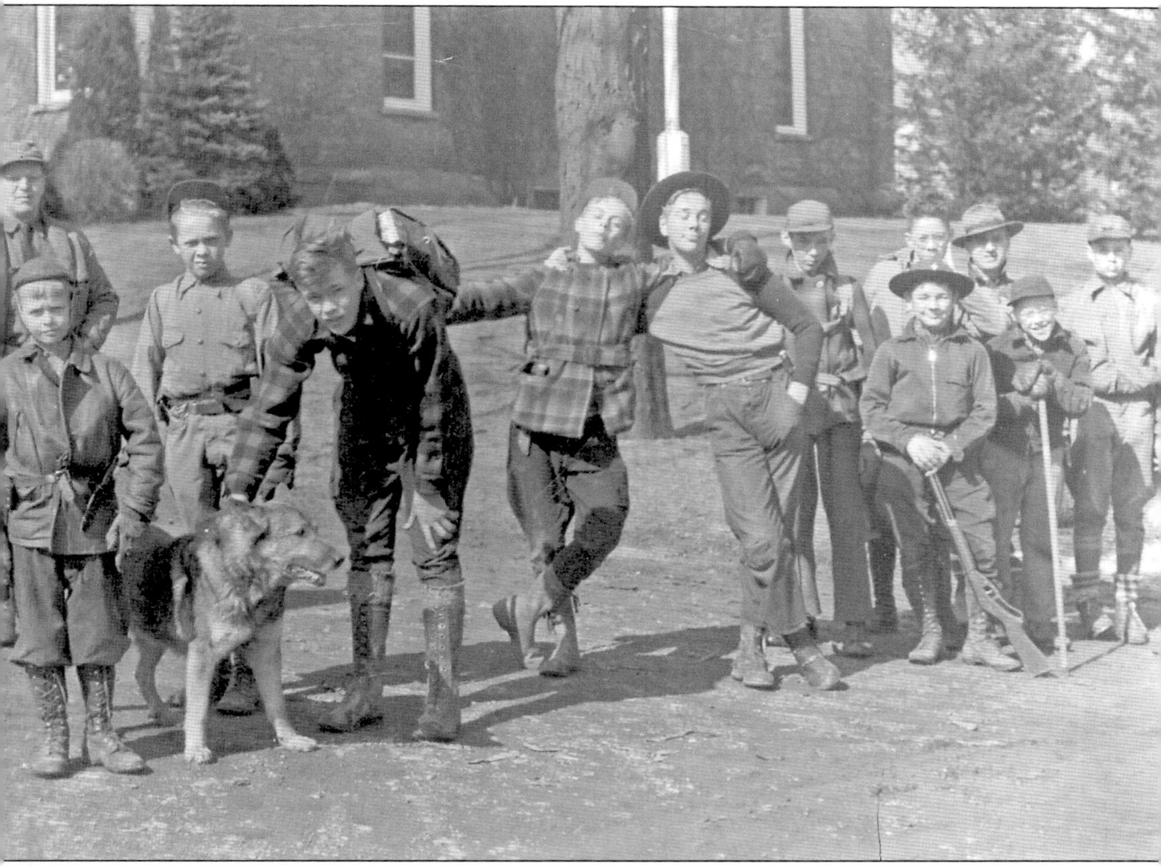

Here is a Boy Scout troop on the grounds of the Niskayuna Reformed Church in 1943. Pictured from left to right are (first row) Charles Walrath, Vincent Duffy, John Witte, James Sutliff, Francis Green, John Sutliff, Ronald Mitchess, Stanley Hickok, and Victor Handy; (second row) Scoutmaster J. W. Macy, Harmon Gillie, and district commissioner William Dimarco. (Niskayuna Reformed Church.)

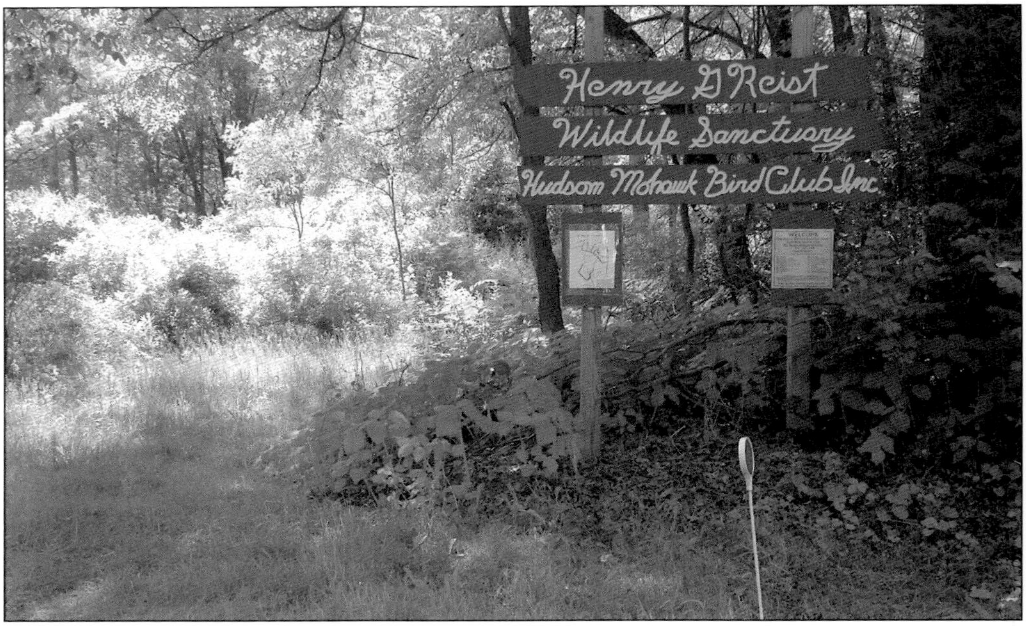

The Henry Reist Wildlife Sanctuary was established in 1965 on land that was once part of the extensive Pearse homestead. The restoration of these 105 acres was overseen by Dr. Henry G. Reist (1862–1942), a General Electric engineer, botanist, artist, and third president of SCHS. Trails lead through the sanctuary, which is maintained by the Hudson-Mohawk Bird Club. Margaret Breed Reist gave the sanctuary to the club in 1965, 24 years after the death of her husband. (SCHS.)

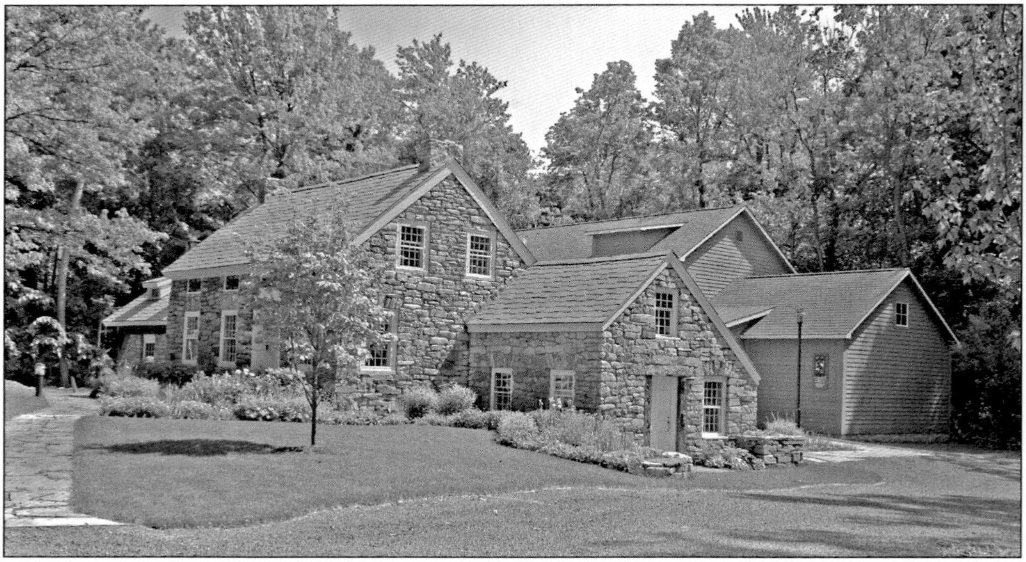

Paul Schaefer (1908–1996) and his wife Carolyn built this home on St. David's Lane in 1935 on three acres of land given to them by Henry Reist in exchange for Paul's work in restoring Reist's nearby Pearse homestead. Paul was a builder, conservationist, and author dedicated to preserving the Adirondacks. In 1999, the house was purchased by the Association for the Protection of the Adirondacks, founded in 1901, and now houses its Adirondack Research Library. (SCHS.)

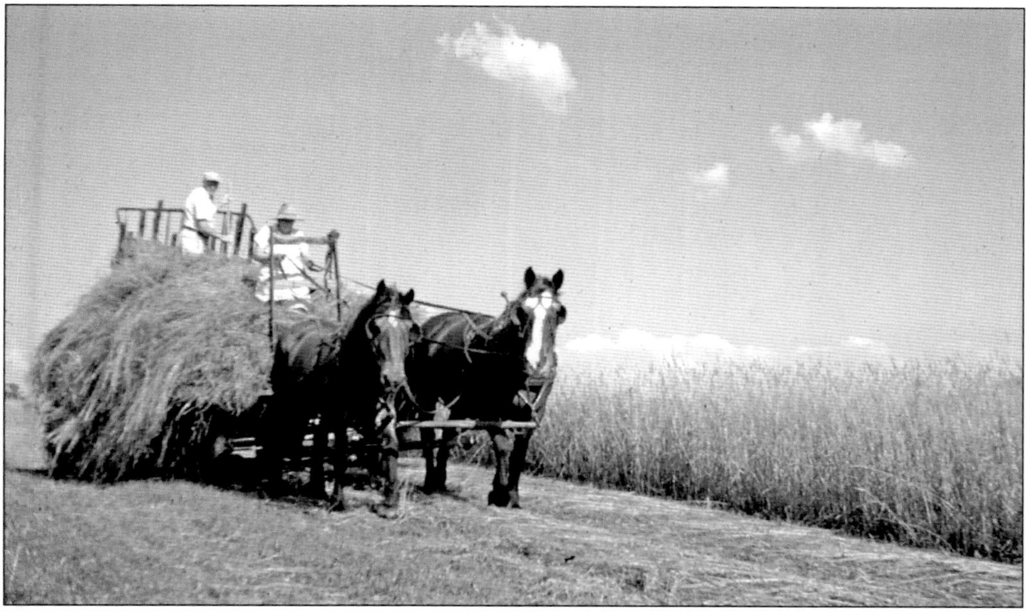

Edna Scheckelman is seen here in 1961, driving a horse-drawn wagon while a farmhand manages its hay load. The hay is being loaded onto the wagon by a mechanical hay loader pulled behind the wagon. Edna and her sister Emma continued to operate the farm after their parents and brother died. The farm on River Road was part of the property once owned by the Shakers. (Rudy Dehn.)

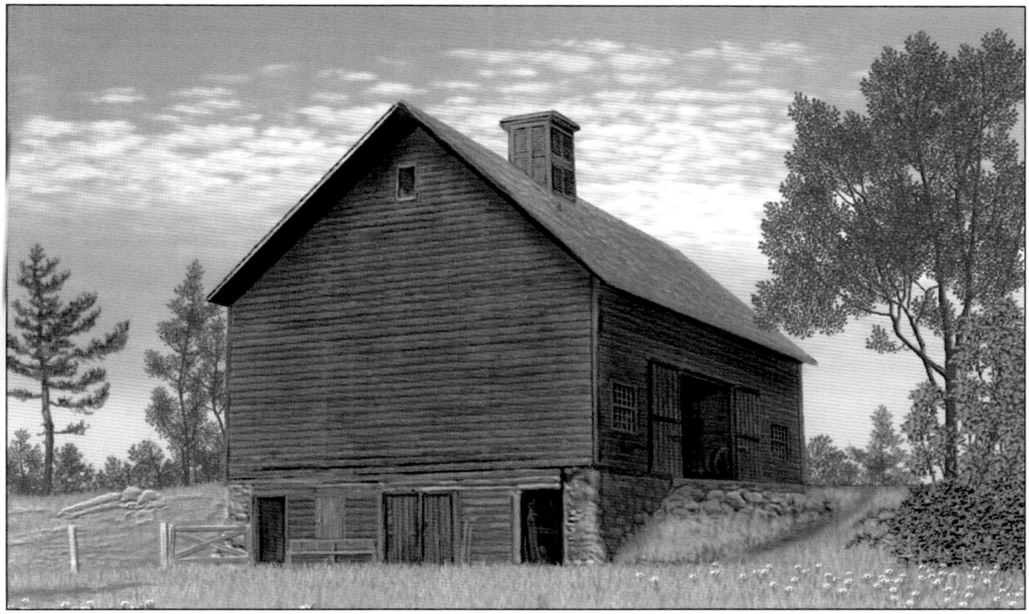

The Scheckelman farm on River Road contained a Shaker barn built in 1890. The parcel containing the barn was purchased by the Town of Niskayuna in 1971. The barn was razed on November 17, 1975, to make room for new tennis courts. Depicted is a drawing by artist Carl Buell, based on an old, unusable photograph. Buell used his artistic license to render the barn as he imagined it to have looked in 1910. (SCHS.)

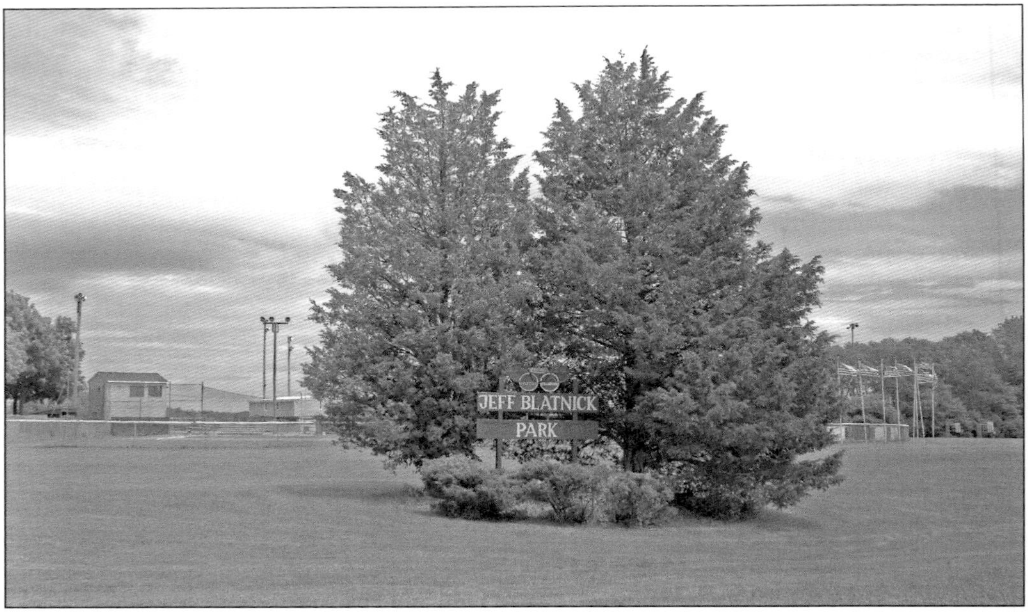

Jeff Blatnick Park was built on the site of the old Scheckelman farm. The park includes baseball fields, a picnic pavilion, a skate park, a playground, lighted tennis courts, a golf driving range, and access to the Mohawk River and the bike path. Originally called River Road Park, it was renamed in honor of Jeff Blatnick in 1984, and a new River Road Park was built on the opposite side of River Road in 1994. (Efner City History Center.)

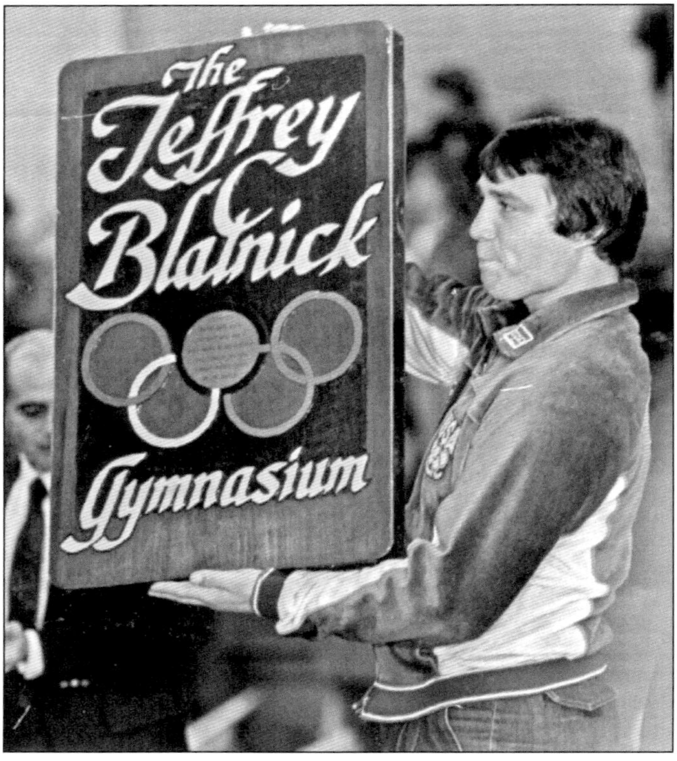

Blatnick began his wrestling at Niskayuna High School and continued at Springfield College. He qualified for the boycotted 1980 Moscow Olympics but then suffered a bout of cancer. He recovered, went on to compete as a super heavyweight in Greco-Roman wrestling at the 1984 Olympics in Los Angeles and won a gold metal. (Efner City History Center.)

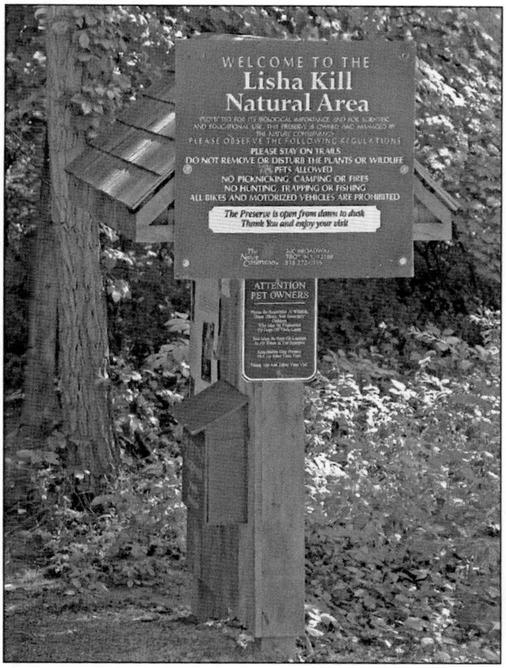

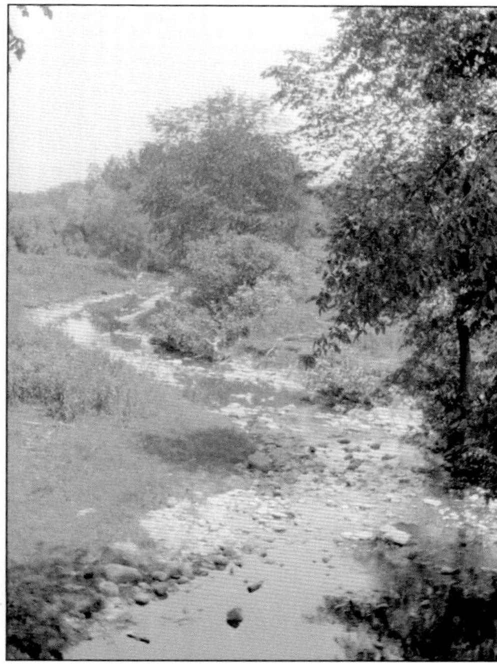

The 112-acre Lisha Kill Nature Preserve in southeastern Niskayuna was acquired by the Nature Conservancy in 1964. Part of the area is old-growth forest similar to those in Colonial times. (Efner City History Center.)

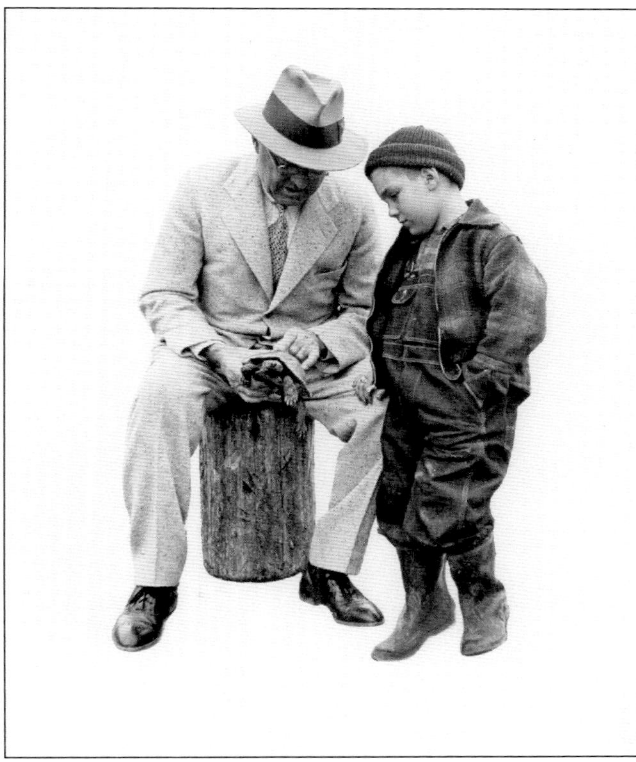

Dr. Willis R. Whitney (1868–1958), founder and first director of the General Electric Research and Development Center, is discussing natural science with young neighbor Paul Gundrum in 1937. Whitney lived in a home he built in 1912 across from what later was formally dedicated as the Nature Preserve six years after he died. He loved to roam that area in search of turtles and other flora and fauna that struck his wide-ranging interest. (Schenectady Museum.)

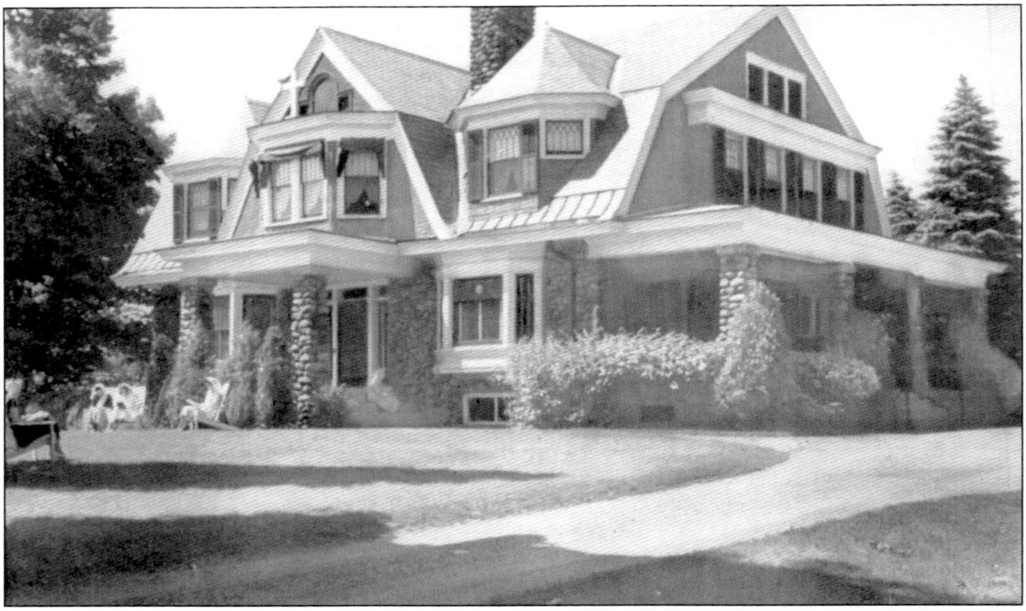

Here is the Dominican Retreat House at 1945 Union Street in Niskayuna. The site was purchased by the Dominican Sisters from the estate of Charles Witbeck in 1948. The manor house was used as a retreat for the first 10 years until a larger, more modern facility was built in 1958. The facility hosts retreats for several hundred men and women each year. (Efner City History Center.)

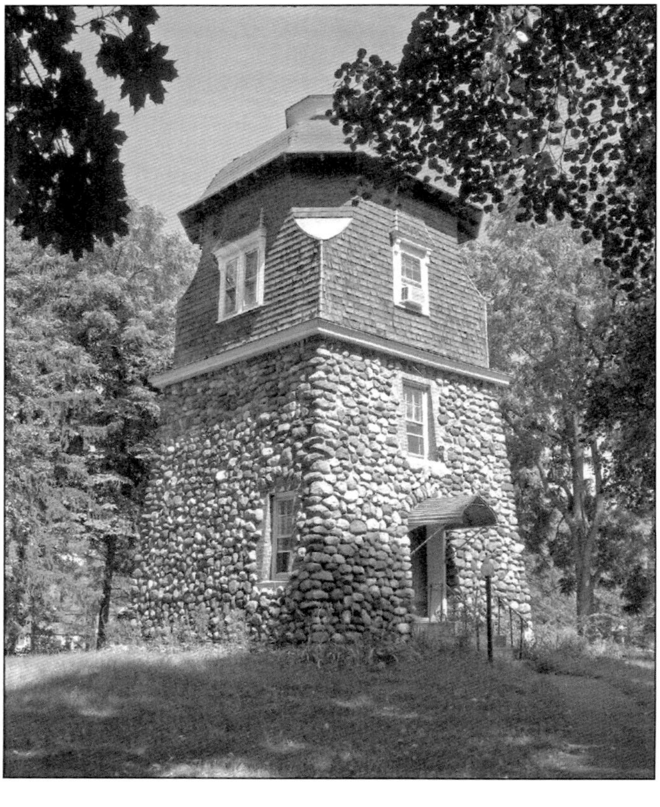

What was once a working windmill on the Witbeck estate at the corner of Union Street and Rosendale Road is now used for retreats for one or two persons. It was refurbished with a living room/kitchenette on the first floor and a bedroom, prayer room, and bath on the second. (SCHS.)

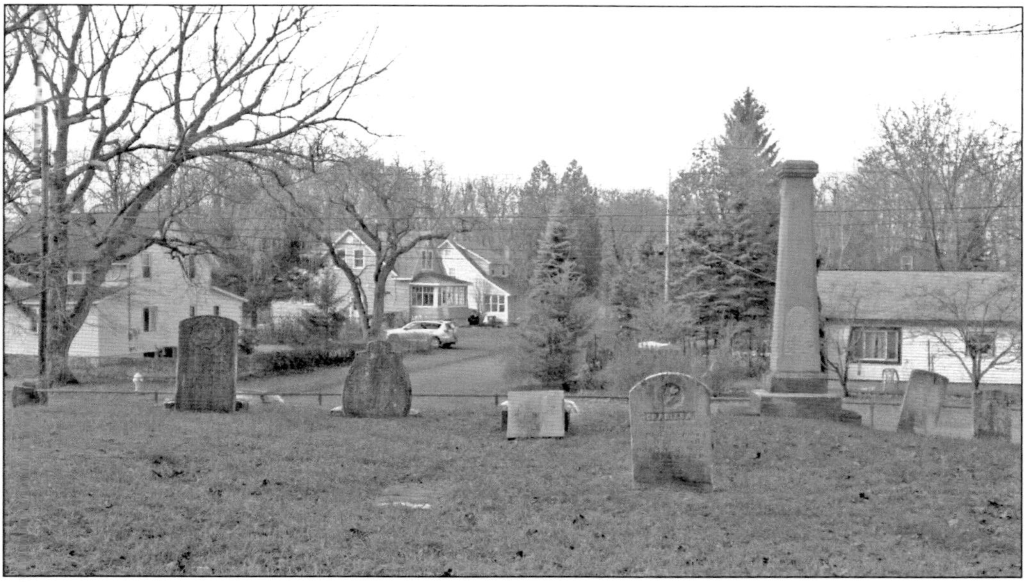

The Vrooman Family Cemetery on Fillmore Avenue, once part of the extensive Duncan holdings, also includes the graves of several other early Niskayuna families with surnames such as Hand, Hildebrand, Sitterley, and Quackenbush. Three John I. Vroomans were once buried here—a grandfather, a father, and a son—but the father has since been moved to Vale Cemetery in Schenectady. The father and son had been town supervisors in Niskayuna. The last interment at the Vrooman Family Cemetery was in the early 1900s. (SCHS.)

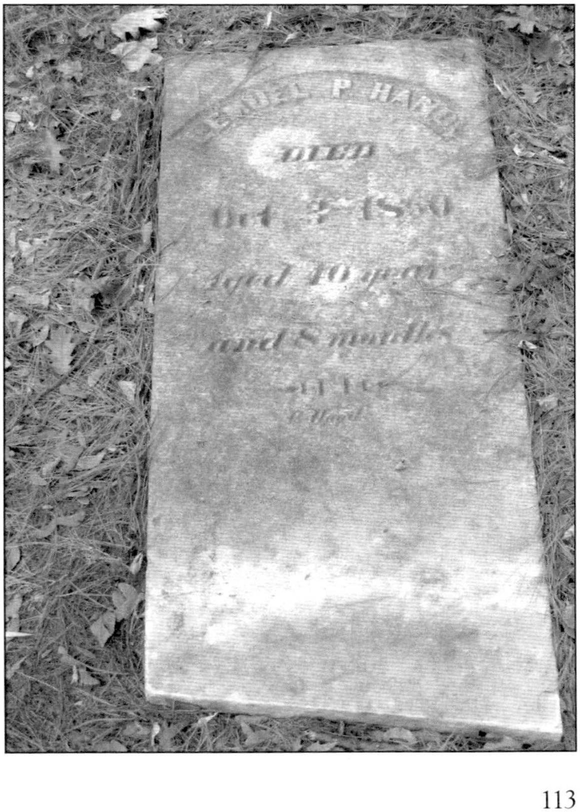

Here is the Vrooman cemetery gravestone of Capt. Lemuel P. Hand (1810–1850), who became the second owner of what is now called the Stanford mansion when he bought it from Hermanus Schuyler in 1839. Hand lost the title of the property, and after being sold at auction to an intermediary in 1849, John I. Vrooman Sr. became its fourth owner until he became town supervisor in 1859 and sold it to Josiah Stanford. (SCHS.)

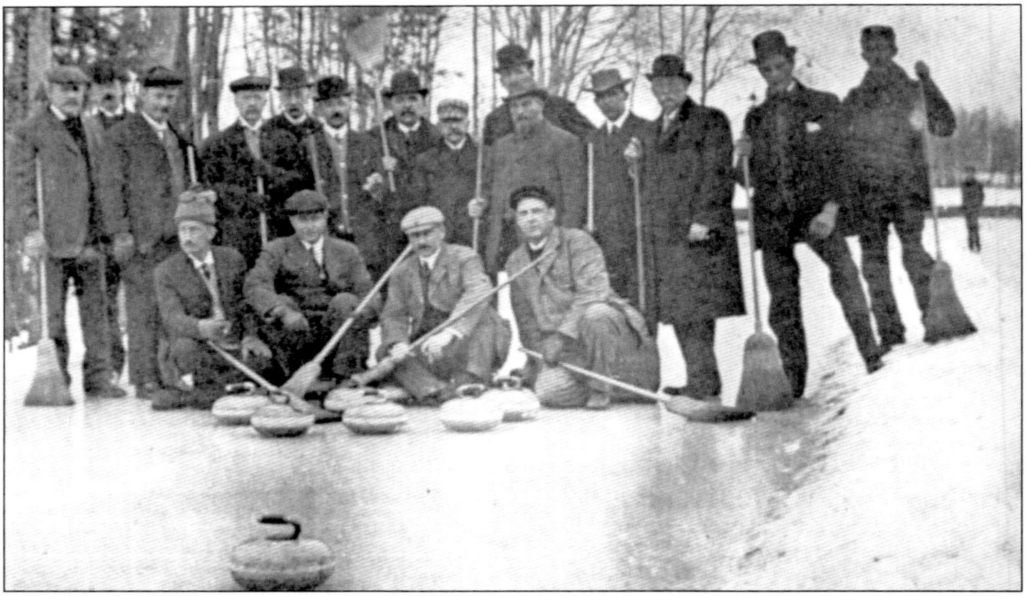

The Mohawk Golf Club Curling Association was formed in 1906 and held its first bonspiel in 1908. Seated are Schenectady team members Charles Langley, R. B. Beale, R. S. Emmet, and B. B. Hull. Standing are Utica, St. Andrews, and Albany team members R. A. S. Brinkerhoff, C. J. Hailes, J. McGregor, Thomas Mickolson, H. I. Johnson, W. B. Wackerhiggan, J. E. Frederick, J. F. Conley, Henry Quinn, John Leslie, N. R. Gurley, Robert Strathdee, Archie West, and in the distance at the right, ice maker Ed Ulrich. (SCHS.)

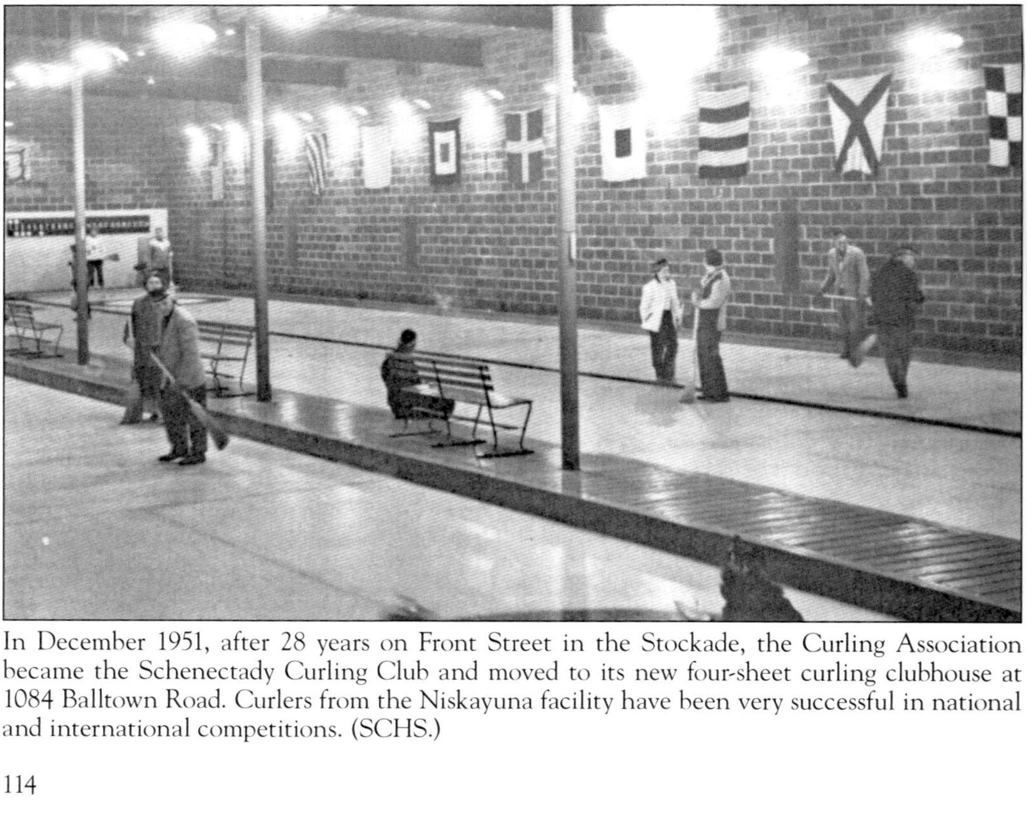

In December 1951, after 28 years on Front Street in the Stockade, the Curling Association became the Schenectady Curling Club and moved to its new four-sheet curling clubhouse at 1084 Balltown Road. Curlers from the Niskayuna facility have been very successful in national and international competitions. (SCHS.)

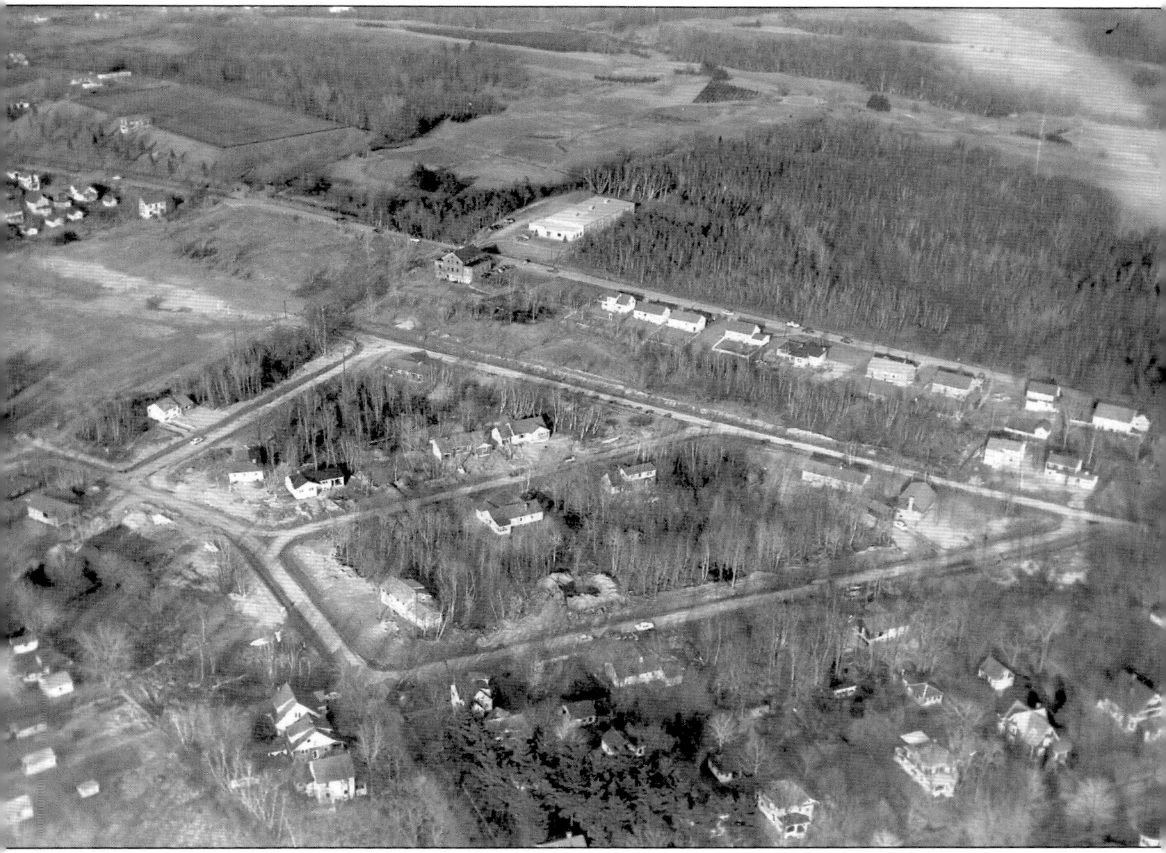

This 1950s aerial photograph shows several of the facilities featured in this book. Balltown Road runs from left to right. On opposite sides of Balltown near the center of the photograph are the Grand Boulevard fire station and the Schenectady Curling Club. To the left of the firehouse is Reid's Field, now the site of the Hillside School at 1100 Cornelius Avenue. Farther to the left along Balltown Road, the raised area is the Bevis Hill Reservoir owned by the City of Schenectady (see page 122). (SCHS.)

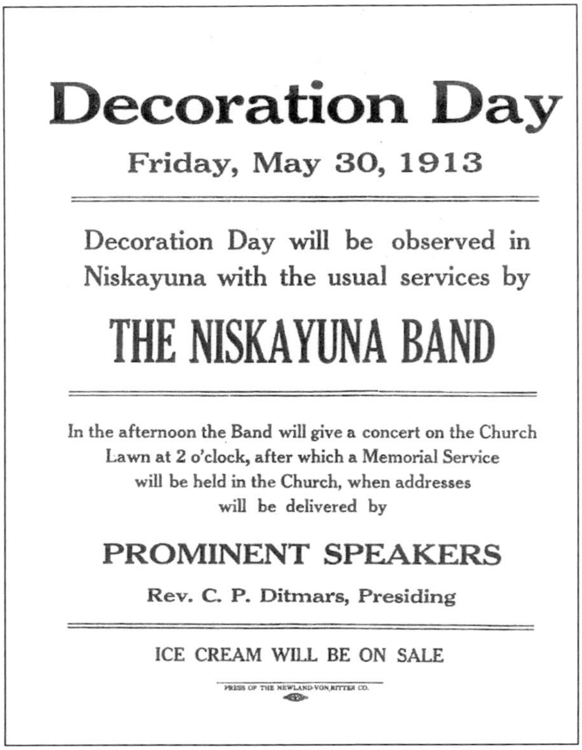

Decoration Day

Friday, May 30, 1913

Decoration Day will be observed in Niskayuna with the usual services by

THE NISKAYUNA BAND

In the afternoon the Band will give a concert on the Church Lawn at 2 o'clock, after which a Memorial Service will be held in the Church, when addresses will be delivered by

PROMINENT SPEAKERS

Rev. C. P. Ditmars, Presiding

ICE CREAM WILL BE ON SALE

PRESS OF THE NEWLAND-VON RITTER CO.

Decoration Day was initiated after the American Civil War to "decorate the graves" of the fallen soldiers. Later the holiday became known as Memorial Day. Town bands such as the one from Niskayuna advertised in this flyer were common in the early 20th century. Presiding at the May 30, 1913, event was Rev. Cornelius Peterson Ditmars, pastor of the Niskayuna Reformed Church from 1883 to 1929. (SCHS.)

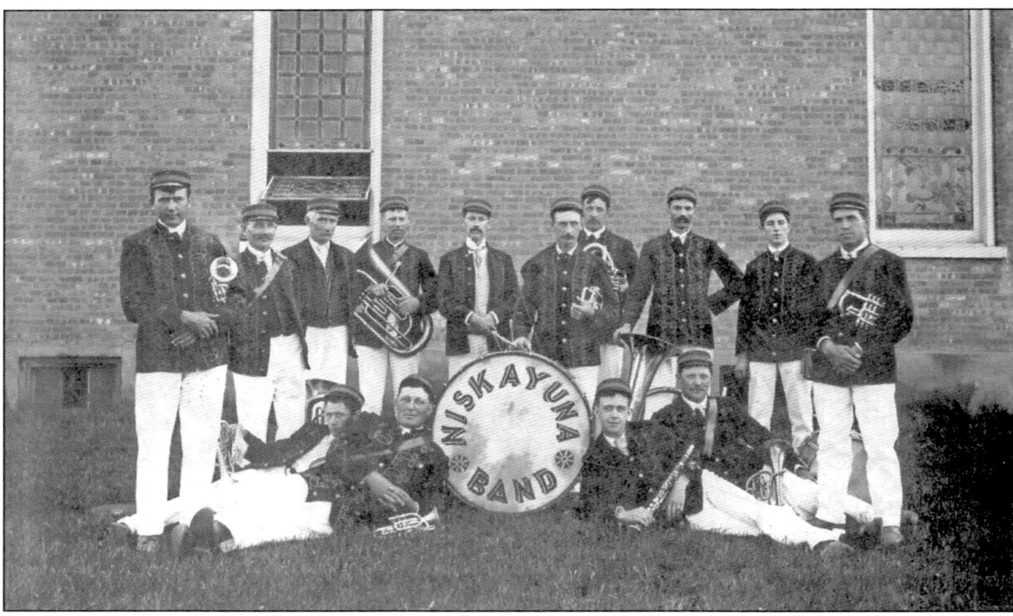

The east wall of the Niskayuna Reformed Church on Troy Road was the scene of this Niskayuna Band photograph taken in 1902. From left to right are (first row) Edward Burger, John Henry Male, Charles T. Male Sr., and Willoughby Male; (second row) William Alheim, George Woods, Lewis Burger, William Lawrence, Frank Male, Charles W. Male, director William Lye, Walter Russell, Lewis J. Male, and George Lye. (Niskayuna Reformed Church.)

Six

Community Services

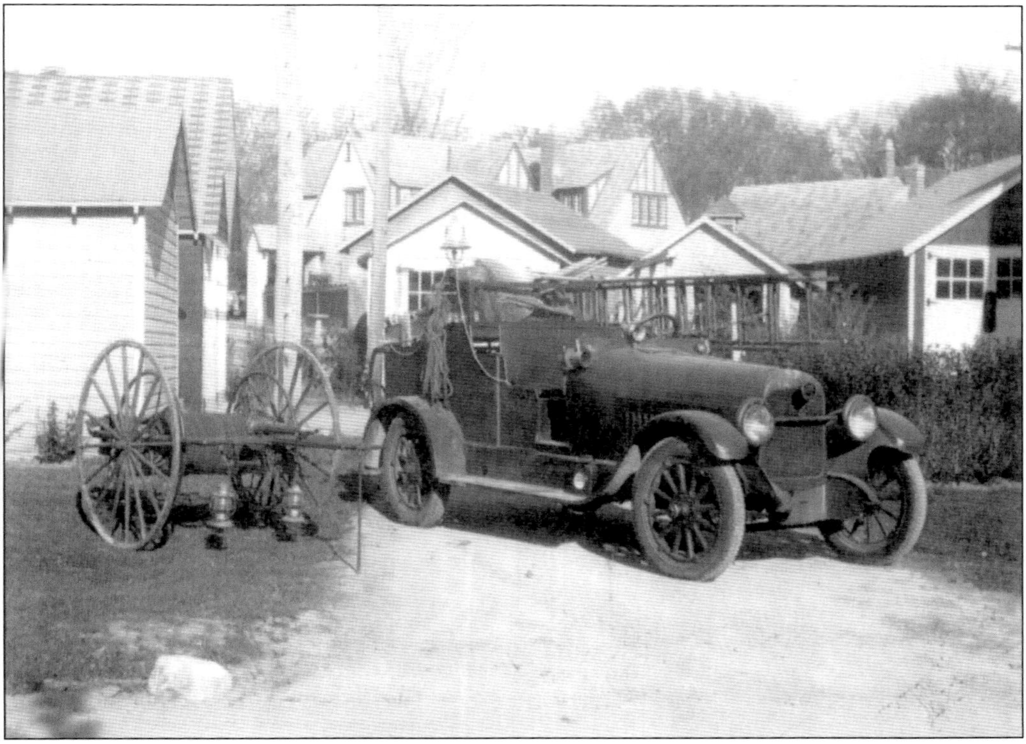

The Grand Boulevard Fire Company, now part of Niskayuna Fire District No. 1, was formed in 1920. It gradually expanded to serve a much larger section of the town. The company's first motorized vehicle, shown here, was a converted Studebaker touring car placed in service in 1930. It was housed in a garage on Myron Street. (SCHS.)

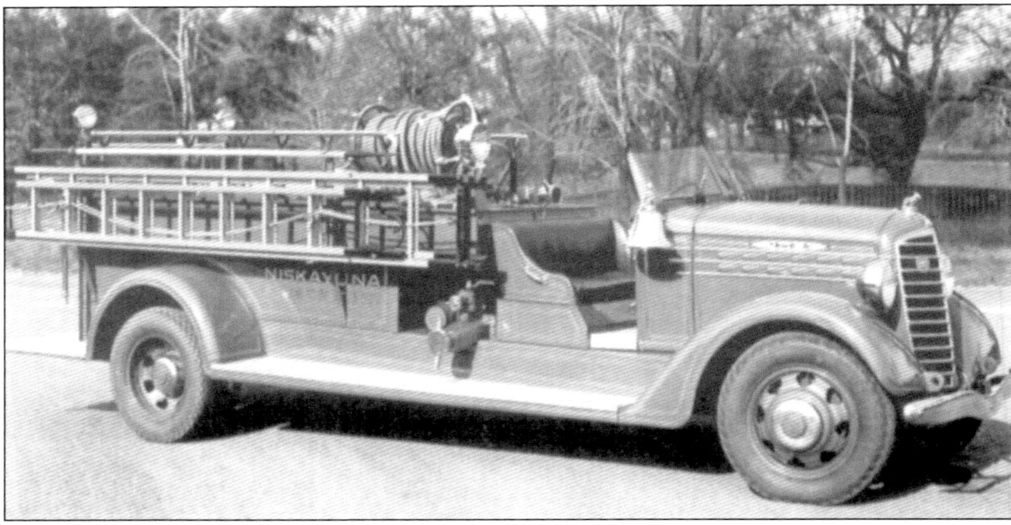

As plans were being made for a new firehouse, Grand Boulevard Fire Company purchased its first real piece of apparatus in 1936. Shown here is a 250-gallon-per-minute Mack Jr. pumper, purchased for $4,200. Like the Studebaker before it, it was housed in a garage on Myron Street until the new station was built. (SCHS.)

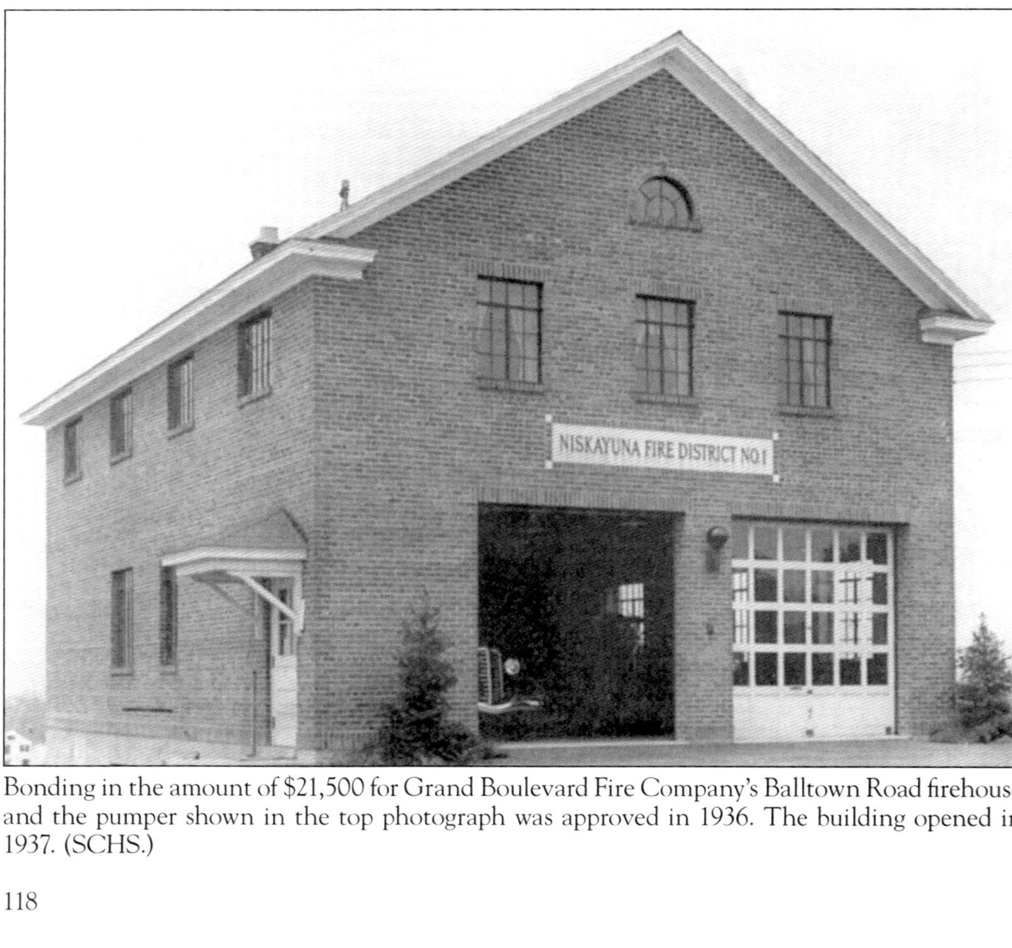

Bonding in the amount of $21,500 for Grand Boulevard Fire Company's Balltown Road firehouse and the pumper shown in the top photograph was approved in 1936. The building opened in 1937. (SCHS.)

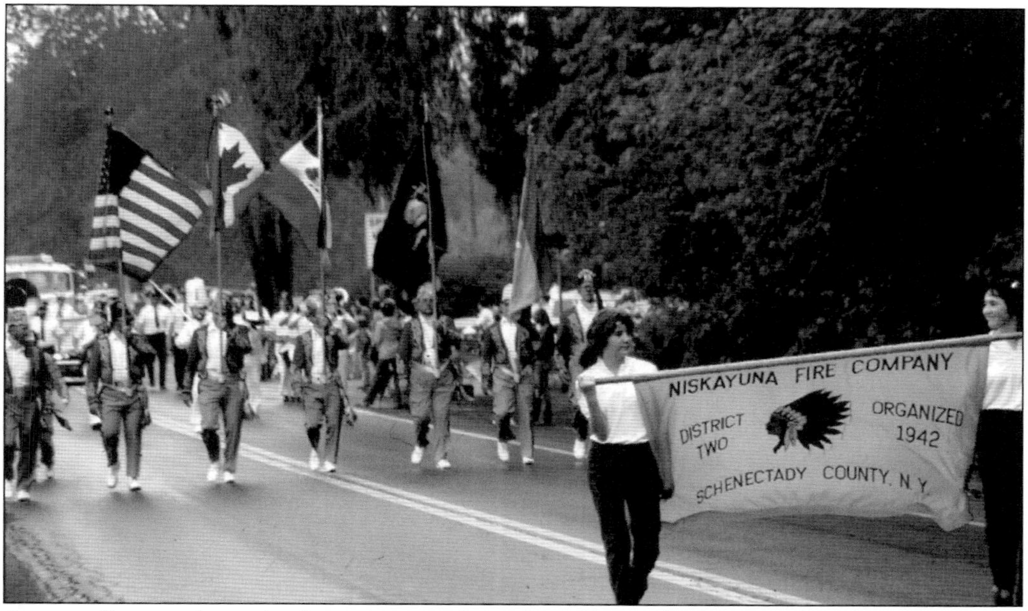

As proudly stated on the banner carried in the 1982 Niska-Day parade, the all-volunteer Niskayuna Fire District No. 2 was organized in 1942. This district serves the eastern end of the town from its station at 2772 Troy Road. The portion of the town not covered by either district No. 1 or No. 2 is served by the Stanford Heights Fire Department from stations in Colonie and Schenectady. (Rudy Dehn.)

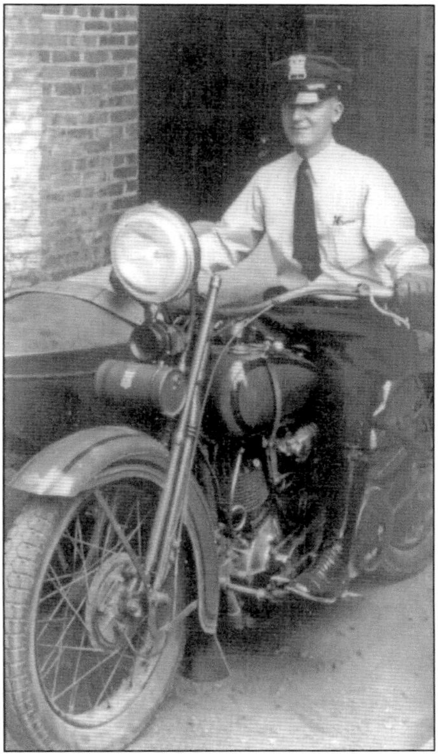

The Niskayuna Police Department was founded in October 1928 through the appointment of its first officer, John T. McGovern, who ran the one-man operation from his home on Myron Street. He is shown here on his cycle during his first year of service. As additional officers were added in later years, he became chief and served in that capacity until his retirement in 1968. (SCHS.)

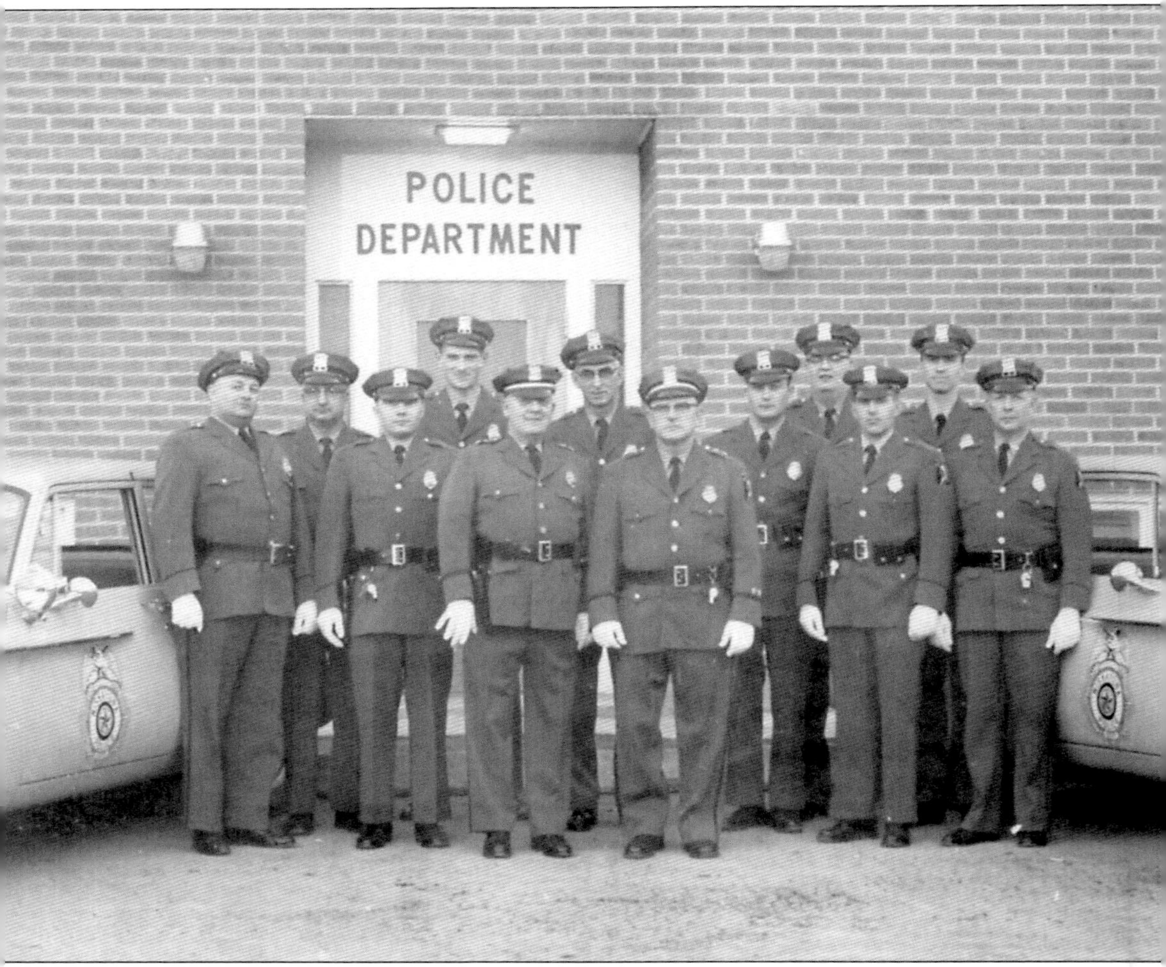

By the time this photograph was taken in 1962, the Niskayuna Police Department had grown to 13 men. The first female officer, Frances Wall, was appointed in 1985 and promoted to sergeant in 1990. Pictured from left to right are (first row) patrolman Warren Danis, patrolman Alpheus Smith, Chief John T. McGovern, Deputy Chief Thomas Sims, patrolman Arthur Nitchman, and patrolman Warren Kelts; (second row) patrolman Wilbur Dickinson, Sgt. Lloyd Wyman II, Sgt. Clifford Crookes, patrolman Michael Masterpolo, Sgt. John J. McGovern, and patrolman J. Richard (Dick) Waterfield. Patrolman John Arnow was not available for the picture. In later years, John T. McGovern was succeeded as chief by Sims, Crookes, and John J. McGovern, respectively, and Waterfield became deputy chief to John J. McGovern, the son of the town's first chief. (SCHS.)

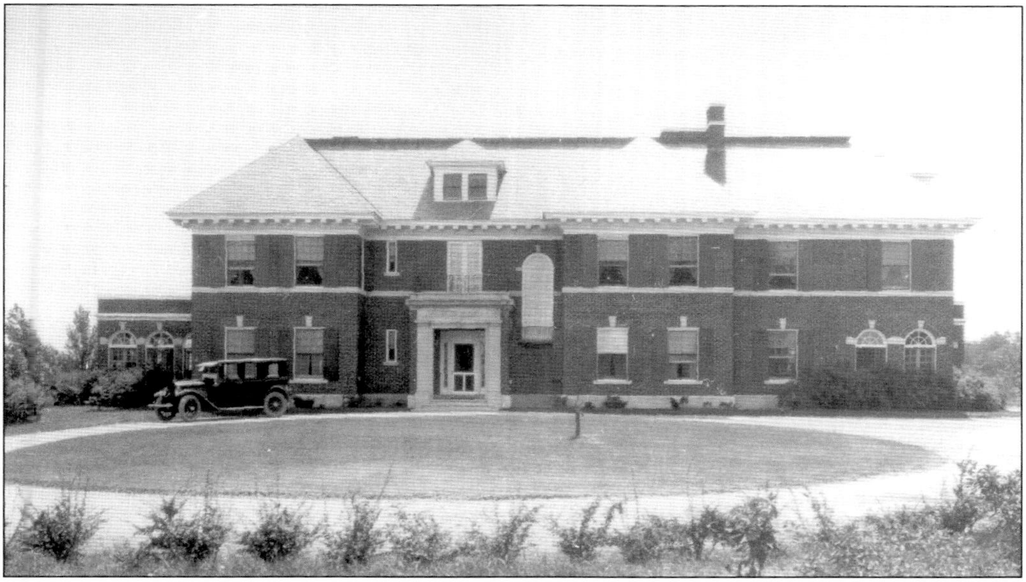

Here is the Bellevue Woman's Care Center of Ellis Hospital at 2210 Troy–Schenectady Road. Built in 1920 as a summer home by Charles W. Stone (1874–1938), this elegant Georgian manor was converted into a women's hospital in 1942 by M. Grace Nordlund Jorgensen, RN, who founded the Bellevue Maternity Hospital in 1931. After a newer building was erected in 1973 to serve as a birthing facility, this structure was divided into offices for the hospital's doctors and administrators. (Schenectady Museum.)

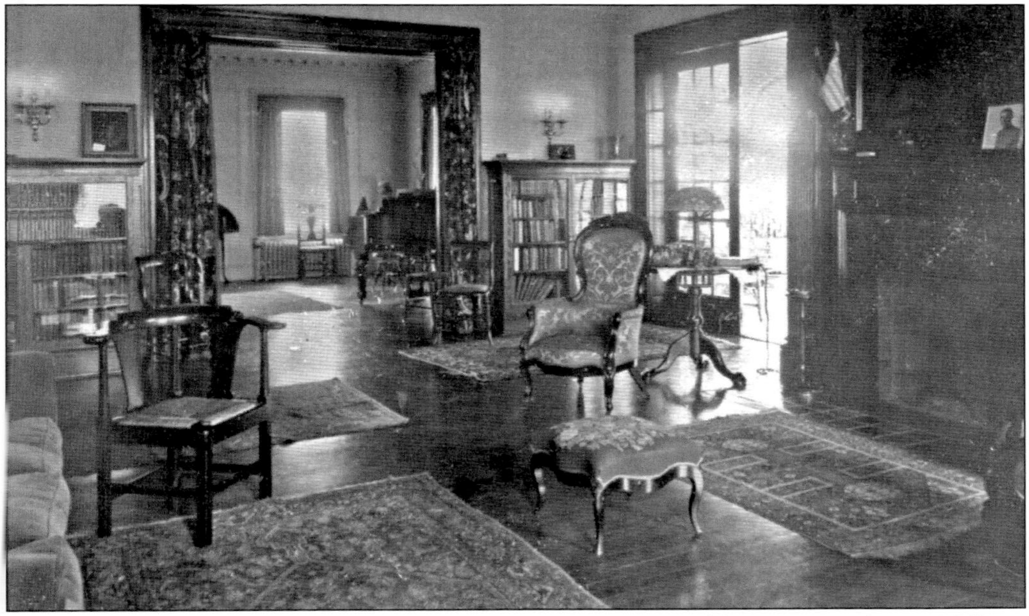

This is the interior of Stone Ridge, the summer home designed by Scotia architect William Mynderse for engineer and inventor Charles W. Stone. Stone started work in the drafting department of General Electric in 1900 and rose to become manager of its lighting department. The spacious lower rooms of Stone Ridge, built in 1920, made an open, graceful entry to the Bellevue Maternity Hospital of 1942. (Efner City History Center.)

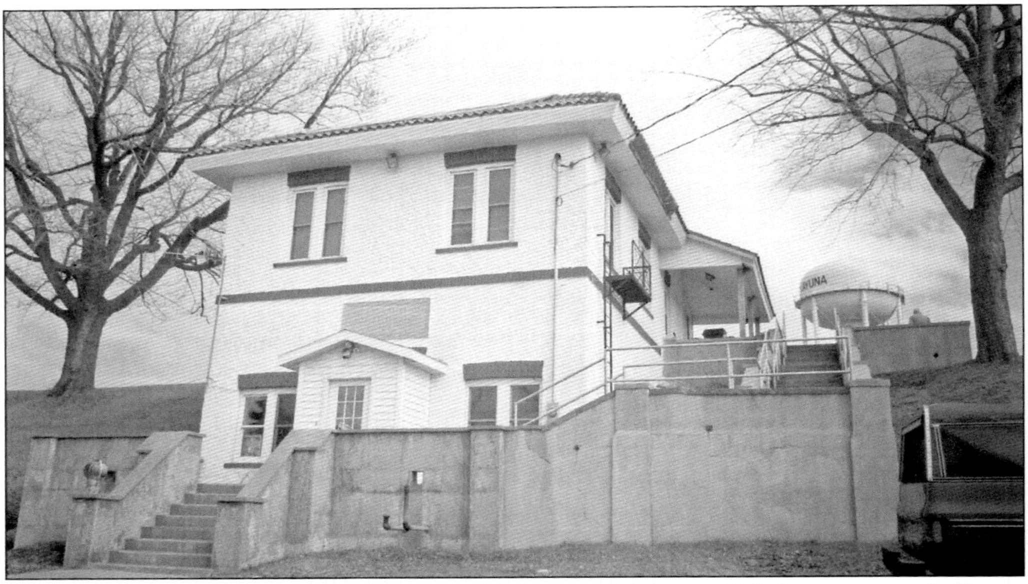

This is the control building at the City of Schenectady's Bevis Hill Reservoir on Balltown Road. Water from the reservoir flows back to the city as needed, and the height of the reservoir provides excellent water pressure for its residents. Water in the pictured tower supplies Niskayuna. Niskayuna purchases roughly half of its water from Schenectady, whose wells are in the town of Rotterdam, and supplements it with water from its own wells off Lock 7 Road. (Efner City History Center.)

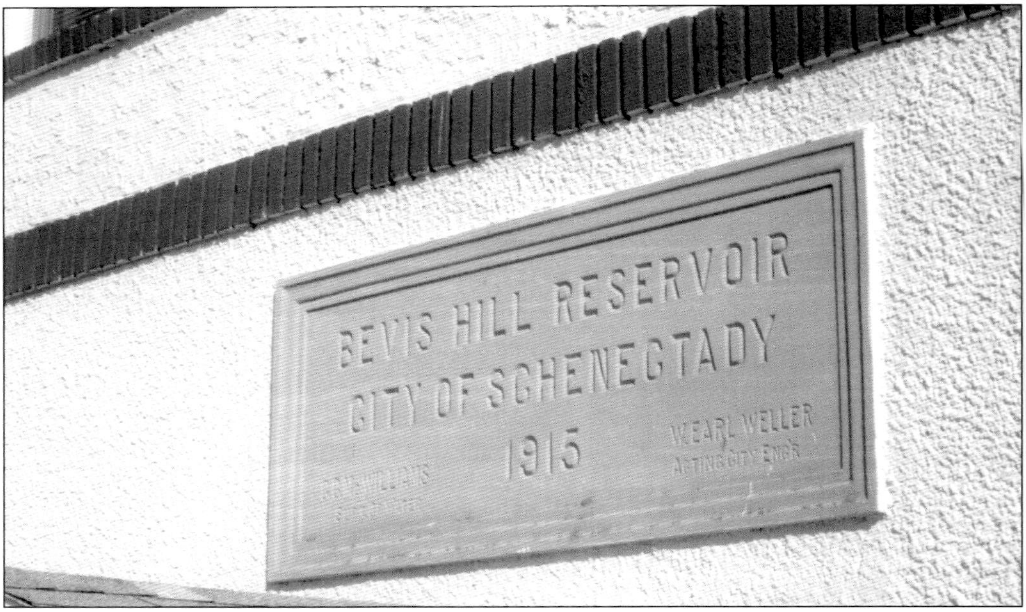

Shown is a plaque commemorating the construction of the Bevis Hill Reservoir in 1915. The reservoir was built on land purchased from the Bevis family, who had owned the land dating back to at least 1864, in order to supply water at good pressure to the rapidly expanding population of Schenectady. The 20-million-gallon reservoir replaced the need for water towers on Albany Street and Rugby Road. (Efner City History Center.)

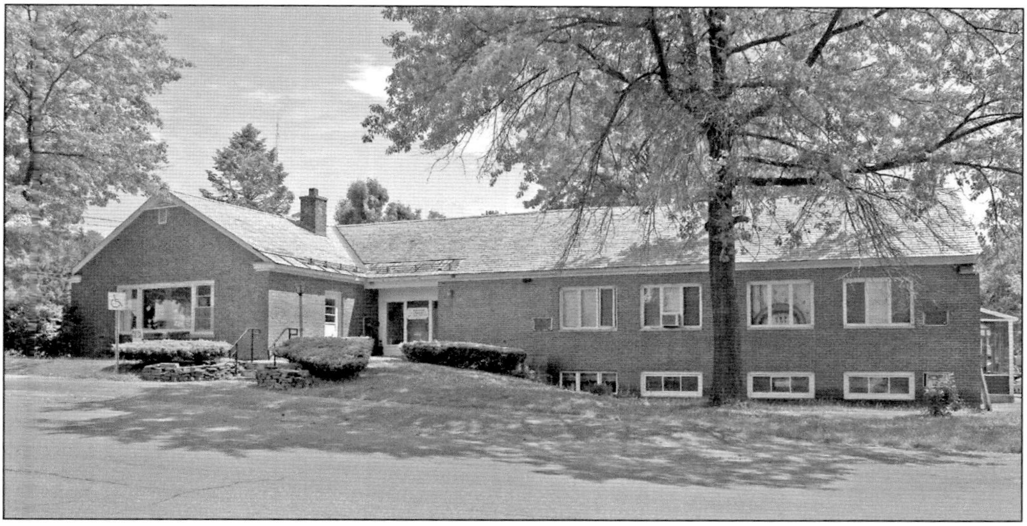

Niskayuna's first town hall was built on Balltown Road at Alton Street in 1950. Additions were built in the years 1961, 1972, and 1975, until increases in the town's population and an expanding police force necessitated a move to larger quarters. In 1994, the building was sold to Niskayuna resident Linda DeFilippo for use as her Plaza Day Care Center. The proceeds were used to furnish the new town hall that had just been completed. (SCHS.)

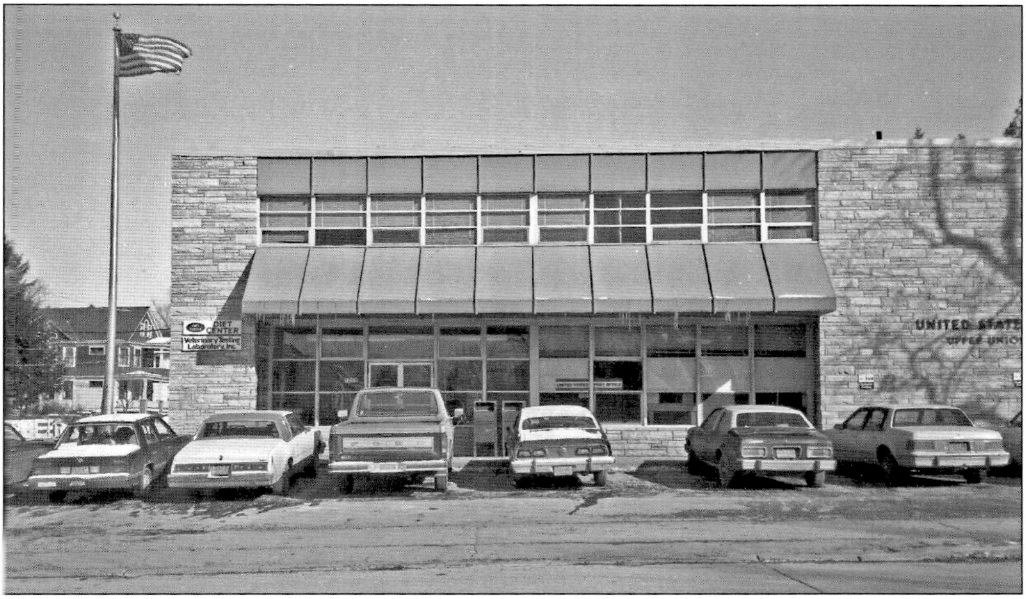

The upper Union Street branch of the Schenectady Post Office, located at 1759 Union Street, served Niskayuna until 1989 when a new post office was opened on Nott Street East. When Van Antwerp School reopened in 1993, necessitating displacement of the Niskayuna Community Center, the town leased the first floor of the building depicted and used it for a community center until it purchased the former Girling Center on Aqueduct Road in 1998. (SCHS.)

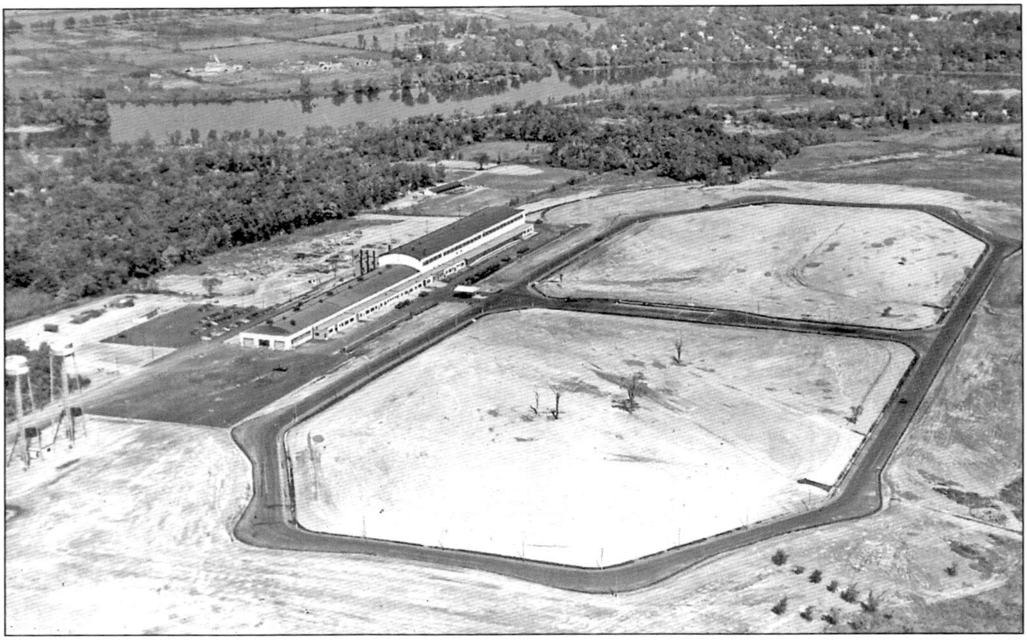

This test track for American Locomotive Company (ALCO) tanks was located off Hillside Avenue. Known for building locomotives, ALCO was awarded a government contract to produce medium tanks in November 1940. In just five months, the first tank was successfully tested before government officials. (Efner City History Center, Legere Lantern Slide Collection.)

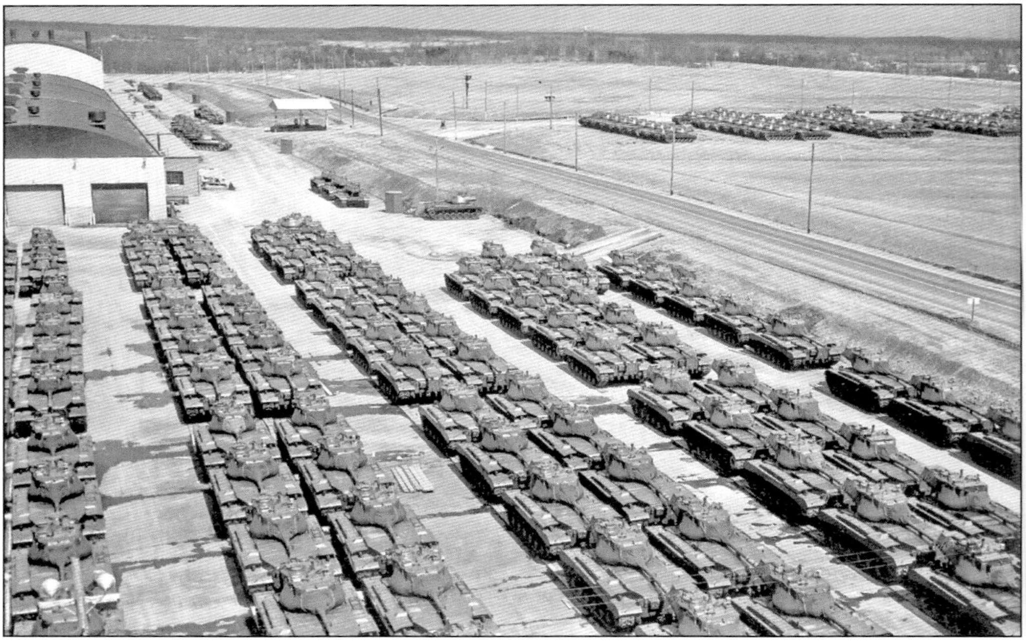

Tanks lined up at the ALCO testing grounds in Niskayuna in 1952. Thousands of square feet of manufacturing space at ALCO were converted to military use during World War II and the Korean War. When combat ended in 1953, production of both tanks and locomotives dropped precipitously, and ALCO went out of business. (Efner City History Center, Legere Lantern Slide Collection.)

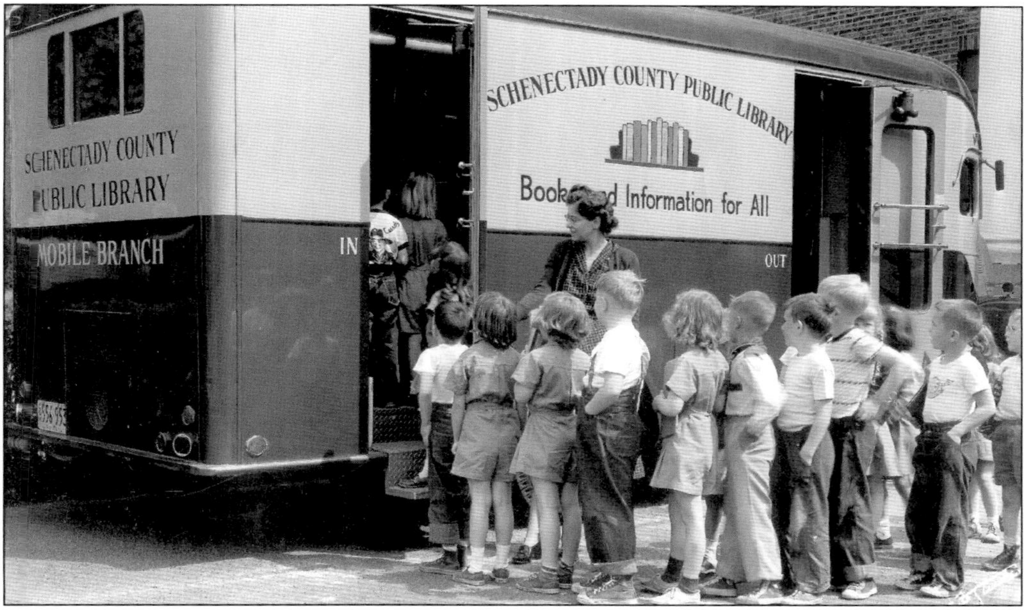

Students from Van Antwerp School line up to visit the Schenectady County Public Library's Bookmobile in 1951. This was the way the large central library in downtown Schenectady extended service to the outlying parts of the county until its complement of nine branch libraries was completed in the late 1990s. The Bookmobile made weekly stops at neighborhoods throughout Niskayuna in addition to school sites. (Schenectady County Public Library.)

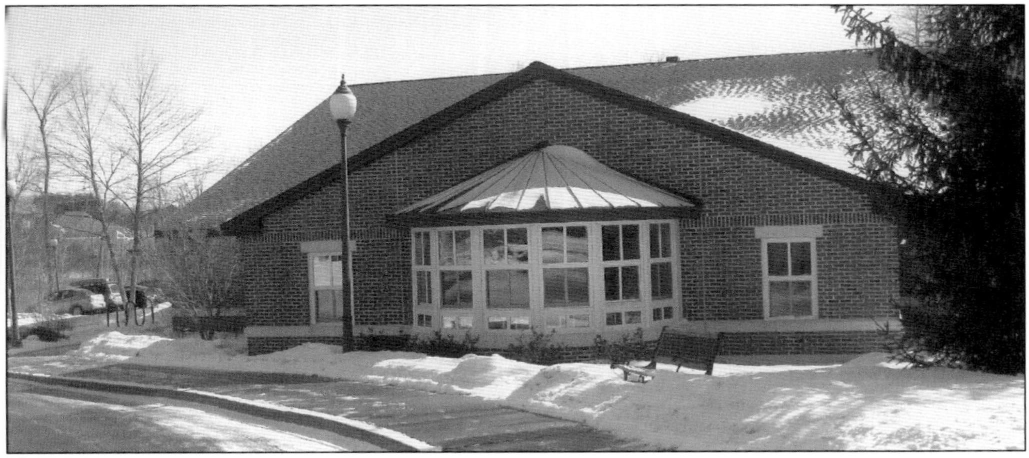

This branch of the Schenectady County Public Library opened in 1995 on Nott Street East across from the town hall on land that the town gave to the county. Previously Niskayuna was served by a bookmobile and then by a small branch library located first at Van Antwerp Middle School and later at the original Mohawk Mall. The new library branch is named for county legislator Elizabeth Harriman Bean (1923–1990). (SCHS.)

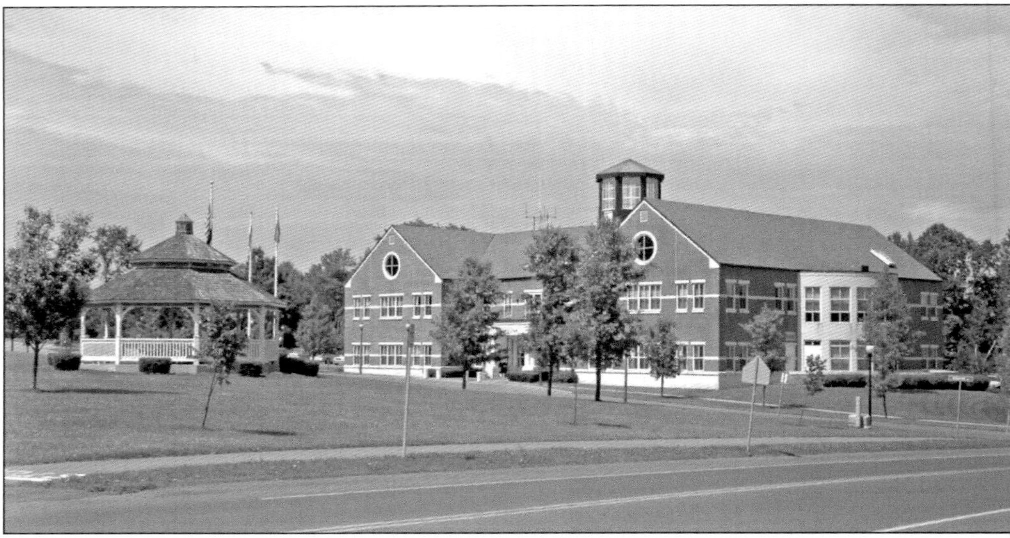

Ground was broken in early 1993 for the current town hall at One Niskayuna Circle off of Nott Street East. Designed by the Einhorn, Yaffee and Prescott architectural firm with Niskayuna resident James McKinney as project director, the building was opened to the public and dedicated on April 30, 1995. A substantial portion of the town hall houses the Niskayuna Police Department. Niskayuna is governed by a town board consisting of a town supervisor and four councilmen. (SCHS.)

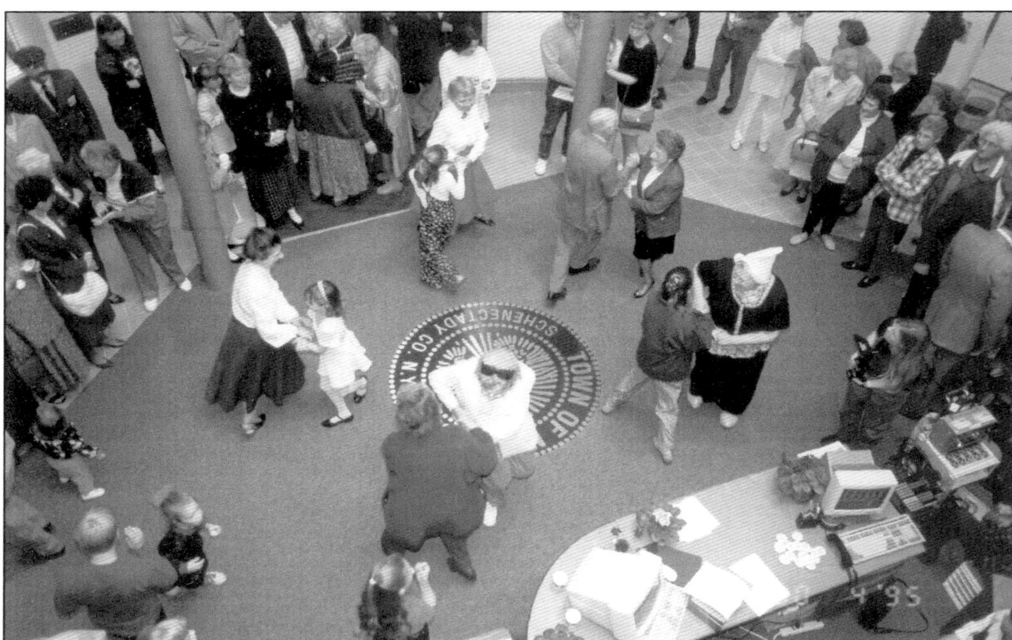

A costumed Maryde King leads a Dutch folk dance in the rotunda of the new town hall at the formal dedication of the building on April 30, 1995. The five couples are circling the metallic representation of the town's official seal of 1809. (Edwin D. Reilly Jr.)

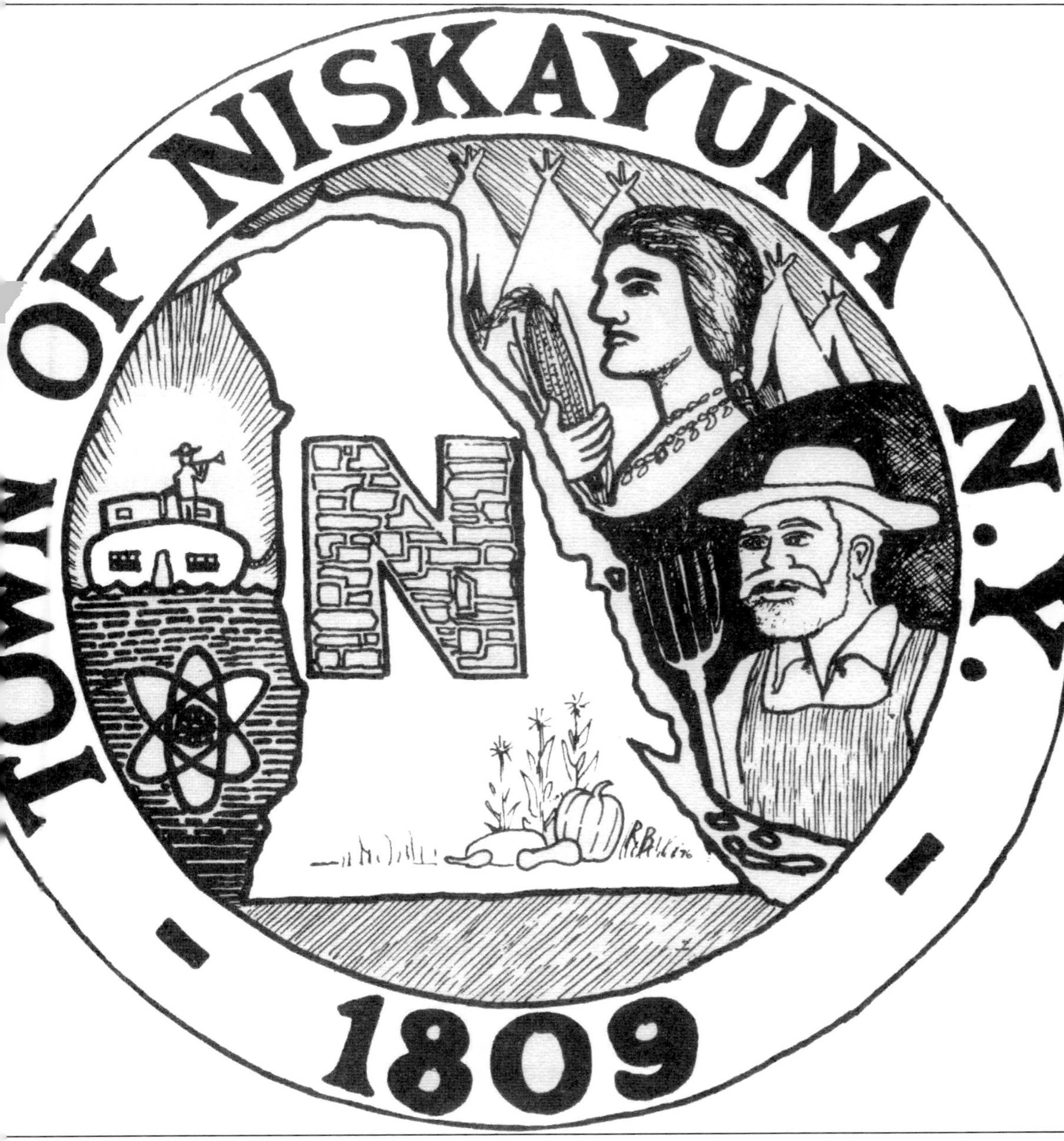

This seal was designed by Robert Banks for use at the Niskayuna celebration of the national bicentennial of 1976. The cost of the associated dinner was set at $17.76. (Town of Niskayuna.)

Discover Thousands of Local History Books Featuring Millions of Vintage Images

Arcadia Publishing, the leading local history publisher in the United States, is committed to making history accessible and meaningful through publishing books that celebrate and preserve the heritage of America's people and places.

Find more books like this at
www.arcadiapublishing.com

Search for your hometown history, your old stomping grounds, and even your favorite sports team.

Consistent with our mission to preserve history on a local level, this book was printed in South Carolina on American-made paper and manufactured entirely in the United States. Products carrying the accredited Forest Stewardship Council (FSC) label are printed on 100 percent FSC-certified paper.

MADE IN THE USA